MARY STEWART'S PEOPLE

Life in Mary Stewart's Scotland

MARY STEWART'S PEOPLE

Life in Mary Stewart's Scotland

MARGARET H.B. SANDERSON

1987

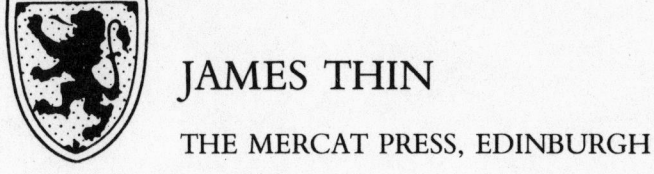

JAMES THIN

THE MERCAT PRESS, EDINBURGH

Published by
JAMES THIN
The Mercat Press
53-59 South Bridge, Edinburgh

First published 1987

© Margaret H.B. Sanderson

Design, typography, jacket, and layouts by
T.L. JENKINS, Edinburgh.

Jacket illustration:
The Arrival of Mary Queen of Scots in Scotland, 1561,
painting by William Hole, reproduced by courtesy of Edinburgh City Museums and Art Galleries,
Photograph by Antonia Reeve.

ISBN 0 901824 81 X

Printed and bound in Scotland by
Spectrum Printing Company Limited

CONTENTS

PREFACE ix

INTRODUCTION 1

MARION OGILVY : Lady of Melgund 3

JOHN SHAIRP : Advocate and Laird of Houston 22

JANE GORDON : Countess of Sutherland 34

SIR WILLIAM DOUGLAS : Laird of Lochleven and Earl of Morton 55

PATRICK NIMMO : Tailor 75

JANET FOCKART : Merchant and money-lender 91

THE FARMERS OF MELROSE : Life on the land 103

WALTER MORTON : Shipmaster 120

CHARLES MURRAY : Messenger-at-arms 135

ROBERT LEGGAT : Parish priest, and the parishioners of Prestwick 149

MARK KER : Metamorphosis 166

GLOSSARY 179

SELECT BIBLIOGRAPHY 183

INDEX 185

ILLUSTRATIONS

These plates are grouped together between pp.14-15

1.   HOUSTON HOUSE, WEST LOTHIAN

2.   LOCHLEVEN CASTLE, KINROSS-SHIRE

3.   A SIXTEENTH CENTURY TAILOR AT WORK

4.   JANE GORDON, Countess of Bothwell

5.   THE SO-CALLED 'ARMADA JEWEL'

6 and 7.   MARK KER and HELEN LESLIE

8.   ST. NICHOLAS'S CHURCH, PRESTWICK, AYRSHIRE

SKETCH-MAP: showing ports visited by the *Antelope* 1589-1600   124

for
my sister, Betty,
a fellow-labourer
in the records

ABBREVIATIONS USED

N.L.S.   National Library of Scotland

S.H.S.   Scottish History Society

S.R.O.   Scottish Record Office

S.R.S.   Scottish Record Society

PREFACE

I am grateful to the Earl of Airlie, the Earl of Dalhousie, the Marquess of Lothian and Sir David J.W. Ogilvy, Bt, for permission to make extensive use of and quote from manuscripts in their family papers deposited in the Scottish Record Office and to the Countess of Sutherland for permission to quote from papers in the Sutherland Muniments deposited in the National Library of Scotland. Thanks are also due to Dr A.L. Murray, Keeper of the Records of Scotland, with whose approval I have made use of public and legal records and of private archives gifted to or owned by the Scottish Record Office. I am happy once again to thank my friend and colleague, Miss M.M. Baird, for giving me the benefit of her editorial advice, especially for reading the typescripts of the essays on Marion Ogilvy, John Shairp, Jane Gordon, William Douglas, Patrick Nimmo, Walter Morton and Charles Murray.

On a technical level, quotations from letters and documents have been retained in the original Scots, the 'lively voice' of Mary Stewart's Scotland. The slightly distracting element of square brackets round the English translation of particularly difficult spellings is, I hope, a small price to pay for being able to catch the sense at the time of reading without having continually to consult a dictionary. The Glossary contains only words with a technical meaning, not common Scots words. Dates are given according to new-style, that is, beginning the year on 1 January. All sums of money are in Scots currency unless otherwise stated; in the later sixteenth century £1 Scots was equivalent to about £12 sterling.

Three excellent tools are now available to help those who are exploring the records of the sixteenth and seventeenth centuries for the first time, whether for general historical research, family history, local history or for the purpose of using archives from the earlier period in school. These are *Scottish Handwriting*, by G.G. Simpson (1986), *The Concise Scots Dictionary*, ed. M. Robertson (1985) and *A Formulary of Old Scots Documents* by P. Gouldesbrough (Stair Society, 1985). A Select Bibliography of books which fill in the background to the themes of the essays in this book is given at the end.

MARGARET H.B. SANDERSON

INTRODUCTION

MARY, QUEEN OF SCOTS is one of the most familiar figures in Scottish history, although she spent only seven of her adult years in her native kingdom. In his book, *Scotland in the Time of Queen Mary*, published in 1904, Peter Hume Brown asked the rhetorical question, 'Who can think of the times of Queen Mary without thinking of her as the central figure to whom all contemporary persons, events, and circumstances form but the setting in which she works out her destiny?'. Those of her contemporaries who are well known to the general reader tend to be the supporting cast in her personal drama – John Knox, Darnley, Rizzio, Bothwell, and a handful of politicians led by her half-brother, Lord James Stewart. In the older histories not much took place outside the Queen's court, and hardly anything, except battles, outside Edinburgh. Modern research is gradually providing Queen Mary with a context as well as an entourage. Whereas at one time her subjects appeared only in the crowd scenes in her story, attention is now being given to what they were doing at other times. The older notion that not much information was available about the lives of the ordinary Scots of her times has given way as records have become increasingly accessible, and the Select Bibliography at the end of this book shows how many aspects of the sixteenth century have been studied in the last two or three decades.

This group of pen-portraits, drawn from different walks of life, affords a glimpse of life in the sixteenth century. A look at the experience of particular individuals, families and communities is an antidote to too much generalisation and helps us to discover something of the *quality* of life in the past, not simply to quantify certain aspects of it: letters can reveal personal attitudes; working records show how people coped with the practical business of living and how they became involved with one another; property documents remind us of the vital dependence of all classes on the land itself; the rich detail in many records helps to build up a picture of everyday life and the material culture of Scotland for a period from which not many artefacts have survived.

Studied in context the source material creates a 'feel' for the period and an ear for the sound of its speech. It also brings an awareness of the element of change which is the heart of history; John Shairp's working life saw the development of his chosen profession of advocate; the farmers of Melrose turned from tenants into owner-occupiers within a generation; Robert Leggat found himself at the centre of changes in religious life; William Douglas had to learn to accept the traditional 'auld enemy' of England as a new ally; Mark Ker was able to get the best out of two successive worlds. This handful of Queen Mary's subjects has been chosen to demonstrate that their story no less than hers is of lasting interest, but none of them is exceptional, nor should the information that has been gleaned about them be regarded with purely antiquarian attention. Although few sixteenth-century Scottish shipmasters, tailors, and messengers-at-arms have left behind them account or memorandum books like those of Walter Morton, Patrick Nimmo and Charles Murray, the records of the period are full of the stuff that life was made of in their day.

Above all, there are reminders here that Queen Mary's small northern kingdom shared a European heritage: the regular voyages of Walter Morton's ship, the *Antelope*, the imported cloths and finery sold by the merchants and handled by tailors like Patrick Nimmo, the customary inheritance practices of the farmers of Melrose which had their parallels in Western Europe, as well as the picture of the earl of Sutherland's daughters in Dornoch learning to sing and play the virginals bought for them in London, the glimpse of the minister of Monedie's library of modern European and classical authors, even Janet Fockart, the merchant, wearing a jewel the design on which echoed that used on English and European examples are all in their way evidence of contact with the wider world to which Scotland belonged.

MARION OGILVY

Lady of Melgund

1490s-1575

MARION OGILVY, who sometimes gets a minor mention in the history books as the mistress of Cardinal David Beaton, was a remarkable woman in many ways. To begin with, she lived a very long time by the standards of her own day, being born in the last decade of the 15th century and dying in 1575. Besides, through force of circumstances she was in daily charge of her own affairs throughout her lifetime and for much of it of those of her family. A lord's daughter though she was, her early circumstances, as a child of her father's old age and poorly provided for at his death, must have been those of many girls in humbler walks of life. Her father, Sir James Ogilvy of Lintrathen, an influential and respected figure in Angus as well as a trusted royal servant and diplomat, was created Lord Ogilvy of Airlie by King James IV in April 1491 on the eve of being sent as ambassador to Denmark[1]. Marion's mother, whom her father married as his fourth wife shortly after 1490, was Janet Lyle, probably the daughter of Robert, second Lord Lyle, whose landholdings were mainly in Renfrewshire and who was also experienced in the King's service, acting as ambassador to Spain in 1491, the same year as Lord Ogilvy went to Denmark.

Marion and her elder sister, Janet, probably grew up at Airlie castle which their grandfather had had a licence to rebuild around the old tower of Airlie[2], but they may also have been familiar with the family's lodging in Arbroath which Lord Ogilvy used as a base from which to discharge his duties as the abbey bailie (chief executive officer of the abbot), such as holding the court for the abbey tenants. If Marion remembered her father at all it must have been as an old man for he was about sixty when he married her mother. Apart from her full sister, Janet, she had no close relatives in her own age-group although she belonged to a family whose ramifications were vast and among whom she may have chosen her friends. Her oldest half-brother, John, who became the second Lord Ogilvy, was almost forty years older than her and even the children of her father's second marriage were considerably her seniors. There appear to have been no surviving children of his third marriage. Marion's slightly younger contemporary, John, later fourth Lord Ogilvy, was actually her great-nephew. At the time of his death Lord Ogilvy had made only partial provision for his two youngest daughters, not formal marriage contracts but an arrangement with Sir Alexander Gordon of Midmar which was partly a land-settlement into which the future marriages of Janet and Marion were to be fitted. In 1503, Sir Alexander, who owed Lord Ogilvy 600 merks, had alienated the lands of Old Midmar to his creditor, Ogilvy promising, however, not to lift any revenue from them until the heir of Midmar was of an age to marry Janet or, in the event of her death, her younger sister, Marion. Should the marriage not take place the Ogilvys were to retain the lands until the Gordons paid their debt[3]. So far as is known, this was the only provision made for his daughters by Lord Ogilvy who died the following year.

Janet Lyle, who remained a widow for the rest of her life, may have continued to live with her daughters at Airlie castle of which she would have the liferent use. As a woman who had learned to manage her own affairs, her example must have had an effect on Marion's outlook and capabilities. Even during Lord Ogilvy's lifetime Janet had appeared personally before the lords of council in pursuing a legal action over land to which she laid claim, and long after his death she continued to be involved in lawsuits concerning her rights. When her mother died in about 1525, Marion found herself in a lonely situation. The fact that she acted as executor of both parents suggests that Janet was already dead and that there had been no attempt to implement the contract of 1503 with the Gordons of Midmar. As an unmarried woman of about thirty, poorly provided for, she looked like being dependent upon the household of her great-nephew, John, fourth Lord Ogilvy, who had come of age in 1524 and was now head of the family.

We cannot tell when or how Marion Ogilvy met David Beaton, a younger son of the laird of Balfour in Fife, who in 1524 became abbot of Arbroath, the first major appointment in what was to be a remarkable career. They had an overlapping circle of friends and acquaintances among whom they may have met, while members of their families had long been associated in government and on the King's council. James Beaton, David's uncle, while archbishop of Glasgow, had arranged the marriage of his niece, Grizel Beaton of Creich, to John, fourth Lord Lyle, who was probably Marion's cousin. It is possible that they may have met in Lord Ogilvy's household in Arbroath and their association may date from after David's return to Scotland at Christmas 1524, after a period at the brilliant French court of King Francis 1. It is perhaps unfair to Lord Ogilvy to suggest that he turned to David Beaton, who as bailie of Arbroath he knew well, to help him solve the problem of his youngish, unmarried great-aunt. Perhaps it was Marion who saw a way out of becoming a dependent member of her great-nephew's household. The fact that they were about the same age and remained together until the end of David Beaton's life, when they were both over fifty, suggests that their association was mutual rather than arranged. At any rate, she was at Airlie castle on 6 April 1525 winding up her mother's affairs, granting Lord Ogilvy a receipt for the price of horses that had belonged to Janet Lyle[4], but by February 1526 she was with David Beaton in Edinburgh.

Certain aspects of their circumstances at this time fail to be explained. In the first place, although he is called abbot or, sometimes, commendator of Arbroath, David Beaton was not a monk. He never became a professed member of the Benedictine order or took the monastic habit. The practice of appointing non-monastic commendators as heads of religious houses was quite common in the first half of the sixteenth century, making the head of an abbey or priory a kind of financial and legal administrator who, because he was normally following a public career, probably took little to do with the internal spiritual life of the house. Secondly, although he was a churchman and was destined to hold high ecclesiastical office, David Beaton was not in full priest's orders for more than half his life with Marion Ogilvy. Many like him petitioned the Pope to be allowed to postpone full ordination, while drawing ecclesiastical revenues to finance the career of their choice. They thus belonged to a class of 'managers' of the church's temporal assets who paid deputies to do the spiritual work associated with their livings; to occupy a stall in the cathedral or undertake the cure of souls in a parish. Many of them carried out their management duties efficiently, some made sure that the deputies discharged their spiritual duties responsibly, but many simply regarded their livings as income. This delegation of spiritual duties to the bottom of the clerical scale and the concentration of revenue at the top had debased the system of church livings, or benefices, tending to draw many unspiritual men into the ranks. Although some descriptions of the late-medieval church as spiritually bankrupt are exaggerated, it is clear that it had lost much of its commitment to the parish service and had become a market place in which the trade in benefices was carried on in a competitive atmosphere.

David Beaton was trained in Scotland and France for royal and diplomatic service, and had taken a post-graduate training in civil law at the university of Orleans to enable him to take his place on the bench among the lords of council in judging civil court actions. Like others of his kind he behaved less like a churchman and more like an exempt layman, protected with the minimum of technical distinctions – minor orders – which placed him in the privileged ecclesiastical ranks. These minor orders, which began with the tonsure in boyhood, would have been conferred on him even without the practical training for the priesthood in which they were meant to be landmarks. One of the most conspicuous ways in which clerics, in spite of church censures, lived like the laymen among whom they lived and worked was in the practice of concubinage – forbidden clerical marriage gone underground. This was the answer of many churchmen to the centuries-long pressure from the papacy and church councils to apply the rule of clerical celibacy, which had been extended to the secular clergy from the monastic orders by Pope Gregory VII in the late eleventh century. The practice was found among the highest and lowest ranks of the clergy, from archbishops to parish curates, although it is fair to say that the many priests who practised the spirit as well as the rule of celibacy – non-marriage – earned the greater respect of the people. It is also likely that many of the clergy who lived with women in more or less constant relationships were dissenting from rather than flouting the rule. Historians have not always identified this attitude which, admittedly, is implied rather than explicit in the records, and have not always recognised that not all women in this situation were of ill-repute. Dissent from the rule of clerical celibacy, however, had to be silent, for to oppose it openly might invite a charge of heresy. Whatever he privately thought of the rule, David Beaton treated Marion Ogilvy virtually as a wife for over twenty years, although as head of the ecclesiastical courts in Scotland he was to pass sentence on more than one who dared to advocate that priests should marry. It was the application of this hypocritical double standard, as much as the fact of concubinage itself, that angered many lay critics of the church.

Marion's home in the 1520s and 1530s seems to have been at Ethie, the abbot's castle about five miles north of Arbroath, which he appears to have leased to her for her lifetime. There was no question of her simply living on an allowance from the abbot's purse. Rather, she lived on what all people of her social background lived on, rents from landed property. Over the first decade of her life at Ethie she received a number of leases of abbey land which in practice she would let out to sub-tenants, very probably the people who already inhabited it. These pieces of property included the substantial Brunton and Easter Green of Ethie, with the brewland, meadowland, and additional two acres of arable, with the right to sixty loads of turf, for roofing and dyke-building, from the moor of Arbroath. For this she paid a rent to the abbey chamberlain of £6 money and 57 bolls of various types of grain and meal. Her tack, or lease, dated 22 May 1528, expressly permitted her to 'name and remove' subtenants[5]. Four days later the occupant of the Brunton, David Lichton, whose family had held it since 1483, agreed to resign it to the abbot in exchange for part of the Mains of Ethie[6]. So, in this case, the arrival of Mistress Marion Ogilvy in the district caused some dislocation among the tenantry. In July 1530 she was given a life-lease of the Kirktoun of St Vigeans, or Arbroath, which was probably fairly thickly settled with the families who would become her subtenants. The rent for the Kirktoun included the customary payment of 6s to the 'master of the pettycommons' at the abbey, to be shared out among the monks[7]. In February 1534 she received a nineteen-year tack of an eighth of the settlement of Auchmithie and a year later a piece of ground in the 'Sandpottis' against the abbey wall, known as 'the red wall', on which to build a kiln for drying grain, suggesting that she farmed some of her property with direct labour who harvested the crop for her[8].

A more purely financial interest in land is suggested by her life-lease of the feu-duties which William Wood of Boniton owed to the abbey but which were thus diverted to her use; Wood had to grant a public obligation in court that he would guarantee payment to her[9]. The beginning of a lifelong pattern of borrowing and lending money over land as security, an endemic practice among all landed folk, appeared in Marion's case in 1530 when she wadset, or mortgaged, the lands of Balmaddy and Chapeltoun to the abbot's tenants, the Ochterlonies of Kellie, whose castle lay west of Arbroath. She redeemed these lands in due course and kept possession of them all her life. The other characteristic of her business life which showed itself early on in her career was her regular appearance in the central civil courts in defence of her property rights. She was incorrigibly litigious, a habit she may have learned from her mother, her first appearance before the lords of council in Edinburgh being on 23 February 1526 when David Beaton was one of the judges. The case revolved around her attempt to recover the value of livestock that had belonged to her father, Lord Ogilvy, in which she persisted for eight years but eventually lost.

Probably the most stable period of her life was the period from 1524 to 1534 when David Beaton was making a place for himself in the central administration of the country and gaining favour with King James V, and Marion built up the property that was to be the basis of her livelihood. Unlike some women of her social class whom marriage took away from their native district she spent all her life in the same county, Angus. She must have been a familiar figure in Arbroath itself where some of the abbey notaries, including sir William Pettilock, did business for her, where she once redeemed some wadset land at the altar of the Lady Chapel at the Bridgend of Arbroath – redemption money was often counted out on an altar, where it was perhaps felt that people were less likely to cheat – and where she once handed over money unclaimed by her creditor to the keepers of the abbey treasury for safe keeping[10]. Since she had for some time found it necessary to manage her own affairs, Marion had learned to sign her name, leaning heavily enough to split the quill on more than one occasion. It is difficult to say whether women who could sign could write any more, since signing was the basic safeguard in controlling documents in one's own name and therefore of greatest importance. It is possible that some women could read without having much mastery of writing skills.

It was also in the 1520s and 1530s that Marion Ogilvy, now over thirty, bore her large family in quick succession. It is largely his eight recorded children who have earned the Cardinal his notorious reputation in private life, although it is not usually explained that they were all Marion Ogilvy's sons and daughters, which they were. Margaret, whose name was a variant on her mother's, who occasionally used it, was the oldest child, 'gotten and born when the Cardinal was young before he was a priest', as Lord Herries later described her. Elizabeth, probably named after David Beaton's mother, Elizabeth (or Isobel) Monypenny, was said to have completed her eighteenth year by 18 September 1545[11]. George, who shared his name with David Beaton's brother who had been at Orleans university with him, is mentioned only once when in March 1531 he had letters of legitimation with his sisters[12]. He presumably, therefore, must have died in childhood. The oldest surviving son, David, and the next one, James, were probably near of age, being sent to France as 'scholars' in 1542[13]. Alexander, who studied in France in the 1550s and who read Greek, probably came next[14]. John, who enjoyed the patronage of James Beaton, last pre-Reformation archbishop of Glasgow[15], went to France with him in 1560. Agnes was probably the youngest child who, like her brother, Alexander, lived on into the seventeenth century[16].

The family's circumstances changed somewhat after about 1537 as David

Beaton's rapid ecclesiastical promotion enabled him to lay his hand on greater territorial resources. In December 1537 the Pope provided him to the French bishopric of Mirepoix on the nomination of King Francis I, and in the late summer of 1538 he crossed to France for his consecration. It was probably on that occasion that he received full ordination to priest's orders. At Christmas 1538 he was raised to the dignity of cardinal, and two months later 'succeeded' his uncle as archbishop of St Andrews and head of the ecclesiastical establishment in Scotland. After an essentially secular career as royal councillor and diplomat he was now also a churchman in the real sense. We do not know whether his crossing of this Rubicon had any effect on how Marion Ogilvy regarded her situation. Apart from the change in his status David Beaton had spent more time away from home since 1534, when he had resumed his role of Scottish ambassador to the French court in order to accomplish long-standing plans for a Franco-Scottish royal marriage; he spent the equivalent of four and a half out of the next ten years in France where he had French citizenship.

From 1539 onwards pieces of land from the archbishopric estates in Angus, chiefly in the barony of Rescobie, were granted to his sons, David, James, and Alexander, liferent use of the property usually being reserved to Marion Ogilvy, rather in the way that a laird would provide for his family. In addition, the Cardinal seems to have planned to settle the family in property which would be held from the crown, as distinct from church land, in order to put the Beatons back among the landed families of Angus, from which part of the country his own forebears, as well as Marion's had come. In 1539 David, and in the event of his death, James, received a royal charter of the Mains and other parts of the barony of Backie which had been forfeited from Lord Glamis by King James V and of which Marion already held a lease. The charter granted permission to rebuild the old tower of Backie[17]. Three years later, while the Cardinal was in France, some of those who were unfavourably disposed towards him persuaded the King to annul the charter on a technical point of law and the Beatons lost this opportunity to acquire a secular property. Characteristically, Marion raised a legal action in the court of session in defence of her lease, in which she was eventually successful.

The early 1540s also saw the first plans take shape for the careers of her oldest sons. This meant their joining the queue for church livings and, in their case, obtaining a papal dispensation to take even minor orders in spite of 'defect of birth'. The petitions of David and James are recorded in the papal register of supplications in the autumn of 1542. In July of that year these two had left for France in the charge of sir David Christison, a priest in the Cardinal's employment. They were described as 'scholars' and must still have been under university age, although that was younger than it is now. They sailed from Kirkcaldy, with wraps and clothes specially bought for the voyage, and may have arrived in France just before the Cardinal left it for home after a long diplomatic mission. Alexander, their younger brother, was then being tutored by Mr Adam Mure, at one time master of Edinburgh grammar school but later a secretary in the Cardinal's household[18]. Mure, who was a Paris graduate and Greek scholar, may have introduced Alexander to that language. For the oldest brother, David, the options were kept open. An academic education and even the holding of a benefice did not necessarily lead to the career of a churchman in those days, nor did they rule-out the possession of property. Although he was 'dispensed to hold clerical character' and in the summer of 1543 was provided to the canonry of Govan in Glasgow cathedral, when it should be resigned by his uncle, Mr Walter Beaton, the Cardinal's brother, he in the event was to become the laird of an Angus barony in assocation with his mother, while it was his slightly younger brother, James, who 'inherited' the canonry of Govan. Petitions to Rome took so long to be dealt with that by the time David's provision to Govan came through the Cardinal had acquired the land and settled it on him, or rather, on Marion Ogilvy for her lifetime and to David after her.

The Angus barony was North Melgund, lying between Forfar and Brechin in Aberlemno parish, of which the heiress, Janet Annand, had married the Cardinal's older brother, James, in the 1520s. James probably died in 1542, for towards the end of that year the Cardinal bought the estate from his widowed and, as it happened, childless sister-in-law soon after his return from France. Shortly afterwards he resigned it to the King, as was the common procedure, for a new charter to David, and his mother in liferent, the charter being confirmed by the crown in January 1543[19]. Melgund castle, on the Mains of the barony, was to all intents and purposes Marion Ogilvy's house. The lands, from which she became known as 'the lady of Melgund', were her direct responsibility for the rest of her life. In a sense it was also the home of the Cardinal and herself. A clear indication of this was the placing of their respective arms over the windows of the hall in the keep, as a laird and his wife might have done on their newly-built house; the shields, which were placed there at the building of the tower, are Marion Ogilvy's lion *passant* over the west window facing towards Airlie, and the Cardinal's arms as they appear on his second seal, used as archbishop of St Andrews between 1539 and 1546, over the south window which looks towards Fife. The castle is an impressive and interesting building even as the ruin it now is. Although the keep, designed on an L-plan and rising to four storeys and attics, has six-feet thick walls, a very high watch turret and shot-holes in the basement, the outer wall of the ground-floor passage leading from the entrance to the cellars is very thin, revealing that the keep is not a genuine ancient structure but built in the sixteenth century to look like one[20]. In spite of its apparent fortifications and 'retrospective' keep, Melgund was definitely a house built for comfort rather than defence, but intended to create an impression of ancient lineage and territorial possession. Even in planning his house, whether he built or substantially rebuilt it, the Cardinal did so, characteristically, for effect.

Inside, the ascent to the private hall in the tower is gradual, by way of an exceptionally wide, shallow-stepped circular staircase, at the foot of which is Marion's heraldic lion and initials, not the narrow, easily-defended turnpike one would normally find in a genuine medieval building. In the hall itself the fireplace is tucked away comfortably into a corner, not given the prominence one would expect in a public apartment. On the north side of the eastern range, which extends from the keep on two floors, are three bedchambers, all with fireplaces, convenient as guest rooms. On the south side of this range are the spacious withdrawing room and hall, the windows of the latter being high enough to take pieces of furniture beneath them. The most pleasant feature is the withdrawing room, measuring 24 feet by 20 feet 6 inches, which has a window on two sides and communicates with the eastern-most bedchamber and its small pentagonal dressing room, and with the circular stair which leads to the garden entrance to the castle. Apart from the architectural evidence there is very little information on the building operations. In the summer of 1543 wood 'to build the place of Melgund' was bought from a citizen of St Andrews, William Mayne, and shipped to Arbroath[21]. It is possible that money from the revenues of Arbroath abbey was used for the building, for which the accounts have not survived.

Ironically, the acquisition of Melgund with its new responsibilities came at the beginning of an unsettling time for Marion Ogilvy and her family. After the defeat of the Scots army at Solway Moss in December 1542 and the death of King James V soon afterwards, the Cardinal was a key figure, on the conservative, Francophile side, in a struggle for the regency with the earl of Arran and the Anglophile party, led by the earl of Angus and his brother, Sir George Douglas, and supported by a group of magnates and professional laymen and royal servants who, among other changes, advocated a positive reform of the church which, at its most radical, threatened the church's property. On 27 January 1543, just four days after the Beatons' charter of Melgund had been confirmed by the crown, the Cardinal was forcibly removed from the privy council and put in detention, while Arran's party began negotiations with Henry VIII for a marriage between the infant Queen Mary and Prince Edward of England and passed legislation through parliament permitting the use of the bible in English. After regaining his freedom in April, the Cardinal returned to St Andrews, and also spent some time at Arbroath, while he waited all summer for the Governor, Arran, to capitulate to him. By the end of the year he was once more in control, both in the council, as chancellor, and in the church's public, reactionary policy. The proposed marriage treaty with England was annulled and earlier laws against heresy reaffirmed, cancelling the Governor's legislation approving the use of the English bible. In the early weeks of 1544 the Cardinal launched an attack against heresy in Perth, where he had repeatedly tried to remove the provost, Lord Ruthven, and those who favoured reform.

In 1544 and 1545, however, he paid the price of his success. Resentment grew among those who had aligned themselves against him, particularly among those who wanted an Anglo-Scottish alliance and who favoured religious reform. The Cardinal was increasingly obliged to buy support through charters of church land or bonds whereby, in return for their promises of support, he maintained members of influential families in his great household at St Andrews; these were chiefly young men such as Lord Gray, Norman Leslie, son of the earl of Rothes, and the son of Sandilands of Calder, from a family with protestant sympathies. Some of his former servants, such as Patrick Crichton of Brunston, now disillusioned, joined a conspiracy to kill him, offering to do so for the benefit of the English king who regarded the Cardinal as the chief obstacle to his plans in Scotland. There was an ambush in Fife, foiled by his bodyguard, and an attack on his baggage train in Perthshire by the servants of the laird of Tullibardine. On top of this came two devasting invasions by Henry VIII's commander, the earl of Hertford, in 1544 and 1545 during which the Cardinal showed signs of concern for his personal safety and interests; he made his will in the comparative security of Stirling in May 1544, and in August 1545 he obtained a second set of letters of legitimation for his sons. It may have been the growing threat to church property that made him anxious to settle his family in possession of land held from the crown. In the summer of 1545 they obtained possession of South Melgund, in security, to complete the holding of the barony, and the lands of Woodend, which were transferred to Marion by a neighbour, William Cramond of Auldbar, in a charter dated at Melgund on 30 June 1545[22]. The estate was completed by David's possession of the kirklands of Aberlemno, of which the Cardinal granted him a charter, as archbishop of St Andrews, in the spring of 1546.

By this time plans were being made for the marriage of Marion's oldest daughters, but a scheme to marry Elizabeth to the son of the laird of Panmure, near Brechin, did not work out. As early as 1533 when Elizabeth was six years old and Thomas Maule twelve, the foundation of a future alliance was laid, as part of which Thomas Maule of Panmure granted Elizabeth the lands of Scryne, to be redeemed on her marriage, or that of her oldest sister, to the heir of Panmure, an echo of the Midmar indenture of 1503 involving Marion Ogilvy and her sister[23]. Thomas Maule, who had been brought up in the Edinburgh household of Robert Leslie of Innerpeffer, a layman trained in the law and David Beaton's legal adviser in Arbroath affairs, was later a member of the Cardinal's household. In April 1541 Thomas granted Elizabeth Beaton a charter of Scryne in his own name, indicating that arrangments for their marriage were nearing completion. However, King James V was reported to have advised him against the match, saying '"marry never ane preistis gett", whereupoun that marriage did ceas'. The Cardinal, offended at the Maules, demanded compensation for breach of the contract, and Thomas remained in the household. On 28 Spetember 1545 Elizabeth, on completion of her eighteenth year, renounced her marriage contract with consent of her mother and her curators, John Beaton of Balfour, the Cardinal's nephew and captain of St Andrews castle, and David Rutherford, his master of the horse.

The marriage of the oldest daughter, Margaret, sealed an alliance with the family of the powerful earls of Crawford. Margaret's future husband was the nineteen-year old David Lindsay, Master of Crawford, the grandson of the eighth earl and son of Alexander, known as 'the Wicked Master', who had been disinherited. David, ninth earl, a cousin of the main line and a widower at this time, had adopted David Lindsay as his heir. The ninth earl had already borrowed money from the Cardinal, in return for which he wadset land to the latter's son, David Beaton of

Melgund. On 10 April 1546 the marriage contract of Margaret and the Master of Crawford was drawn up at St Andrews[24]. The earl agreed to resign all the family's major land-holdings and all his rights to land that was then in wadset in favour of the Master and his heirs, keeping the liferent use of them, within the terms of the charter of entail drawn up after the 'Wicked Master's' disinheritance. The terms of the contract make plain that the Beatons gained more in prestige than in real property as a result of the alliance. Margaret's portion was the liferent of some half-dozen territories, while if the earl and her husband should both predecease her she was to resign the liferent of the central barony and ancestral castle of Finavon to the heir, in exchange for the Mains of Downie as a Dowager's provision. It was also settled that the Cardinal should cause the Master to sign a bond that he would 'stand gude son and servand to the said earle and that na molestatioun sall be made in time cuming to him, his person, tennentis, landis and gudes', a precaution prompted by the experience of the Master's father's improvidence. Margaret's tocher, which the Cardinal bound himself to pay the earl in three instalments over the next year and a half, was the princely sum of 4,000 merks.

The marriage was celebrated in Angus towards the end of April 1546 with considerable pomp and magnificence according to contemporary allusions and may have taken place at Ethie where the Cardinal was on 29 April. The following day at Arbroath he transferred to Marion Ogilvy his own rights to certain debts, for which he held some land in security, a kind of gift on the occasion[25]. The background to the celebrations, however, was one of national and international tension, following the effects of the two English invasions of 1544-5, for which the Cardinal's aggressive, anti-English policy was widely blamed, and during which his attempts to summon realistic French assistance had been humiliatingly unsuccessful. Opposition to him had taken on the aspect of a personal vendetta, fuelled by local quarrels, an Anglo-Scottish conspiracy and a mood of revenge among those committed to religious reform as a reaction to the trial and execution early in March of the preacher, Mr George Wishart, who had gained a widespread acceptance. On hearing of the movements of the English fleet the Cardinal returned south early in May in order to inspect the fortifications of his castle and the Fife coast. He was in Edinburgh by the middle of the month with his household and possibly members of his family, as the Master of Crawford and some of his younger relatives were there. There is no record of whether Marion Ogilvy was in Edinburgh with him at this time, but when he returned to his castle at the end of the month she was also in St Andrews, probably lodging in the city.

Thanks to John Knox, we know that she spent the night of 28 May with the Cardinal in the castle[26]. Much building work was still going on, but the workmen left in the evening to return early in the morning. The captain of the castle, the Cardinal's nephew, John Beaton of Balfour, and his wife, Agnes Anstruther, had living accommodation in the castle but appear to have been away at this time. The absence of the captain may have been one of the circumstances that decided those who conspired against the Cardinal's life to make the attempt at this time. When Marion the castle on the morning of 29th May by the postern gate, she was seen by the assassins who were waiting to enter the castle gateway under cover of a load of building materials. Marion was probably still in her St Andrews lodging when the alarm was sounded and the general uproar erupted, as people tried to find out what was happening. The cause was traced to the castle, where the assassins, in order to satisfy the crowd, had hung the Cardinal's body over the wall-head of the great east blockhouse in which he had been slaughtered. Even although she must have lived with the possibility at the back of her mind for some time, the shock of what had happened must have been traumatic. Added to the personal loss must have been a strong feeling of vulnerability and fear for the safety of her property and possessions, a fear that was to be justified before long. She evidently left for Angus immediately, probably taking the ferry as the most direct means of transport. Local legend used to have it that on 29 May each year the figure of a woman, waving towards the castle of St Andrews, could be seen at Claypotts castle. There was no castle at Claypotts in 1546, but its site was a ferry landing-stage.

The legal records are silent as to Marion's whereabouts that summer, but on 4 August Patrick, Lord Gray, sheriff of Forfar, who had had several years of bad relations with the Cardinal, broke into 'hir place and fortalice of Athy by night and put out hir servants.'[27] It was, of course, her writs and papers he was after, for it was very difficult to defend one's possession of property in court without these. Marion lost the opportunity of pursuing her action against Gray, because when her allegation was read in court on 11 August she did not turn up. Clearly, personal and material insecurity were disrupting her family's lives in these months after the Cardinal's death, as those who resented her accumulation of property tried by various ways to get their hands on it. By November, however, she was in St Andrews, where the Cardinal's body still lay unburied in the castle where his assassins were besieged. On this occasion she pursued Gray for his intention to evict her from her lease of the lands of Backie; the judges decided to take the case out of Gray's hands as sheriff of Forfar and into their own, in the court of session. Meantime, in Fife, the sheriff there, who was Norman Leslie, one of the slayers of the Cardinal, was endeavouring to have Marion's son, David, removed from the lands of Cairnie. David and his curators were unable to turn up in court in January of 1547 due to 'occasioun of certane inconvenientis' – the risk of confrontation with friends of his father's murderer. The lords removed this case also, from the tolbooth of Cupar to that of Edinburgh, and exempted a list of the late Cardinal's relatives and dependants from Norman Leslie' jurisdiction. The Cardinal's legal heir, his brother, Walter Beaton, archdeacon of Lothian and canon of Govan, did what he could for the family's interest by tackling the confused business of the Cardinal's testamentary debts, while Margaret and Agnes Beaton tried to recover £1,000 due to their father by his brother-in-law and nephew, the Grahams of Fintry, which he had assigned to his two daughters before his death, and certain movables stolen from Ethie by Lord Gray and his accomplices.

Whether the pressure of these months told on Marion's nerve or she simply recognised her vulnerability as a single woman, even though the law upheld her rights, she married in the summer of 1547.[28] Nothing is known about her husband except his name, William Douglas; not one that would have commended itself to the late Cardinal who had once sworn that he would drive the whole house of Douglas out of Scotland even if it cost him his life. Someone surnamed Douglas (first name unknown) is found in connection with the administration of the Arbroath abbey estates at this time, and it may have been that Marion sought security in a husband who could defend her properties held from the abbey, which were those most under threat. The marriage was short-lived: she was still unmarried on 15 May 1547 but on 18 September of that year she is referred to as 'Marion Ogilvy of Melgound, relict of William Douglas', perhaps poor William was killed at Pinkie that month. By then Marion was recovering her nerve. In October 1547 she was doing legal business in Dundee, in 1548 she won her case to keep the lands of Backie since this time Lord Gray failed to turn up, and in 1549 her ingenuity in managing her affairs stretched to having a clause in a legal document tampered with by an amenable notary, for which she had some of her stock on the Brunton of Ethie confiscated.

The last attack on her home at Ethie severed her personal connections with the Arbroath area, although she continued to hold land there, and caused her to withdraw entirely to Melgund. The Carnegies of Kinnaird, who were then building up their landed interests in the Arbroath area, had their eyes on Ethie. On 13 February 1550 Robert Carnegie of Kinnaird and his wife, Margaret Gardin, received a feu charter of the barony of Ethie from the new abbot of Arbroath, James Beaton, the Cardinal's nephew, the documents being drawn up at Ethie castle by sir William Pettilock, a notary who often did business for Marion and her family. Carnegie was keen to remove Marion, the sitting tenant, from the castle, even though she had a life-lease. In order to get hold of her title deeds he and some friends broke into both Ethie and Melgund towards the end of 1550, making off with a quantity of legal papers and personal possessions. Nothing daunted, Marion took him to law and had the satisfaction, although not until 21 October 1552, of receiving from him in public court in Edinburgh the bundle of documents which he had stolen, including those granting her son Alexander pensions from the kirks of Monifeith and Abernethy, his appointment as archdeacon of Lothian which he had lately 'inherited' from his uncle, Walter Beaton, and some papers relating to debts which the Cardinal had owed to King James V.[30] From about 1552 Marion's name disappears from the records in connection with Ethie, suggesting that she may have abandoned it to the Carnegies at this time.

As the struggle to defend her property diminished in the 1550s she turned to settling the affairs of her family. Elizabeth married Alexander Lindsay of Vayne, whose castle was fairly near her sister's home at Finavon.[31] Vayne has sometimes been mistakenly identified as a castle built by the Cardinal, and the legend that a son of his called Thomas drowned in a nearby pool may derive from an accident to

PLATE 1

Houston House, West Lothian, which John Shairp began to build
about the year 1600 (Photograph by courtesy of the Royal Commission
on the Ancient and Historical Monuments of Scotland)

PLATE 2: A reconstructed bird's eye view of Lochleven castle, Kinross-shire; J. Begg, 1887 (Photograph by courtesy of the Royal Commission on the Ancient and Historical Monuments of Scotland)

PLATE 3

A sixteenth century tailor at work at his cutting-out board which has a box for off-cuts underneath. Patrick Nimmo, in accounting for setting up his booth, refers to his 'kist and over buird'. (J. Amman and H. Sachs, *The Book of Trades*, 1568)

PLATE 5

The so-called 'Armada Jewel' believed to have been given by Queen Elizabeth to Sir Thomas Heneage after the defeat of the Spanish Armada in 1588; one side shows the Queen in profile, the other the device of Noah's Ark, symbolising, it is said, the Protestant church, with an inscription which (translated) reads, 'calm through the troubled waves'. The device of 'the airk of Noe' was used on a jewel belonging to the Edinburgh merchant, Janet Fockart, who died in 1596, and occurs on a jewel in the Museo Poldi-Pezzoli, Milan. (Photograph by courtesy of the Trustees of the Victoria and Albert Museum)

Plates 6 and 7

Mark Ker, Commendator of Newbattle abbey, and
Helen Leslie (Plate 7 opposite) who became his wife after
the Reformation, painted in the 1550s by Willem Key
(Photographs by courtesy of the Trustees of the National
Galleries of Scotland)

PLATE 7

PLATE 8: St Nicholas's Church, Prestwick, Ayrshire, drawn by A. Henderson and lithographed by D. Allan for *Records of the Burgh of Prestwick*, published by the Maitland Club in 1834 (Photograph by courtesy of the National Library of Scotland)

Elizabeth's son, Thomas. A dispute between Elizabeth Beaton and the Maules of Panmure in 1556 over the lands of Scryne, which had been conveyed to her by the abortive marriage arrangement of over twenty years earlier, was settled at Edzell castle, near the earl of Crawford's home, by a panel of arbiters which consisted of the earl, Robert Carnegie of Kinnaird and Marion Ogilvy herself.[32] The unusual appointment of a woman to such a panel is eloquent of Marion's determined personality. Agnes's husband, James Ochterlonie of Kellie, near Arbroath, died in December 1561, leaving her with a family of six young children. Agnes was seriously ill in the summer of 1562, when she made her will, naming her mother, her brother Alexander, and the laird of Vayne, her brother-in-law, as tutors to her children. The full inventory of her moveable goods preserved in sir William Pettilock's protocol book gives the impression of a comfortable home at Kellie Castle.[33] Agnes recovered, however, and remarried, her second husband being George Gordon of Gight from a recusant family, a connection which drew the Beatons into the circle of the earl of Huntly in the latter part of the century. Many years after their marriage George granted his wife a charter 'in fulfillment of a promise and for kindnessess done to him before his marriage by the late Marion Ogilvy, lady of Melgound'.[34]

In the early 1550s David, James and Alexander Beaton were in Paris studying at the college of Cambrai, partly supported by grants from the revenues of the late Cardinal's French bishopric of Mirepoix in the Languedoc and partly from cash advanced by their mother to the humanist scholar, Giovanni Ferrerio, who had lived in Scotland under the patronage of the Cardinal's colleague, Robert Reid, bishop of Orkney, but was now resident in Paris where he took an interest in the Cardinal's sons. The money was sent to Ferrerio through the Italian banker, Timothy Cagnoli, who visited Scotland 'to do banque' from time to time.[35] David Beaton was back in Scotland by 1557, his career in the church effectively cut off by his marriage to Margaret Lindsay, daughter of Lord Lindsay of the Byres. Two years later he was still arranging to pay back to a friend money which he had borrowed in France. James returned in 1556 when he was incorporated in the university of Glasgow but two years later he was once more in France, with Alexander, when their mother again sent them funds through Cagnoli. A few of Alexander's books, including his Latin-Greek dictionary have survived. His various sources of income in Scotland meant that his mother acted as his 'factrix' while he was abroad; in the autumn of 1557 she went personally to the kirk of Monifeith to demand his teinds from the parishioners, once appearing there at 9.00 am for the purpose, when the vicar of Monifeith and others accompanied her round the various places from which the teinds were due.[36]

Changes were on the way by 1559-60 as the military resistance of the Lords of the Congregation brought to a head the long connection between desire for religious reform and alliance with England which the Cardinal had sought to control in his last years. Of the members of Marion Ogilvy's family, Alexander seems to have come to terms with the new establishment although he did not take office in the Reformed kirk and was loath, as many benefice-holders were, to part with his 'third', a tax lifted from benefices after 1562 which was partly used for the upkeep of the ministers. While in France in 1559 he had leased his parson's manse of Currie to George Crawford of Leffnoris, an Ayrshire laird of reforming sympathies, from whom he had trouble in getting the house back in 1563.[37] James died in the summer of 1560. On 31 July, Marion and Alexander, accompanied by James Ochterlonie, Agnes's husband, arrived at the parish kirk of Govan to warn the parishioners about payment to them as James's executors of certain dues of his parsonage of Govan. The witnesses of their public announcement included Mr Thomas Archibald, chamberlain to James Beaton, archbishop of Glasgow, who had left Scotland only a few days before.[38] Marion's youngest son, John, who shared with her the lands of Spitalfield near Arbroath, had been in Glasgow since at least 1557 and may have left for France with his cousin, the archbishop.

In the 1560s, the years of Queen Mary's personal reign in Scotland, David Beaton of Melgund found himself a place at court. In June 1562 the Queen sent him to France to represent her at a baptism. Randolph, the English ambassador, who reported this to Queen Elizabeth's minister, William Cecil, explained that David was 'named by his father Beton, called with us Monsieur Mildrome [Melgund]', adding that David had told a friend that he expected to see Piedmont before he returned. In their association with France the Beaton sons were following in the footsteps of their father who had spent the formative years of his career in Paris where, so a cousin once remarked, he might easily have been taken for a Frenchman. Their European education showed in David's elegant italic handwriting. In 1567-8 the 'laird of Melgon' was once again in France and according to one informant was one of the 'papists' who had recently replaced protestants in the French King's Scots Guard, partly through the influence of the archbishop of Glasgow who was now living in exile in Paris. This duty at the French court meant separation from his wife, Margaret Lindsay, with whose strongly Protestant family David's relations may already have been strained. In May 1567 the commissary court of Edinburgh tried to enforce a payment of £40 by David to his wife, a sign of the break-up of their ten-year marriage. Alexander Beaton stayed at home after 1560 and married Margaret, daughter of the laird of Allardyce, in Kincardineshire. In the summer of 1568 Marion's family circle was touched by the drama of the Queen's escape from Lochleven castle and the hurried, and extraordinarily successful, attempts to gather her supporters together before the battle of Langside on 13 May. Between her escape on 2 May and the battle many hastily-written letters were sent out from the Queen's headquarters at Hamilton, and others were sent by her chief supporters to friends and allies in their areas. On 8 May, six days after the escape, the earl of Crawford, Margaret Beaton's husband, and James, fifth Lord Ogilvy, met under Marion's roof at Melgund and wrote to the laird of Inverquharity:

> '. . . becaus her grace could not have opertunity to wreit to every
> man in speciall, hes desyrit us to wreit to yow as ane of her knawin

faithfull and constant leges to address yowr selff wythall your kyn, freindis and servandis, bodin in feir of weir [armed in warlike array], to accompany us . . . to meit us in Cuper of Fyff this nixt Fryday at evin to ryd wyth us to hir grace . . .'.[39]

In spite of this appeal, however, and the fact that Lord Ogilvy and others proclaimed Queen Mary at nearby Brechin and Forfar, the laird of Inverquharity joined the King's party.

The periodic absences of the laird of Melgund meant that Marion, by now in her mid-sixties, was running the estates from day to day, as well as supervising her household and keeping an eye on the revenues of her distant properties. She no longer made journeys to Edinburgh to appear personally in court in defence of her rights, so in the 1560s she employed advocates, most frequently Mr Clement Little. Although she regularly paid her contributions from her properties to the stipends of Reformed ministers, such as Mr James Balfour, minister of Idvie, she was probably an important influence in her family's evident adherence to Roman Catholicism. It is a pity that there are no surviving presbytery records for the district to tell us whether she got into trouble with the church authorities for recusancy, as Jane Gordon, countess of Sutherland did. In these years when her life centred more and more on Melgund we find her defending her tenants against charges of theft of stock and lending some of them money. She also acquired property in the nearby city of Brechin. Her sons occasionally dated their legal transactions at her home, reflecting her continuing interest in their affairs. In January 1566, David, Alexander, and John Beaton of Balfour, the Cardinal's great-nephew, were recognised as his executors for gathering in his remaining debts. Two years earlier they had won some compensation from those who had stolen his moveables during the time the assassins had held the castle of St Andrews. Marion had a handful of faithful friends to help her in transacting her business, among them sir William Pettilock, the notary, dene Richard Craik, former monk of Arbroath abbey and keeper of its treasury, and Mr James Balfour, dean of Glasgow cathedral, who belonged to the family of Balfour of Tarrie, near Arbroath.

As she entered the 1570s there were family problems which must have been distressing in her later years. Agnes's second husband, George Gordon of Gight, was at one time forfeited for recusancy. In May 1573 David and his cousin, Graham of Fintry, were arrested at Dundee on their return from France, suspected of bringing Jesuit literature into the country. Their imprisonment, however, did not last long. David's marriage to Margaret Lindsay eventually broke up about this time after he acknowledged the birth of a child to him in France. Elizabeth, lady of Vayne, had died in 1574. Only Margaret, David, Alexander and Agnes were certainly alive at this time. John may have died in France, as his property of Hospitalfield had passed by 1565 to Alexander, who made his home there for a time.

The greatest disappointment must have been the breakdown of Margaret's prestigious marriage to the earl of Crawford, after twenty-six years. Only something fairly serious could have caused this to happen after such a long time. The tenth earl had a troublesome temperament and was often on bad terms with both his Lindsay and Beaton relatives. He had enjoyed Queen Mary's favour in the 1560s, being made provost of Dundee in 1565 on her nomination and witnessing her controversial marriage contract to Bothwell in 1567. Trouble between him and his wife may have had something to do with his weakness for being led into plots which endangered his house and its fortunes, perhaps coming to a head in July 1568, two months after Queen Mary had fled to England, when Crawford, the earl of Huntly and Lord Ogilvy laid an ambush for the earl of Morton as he was on his way to hold the regality court of Kirriemuir for his young nephew, the earl of Angus. According to 'News out of Angus' sent by an informant to Cecil, Morton himself remained at Glamis on hearing of the plot and sent three deputies to Kirriemuir to hold the court. While they were sitting a messenger arrived, 'in great speed on a horse without a saddle', sent by Lady Crawford to warn them that the earl of Huntly with 700 horse was only a mile away. The three deputies sent to Morton telling him to stay away; he withdrew from Glamis to Dundee and with an escort from Lord Gray, the sheriff of Forfar, made his way to Stirling. Meanwhile, on hearing of the escape of Morton, the earl of Huntly went to Finavon where he met Crawford, after which they both left for the Mearns. Margaret Beaton's action in averting the success of the plot, which could have resulted in disaster for her family, may have led to a quarrel with her husband. He turned her out of the house of Finavon and she went to live with her mother at Melgund castle. A year later the earl took ill and died, in February 1573, at his house at Cairnie in Fife, while an action for divorce was pending.[40]

Marion Ogilvy herself became seriously ill in the summer of 1575. David and Alexander, Mr James Balfour, David Lindsay, heir of Vayne, her grandson, dene Richard Craik, and William Henry, vicar of Auldbar, who may at one time have been a private chaplain, were among those with her when her testament was drawn up at Melgund during the last week in June, and Margaret may also have been with her.[41] Marion was comfortably off even at this late date, and at her death her estate was worth over £3,000, £1,000 of which was in coin. Her household goods were valued at £100, when an average laird's might be between £40-50. As was common in sixteenth-century testaments her moveables were not separately listed. The stock on the land suggests extensive farming operations, with 14 oxen at Chapeltoun, 14 on the Brunton of Ethie and 44 on the Mains of Melgund on to which the castle windows looked out. Money had been borrowed from her, for which she held land in wadset, such as £70 by Patrick Gardin of that Ilk, £40 by David Ogilvy of Glenislay and 226 merks by her near neighbours, the Cramonds of Auldbar. Her own debts reflect the pattern of her contacts: these include £400 to John Ogilvy of Kinnordy in terms of a marriage contract to which she was a party, presumably on behalf of a young relative, £20 to John Dempster, litster [dyer] in Brechin, £22 7s 2d to sir John Ritchie, an ex-chaplain who did legal business for Alexander Beaton and herself. She owed rents to the abbey of Arbroath, now the property of the Hamilton family, teinds from the lands of Melgund to the collegiate church of Methven, and £6 to the surviving monks of Arbroath for their 'common victual'. The financial side of life in the sixteenth century could be quite complicated, with overlapping interests in the land and legal owners of certain ecclesiastical revenues still living well on into the second half of the century. Marion's servants were due their fees – £3 6s 8d to her cook, Robert Smith, £4 2s 6d to her servant, Alexander Simpson, £5 6s 8d to Thomas Lyn, 'foreman about the place'. Her latter will began with the non-committal statement, 'I leve my saule to God omnipotent . . .', a phrase used by the Catholic minority in a period when many wills were prefaced with a clear statement of Protestant belief. She asked to be buried in the Ogilvy aisle of Kinnell parish church, leaving £20 and two bolls of meal to be distributed to the poor on the day of her burial. She made bequests to a handful of servants and dependants: £40 to her cousin, Janet Ogilvy, £13 6s 8d to Isobel Greg 'for her lang service', £6 13s 4d each to Katherine Bell, a servant, Willie Haghouse, 'to put him to ane craft', and William Henry, vicar of Auldbar, with 'my goun and doubleit'. She made David and Alexander her executors and Mr James Balfour the oversman of her testament to see that everything was carried out properly. She died during the last week of June 1575.

The Cardinal's family held Melgund for only two more generations. David, like other Catholic gentry and nobility, found himself in the favour of James VI in the 1580s and was for a time a master of the King's household. A few months after his mother's death he married, as his second wife, his cousin Lucretia Beaton of Creich, sister of Mary Beaton, Queen Mary's lady-in-waiting.[42] In 1586 he transferred Melgund to his son by his first marriage, James, the last of the family to make his home there. A son of his marriage to Lucretia, Dr David Beaton, was made physician to Charles I on the occasion of the latter's Scottish coronation in 1633[43]. Alexander Beaton, archdeacon of Lothian, as he was usually called, lived at Hospitalfield near Arbroath in the 1570s, but by the early 1580s was in Edinburgh where he had a protracted tussle with the town council over the resignation of his parsonage of Currie for the endowment of the new 'tounis College' – the university[44]. By 1611 his son, David Beaton of Carsgownie, was on the wrong side of the law for 'non-communicating in his paroch kirk of Aberlemno', perpetuating the family's adherence to Catholicism. Alexander himself died about 1611-12. Margaret was alive in 1583 and on good terms with her own family in spite of the earlier separation from her husband.[45] Agnes probably suffered most in the upheavals towards the end of the century when those known as 'the Catholic earls', led by Huntly and Errol, rebelled against the King, bringing hardship on their followers although they themselves escaped. Agnes's third husband, Sir Patrick Gordon of Auchindoun, whom she married about 1582, was implicated not only in the murder of 'the Bonnie earl of Moray' in 1591 but also in the affair of 'the Spanish blanks', a suspected Catholic plot, in 1592, and was killed at the battle of Glenlivet in 1594. She lived on into the early 17th century, dependent on the kindness of friends.[46]

It is not difficult to see Marion Ogilvy, having made good the disadvantages of her youth, as the unifying force in her family's lives, or her home at Melgund as the centre of many of their activities. Her influence on their outlook must also have been considerable. Margaret's spirited action in averting disaster from her family suggests inherited initiative, even when it recoiled on herself. The fact that different members of the family, to the second generation, were out of sympathy with the Reformed kirk was probably partly due to Marion's attitude. It is significant that not until she was gone did her family make their peace with their father's surviving murderer, John Leslie of Parkhill. Of course, the involved business of settling on the assythment, the ancient compensation for the loss of a blood relative, and the drawing up of the letters of slains, or formal deed of remission by the injured family, not to speak of the protracted business of settling the Cardinal's debts, took some time to finalise. However, it may be more than coincidence that the letters of slains, signed by the Cardinal's relatives, were granted to Leslie of Parkhill within days of Marion Ogilvy's burial. She died between 22 and 30 June and the letters of slains are dated 3 July, at most thirteen days after her death.[47] Perhaps it was done after her funeral; a family contract drawn up in the kirk of Kinnell in 1577 may suggest that they regarded the Ogilvy burial aisle as the next best place to her living presence at Melgund in which to do family business. [48] The letters of slains of 3 July 1575 were signed by her grandson, David, eleventh earl of Crawford, John Beaton of Balfour, the Cardinal's great-nephew, and Robert Beaton the latter's brother, David Beaton of Melgund and his brother, Alexander, David Beaton of Creich, who was shortly to become the laird of Melgund's brother-in-law, and Mr James Beaton, the laird of Creich's brother, Sir David Graham of Fintry, the Cardinal's nephew, John Beaton of Capildrae, son of his cousin, Archibald Beaton of Capildrae, William Ochterlonie of Kellie, Agnes's son, and David Lindsay of Vayne, son of Elizabeth. They, – 'having consideratioun to the repentance of John Leslie of Parkhill . . . declared unto them manifestly for the slaughter of the said David, Cardinall, thair maist tendir freind', (that is, blood relative), forgave him the 'rancour of their wrath and deidlie feid [feud] and malice'. The deed was signed at St Andrews where the crime had taken place. We cannot help wondering whether respect for, or obedience to, Marion Ogilvy's wishes was one reason why it had been delayed for almost thirty years.

MARION OGILVY

NOTES

1 J.B. Paul *The Scots Peerage*, I, 114; *Accounts of the Treasurer of Scotland*, I, 200

2 Airlie Muniments, (S.R.O.), GD16/1/1

3 *Records of Aboyne* (New Spalding Club), 220

4 Airlie Muniments, GD16/42/5

5 *Liber S. Thome de Aberbrothoc* (Bannatyne Club), II, 692

6 *Ibid.*, II, 230, 341, 697, 698

7 *Ibid.*, II, 747

8 *Ibid.*, II, 797, 804

9 Acts of the Lords of Council and Session (S.R.O.) xxxiii, fo 194

10 Register of Acts and Decreets (S.R.O.), vi, fo 227

11 Dalhousie Muniments (S.R.O.), GD 45/16/619

12 *Register of the Privy Seal*, II, 843

13 R.K. Hannay, ed., *Rentale Sancti Andree: Accounts of the Archbishopric of St Andrews, 1538-46* (S.H.S.), 139

14 Register of Deeds (S.R.O.), ii, fo 347

15 *Registrum Episcopatus Glasguensis: Episcopal Register of Glasgow* (Bannatyne Club), II, 364, 365

16 *Register of the Privy Council*, V, 406

17 *Register of the Great Seal*, III, 1931

18 *Rentale Sancti Andree*, 199

19 *Register of the Privy Seal*, III, 50

20 D. MacGibbon and T. Ross, *The Castellated and Domestic Architecture of Scotland*, IV, 311-16

21 *Rentale Sancti Andree*, 168-9

22 *Register of the Great Seal*, III, 3108, 3138

23 Dalhousie Muniments, GD45/16/575

24 *Ibid.*, GD45/17/9

25 Acts of the Lords of Council and Session, xxviii, fo 85v

26 J. Knox, *History of the Reformation in Scotland*, ed. W.C. Dickinson, (1949) I, 76

27 Acts of the Lords of Council and Session, xxvi, fo 16v

28 Court of Session processes, first series, (S.R.O.), CS 15/1 (1548)

29 *Accounts of the Treasurer of Scotland*, IX, 357, 390

30 Register of Acts and Decreets, vii, fo 1

31 *Ibid.*, xii, fo 470

32 Register of Deeds, i. fo 292v

33 Miscellaneous Collections (S.R.O.), GD 1/311/2

34 *Register of the Great Seal*, IV, 2740

35 Protocol Book of James Harlaw (S.R.O.), fos 61, 75v; Register of Deeds, RD ii, fo 347

36 Protocol book of William Pettilock (S.R.O. Microfilm), RH4/96, fo 32v

37 Register of Acts and Decreets, xxvii, fo 350; Currie parish was appropriated to the archdeaconry of Lothian, so that Alexander had the right to parsonage teinds and the parson's manse.

38 *Protocols of the Burgh of Glasgow* (Scottish Burgh Records Society), V, 1384

39 Ogilvy of Inverquharity Muniments (S.R.O.), GD 205/1/7

40 Diligence records, Forfar (S.R.O.), DI 57/1, fo 42-4

41 Edinburgh Commissariot Records, Register of Testaments (S.R.O.), CC8/8/3 fo 260

42 *Register of the Great Seal*, V, 2251

43 *Roll of Burgesses of Edinburgh, 1406-1707* (S.R.S.)

44 *Extracts from the Records of the Burgh of Edinburgh* (Scottish Burgh Records Society), IV, 311, 321

45 Register of Deeds, xxiv, fo 91

46 J Durkan, 'William Murdoch and the Early Jesuit Mission in Scotland', *Innes Review*, XXXV, 1 (1984), 6

47 *Historical Manuscripts Commission Report IV*, 492

48 Register of Deeds, xvii, fo 27v

JOHN SHAIRP

Advocate and Laird of Houston

d. 1607

Although the name of John Shairp turns up continually in contemporary records he is mentioned only briefly in biographical dictionaries[1]. Clearly, however, he was successful in his chosen career of advocate and influential in the affairs of his day, a figure to whom both civic and royal authority turned for advice and, at times, financial help. He became the owner of considerable property, in different parts of Scotland, was knighted by King James VI in 1604 and died a rich man by the standards of his day, leaving moveable estate of the then colossal sum of £58,000 Scots, or over £4,800 sterling. He saw many public changes during his lifetime: the Reformation settlement of 1560 and the events that surrounded it, the civil war that followed the deposition of Queen Mary in 1567, and, near the end of his life, the departure of the royal court from Edinburgh on the accession of King James VI to the throne of England. A year later, in 1604, as one of the Scottish commissioners in London for discussions on the projected parliamentary union of the two kingdoms, he was knighted at Whitehall.

It is possible to piece together a picture of his private and public life from surviving records, which include, fortunately, the archives of the family he founded, the Shairps of Houston, with a great many papers dating from the sixteenth century, a quantity of which is his incoming correspondence. Very little is known about John Shairp's early life or family background except that he may have been born about 1504 and that his father was a burgess of Edinburgh and had property in Borthwick's close. John matriculated in St Leonard's college in the university of St Andrews in 1553, later graduating Master of Arts, and probably studied law as well. Like its sister colleges St Leonard's had been founded, in 1512, to strengthen the authority of the late-medieval church in Scotland and loyalty to its teaching through an educated clergy. Long before Shairp arrived, however, St Leonard's had a reputation for fostering Protestant beliefs and in 1545 it broke free of the paternalist control of the priory of St Andrews, under which it had operated since its foundation, acquiring the character of an independent college. In the decades before the Reformation the contemporary phrase 'to have drunk of St Leonard's well' meant to incline towards heretical beliefs. From his later actions it is clear that during his period of study John Shairp came to support the Reformed teaching. On his return to Edinburgh he was sufficiently versed in Protestant doctrine to be one of those set aside by the General Assembly of 1560 to be ministers under the new church order, who were to await a parish. At that point, however, he decided to change careers. It is John Knox in his *History* who remarks bitterly that by the summer of 1562 'some ministers had left their charges and entered into vocations more profitable for the belly; against who were acts made, although to this day they have not been put into execution'. His marginal note 'Sharp left preaching and took him to the law', carries the feeling that the law's gain was the kirk's loss.[2]

Although originating in the 15th century, the profession of advocate, to which John Shairp was admitted on 8 January 1562, had grown in consequence since the endowment of the college of justice, or court of session as it came to be known, in 1532, when eight men were selected by the lords to be 'general procurators'.[3] These advocates were appointed by the lords of council and session on petition from applicants, who usually mentioned their academic qualifications and/or practice in the law. The profession became increasingly competitive as the numbers rose with time, from nine in 1549 to sixteen in 1565 and over fifty by 1586. It would appear that some Edinburgh advocates were richer than a number of merchants and much richer than many lairds. It was not long before they began to seek privileges as a body and in 1549 Mr Thomas Marjoribanks obtained an order from the crown that their personal causes should enjoy the precedence in court already granted to prelates and the judges themselves. In 1582 Shairp is referred to as 'dene of the advocattis of the sessioun' and later in the century advocates were included with writers to the signet in a contribution from the college of justice to the chair of laws in the new university of Edinburgh, a transaction in which they were again represented by Shairp.[4]

Not only did advocates become more prosperous and influential but the vocation became more professional. Originally drawn, as was the bench, from the pre-Reformation clerical establishment, the faculty of advocates became increasingly recruited from men without an ecclesiastical background but trained in the law, some of them in European law schools. The profession tended to become hereditary, and between 1601 and 1660 as many as a quarter of practising advocates were sons of lawyers. Indeed, John Shairp's second son, and subsequent generations of the family, were to follow in his footsteps to the Scottish bar.

In 1565 Shairp appears in the fifth out of seven tax categories of advocates lending money to the crown; he would certainly rate nearer the top before the end of his successful career.[5] Employed to act for the town council in the role of intermediary as early as the winter of 1560-1, that is before his admission as an advocate, he may have done part of his legal training in the civic service.[6] About this time he is found taking delivery of some of the council's 'books' from workmen in the castle, which had presumably been put there for safety during the recent military operations, and writing out legal documents on the council's behalf. He appeared as a procurator for the town on many subsequent occasions in the civil court, in all kinds of causes from disputes with the craft incorporations to the case of a Leith skipper accused of evading his porterage fee. The town council also continued to employ him in an advisory capacity, on matters, for example, concerning the custom and impost, and on the burgh's rights to land belonging to a chapel in Newhaven; and, in December 1596, he was paid 'to pass to Linlithgow' with others to pacify the King over recent riots in Edinburgh. His position of trust with the burgh council may account for the fact that not until 16 October 1590 was it felt necessary to admit him formally as a burgess and guildbrother, free, 'for his services to the toun and by right of his late father'.

He had other clients, of course, for whom he appeared in court as procurator in their names, or as prolocutor, or forespeaker, in company with them if they wished to appear personally in court. His clients were many and varied: John Hamilton, archbishop of St Andrews, Lord Robert Stewart, Queen Mary's natural brother, Lord Oliphant, the son of the laird of Urie in Kincardineshire, the earl of Athol in his suit against the earl of Argyll over their claims to the office of justice general, the earl of Eglinton against the commendator of Kilwinning abbey, the widow of Crichton of Cluny over the abduction of her daughter, and Robert Wilson, a money-lender in Leith. To determine how successful Shairp was in practice would necessitate combing the registers of acts and decreets (nearly 200 volumes for his lifetime), but these would tell us little about his expertise as a lawyer since the reports of the cases are terse and relate only to their final stages and the decisions reached. What we would need would be the papers compiled by the advocate in preparing his brief, and these have gone. Perhaps Shairp's prosperity is, after all, as Knox implied, the best indication of his professional success.

From letters he received we may get some idea of the kind of advice people asked him for, which may or may not have turned into a brief. Some of it was on general legal business, as when Alexander Bruce, the laird of Earlshall in Fife, asked for his advice on 'framing', or drafting, the charters of his daughter's settlement and on revising some security writs.[7] Another correspondent asked the advocate to delay instigating letters of horning for the recovery of a debt until the writer and his debtor had had a chance to meet, 'at the quhilk tyme I doubt not bot ane end salbe put to thir materis freindfullie'.[8] Good for social relations, no doubt, but bad for legal business. One grateful client, the laird of Minto, congratulated Shairp on his handling of a case:

> 'we maun all thank yow and reward yow as we may . . . As to my awin part I am content ye haif fyve merkland of the best I haif, as I wrait to yow, for ane werkman is worth his waige'.[9]

It would not have been the first merkland to fall to John Shairp, not always as a 'thank you', one suspects, but in lieu of a debt that could not be paid.

In the 1570s Shairp is found witnessing charters, not just in Edinburgh, but at Byres in Fife for Lord Lindsay of the Byres, out at Gosford in East Lothian for Alexander Acheson, the rich landowning merchant who became his father-in-law in 1574, at Duns in Berwickshire for George Hume of Spott, on that occasion with Mr Thomas Craig, advocate, and in Edinburgh itself, in company with his servant, Mr Thomas Scroggie, for John Dunbar of Mochram.[10] It is possible that he had advised on the framing of the charters concerned. People sometimes used his services in handing in documents for registration. Younger 'men of law' at the beginning of their careers trained in his office: Mr John MacCalzean, probably the son of the judge, Mr Thomas MacCalzean, was called his servant in 1578, as was Hugh Adamson, son of William Adamson, writer to the signet, in 1588. Mr Thomas Scroggie, his servant who remained with him till the end of his life, writing documents and letters and dealing with Houston estate business for him, later became an advocate himself. Shairp's second son, also called John, is found writing a charter for Alexander Bruce at Earlshall in 1597, and one for the master of Rothes at Leslie in 1606, a year before Shairp's death. John Knowles, a notary, was also in his service. We can see here some kind of apprenticeship, even career structure, in the practice of the law. It is also interesting that through the labours of these younger men Shairp's office was doing a certain amount of general legal practice, like a writer, in addition to his own practice of advocate in the courts; as in other contemporary 'crafts' the lines of demarcation were more loosely drawn than they were later to become.

He had other sources of income. The business of money-lending was one in which many lawyers and merchants dealt, and Shairp was no exception. In February 1574 he had a brief note from Lord Glamis:

> 'I have ado with money at this tyme, being disapointit of sum that I luikit for, and thefor will put yow to charge to gif to the berar hereof, David Falconer, four or five scoir pundis, quhilk salbe delyverit to yow at my returnyng, or sooner gif ye desir'.[11]

The advocate sent him the five score, for which the servant signed the receipt on Lord Glamis's note, the following day. The abrupt form of the request suggests that it was not the first from Glamis – almost like a note to a merchant asking for an other ell or two of cloth. In March 1574 William Campbell of Cessnock, in Ayrshire, wrote to Shairp asking his advice about feuing land belonging to a chapel at Galston, a property asset which Campbell wished to exploit. The servant who brought the letter to the advocate also carried £30, part-payment of a loan which Campbell promised to repay in full by the appointed day, adding, 'I pray yow becaus it is the tyme of labour, spair my furthcuming as lang as is possibill'.[12]

An advocate with a busy practice would have the cash in hand to lend at interest. In 1581 there were twenty-nine 'men of law' including Shairp, who could lend the King 1,000 merks each (£666–13s–4d). Ten years later Shairp himself lent the King's comptroller £500. The sums revealed in Shairp's testament as being owed to him on the basis of bonds with interest are sometimes staggering: 20,000 merks from the earl of Linlithgow, 15,000 from Sir Patrick Hepburn of Wauchton, 12,000 from the earl Marischal, for example. Interestingly, the debts owing to Shairp at the time of his death were more than four times the amount of money that he owed to others. Repaying such loans meant for the debtors virtually mortgaging incoming rent or even parting with their property. Some would wad-set, or pledge, their property or rents to Shairp in return for the loan, a common practice and a dangerous one because if the debtor was eventually unable to pay, his property might be adjudged to belong to the creditor for good. These arrangements brought in considerable annual income to the advocate, provided, that is, the dues were promptly paid: half the grain rents from Wester Cowden, for example, from the earl of Morton, half those of Halton from the earl of Mar, worth £260, 200 merks annualrent, or interest, from the lands in Fife belonging to Balfour of Burleigh, and other lands held in wadset from Lord Glamis, David Wood of Craig, near Montrose, and from Nicol Cairncross, the Edinburgh merchant, from land in his native Roxburghshire. If John Shairp, advocate, had ever been called upon to fill up an income-tax return he would certainly have needed a separate sheet for his 'any other income' information. He also drew annual rents from Edinburgh property, including £120 from what had formerly been the town mansion of the archbishops of St Andrews but which was now occupied by a merchant, Samuel Burnet, as well as annual 24 bolls of barley from Duncanlaw in East Lothian from Lord Hay of Yester, and 4 chalders of oats from the kirklands of Currie from Patrick Adamson, archbishop of St Andrews (the vic-tual probably being sold for cash). In addition to all this he had after 1598 a gift of a barrel of salmon at Lammas each year from the provost and baillies of Elgin; when we note that the provost of Elgin was also the Lord President of the college of justice, Lord Fyvie, we can see the reason.

In addition to his advocate's practice and the income which it gave him the opportunity to acquire, Shairp also became a considerable landed proprietor in his own right. He purchased a property as far away as the Isle of Whithorn through his connection with another judge, Mr Patrick Vaus of Barnbarroch, which brought him in around £30 a year, and in Angus, from which part of the country his family is said to have originally come, he bought the lands of Ballindoch in 1585 for 9,000 merks from John Lovell, and Hiltoun of Cragy, near Dundee, the previous year for 4,500 merks from Scrymgeour of Glaswell and his wife. These widely scattered property interests needed a factor or other representative on the spot. At Ballindoch John Lovell, the man from whom Shairp bought the land, stayed on as tenant, transmitting the rents from the subtenants to Shairp's factor, John Baxter, a Dundee merchant, and writing to the owner himself from time to time on local business. We can see how complex things could become; there were two men between the cultivators of the ground at Ballindoch and their landlord –

the main tenant and former owner, John Lovell, and the factor in Dundee to whom their rents were sent to be forwarded to the advocate in Edinburgh. In addition a 'bailie' was employed for general oversight of Shairp's interests.[13]

In the summer of 1587 Lovell wrote to Shairp about the letting of the ground and the eviction of a tenant, one John Henderson, 'quha hes waistit in drinking all his gear', adding that he had been replaced by Robert Dog, 'ane young man dwelling presently in the toun [i.e. of Ballindoch]'. Letters like these certainly help to put some flesh on the bare bones of an estate rental. Money was due to come in the opposite direction, too; Lovell reminded the landlord that he was waiting for a remittance from him, saying, 'we haif had gryt skaith in wanting [lacking] of that siller as lang'. In 1595 the grain rents from the Angus tenants were sold back to them for £2,800, giving us some idea of the scale of the annual income from these lands. Ballindoch was later settled on one of Shairp's younger sons, William. We have to remind ourselves that Shairp acquired these properties not by taking a fancy to them in the property columns of a newspaper, but through social and professional contacts with landed men in Edinburgh, where many of them spent some time during the year, often during the progress of a 'guid ganging plea' in the the law courts.

However, Shairp may have bought the estate of Houston in the parish of Uphall, then called Strathbrock, in Linlithgowshire, largely with a view to providing himself with a retreat from Edinburgh during the court vacations, as well as furnishing himself with a territorial designation as he became prominent in his career. It would also become an inheritance for his family. He bought the estate in 1569, fairly early in his career, from James Robertson, burgess of Linlithgow, who had acquired it through the Hamiltons of Milburn.[14]

Biographical information in *The Faculty of Advocates of Scotland* states that Shairp was twice married, first to Euphemia Acheson and then to Margaret Collace of Muirtoun in Morayshire. However, his testament –and in particular those passages in which he details the provision for his family – makes clear that he had been married three times. He refers to the children of his first and second wives, all of whom were of marriageable age and were in most cases settled, this being in 1607. Since he married Margaret Collace only in 1591 it is unlikely that any of these would have been her children. His first wife Agnes Moffet bore him three sons, James, John and Patrick, and two daughters, Anna and Agnes.[15] She must have died when her family were fairly young, for in 1574 Shairp married Euphemia, the daughter of the wealthy Alexander Acheson of Gosford, merchant and master of the King's mint.[16] Euphemia also had three sons, Alexander, Andrew and William, and three daughters, Euphemia, Isobel and Helen. Houston would certainly be a more convenient place for a large, double family to grow up in than a cramped lodging in the crowded burgh of Edinburgh. It is not certain what kind of house was on the lands when Shairp bought them. The earliest document which definitely mentions a dwelling is that of 1526, when Sir James Hamilton of Finnart, the King's master of works, acquired the property, being 'bound' to build a mansion upon it.[17] John Shairp's charter of 1569 mentions 'the manor place', but this standard legal form tells us nothing about the building itself.

Although in 1576 the lands were erected into a barony, thus enabling the advocate-laird or his representative to hold courts which the tenants would attend, the advocate's possession of his new estate was not at first peaceable since several other families claimed title to it, or to an interest in its revenues. It is ironic that Shairp, lawyer that he was, had to put up a protracted defence of his title to full possession of the property, against the heirs of Matthew Hamilton of Milburn, relatives of Alexander Stewart, captain of Blackness castle (a state prison) who claimed right to a gift of the feu-duties of Houston, and against a family named Steel, who seem to have been middlemen-tacksmen of the lands, under whom the local inhabitants would have been subtenants. Shairp persisted until he succeeded in getting the middle layer of interest removed. Not until 1590 did he get a crown confirmation of his title, and in the spring of 1600 he transferred the property to his second son, John, reserving the liferent to himself. It is in this transaction that mention is made of 'the fortalice of which the building is begun and with God's help will shortly be finished'.[18]

What difference did the presence of a new landlord make to the people of Houston in Strathbrock, or Uphall, parish? They may not have seen much of him employed in the capital as he was, but it is doubtful if they could have seen any more of James Robertson, burgess of Linlithgow, or of Matthew Hamilton of Milburn. They must have been used to paying rents to a factor, or to someone collecting rent locally on his behalf, but after Shairp began to build the new house the landowner's presence may have been more felt. The parish in which Houston lay had about 400 communicants at the end of the century and the barony itself may have had a fair number of tenants. Only fragments of what can be called estate papers have survived. Here and there they preserve the names of inhabitants: John Gudlat, David Frame, weaver, who was Gudlat's subtenant, and George Carfin who was his servant, William Clarkson, James Todd, Adam Forsyth, smith, his son, Robert, Charles Everar, James Douglas, Alexander Aitkenhead, John Cunningham and David Halket, all at Houston; George Brock in the Eastertoun of Strathbrock, surely an indigenous family, Michael Barton and his servant, John Hall in Stankards; John Ranald in Kirkhill and Thomas Hodge, miller at Houston mill.

The tenants paid rent in a mixture of money and grain – maill and ferme, in contemporary terminology. Once or twice Shairp is found pursuing some of them for arrears, but it was difficult to extract payments. The Clarksons received a warning to pay arrears in January 1599, yet three years later a precept warning them of imminent removal had to be served on them.[19] Still in occupation six months later, they signed a contract with their landlord by which they agreed to remove and Shairp promised to write off their bad debts, amounting to £50 and six bolls of grain.[20] By then they had got themselves a lease of another holding.

The belief that Scottish peasant farmers were summarily evicted is something of a myth, and this document is nothing less than a bargain between the Clarksons at Houston and their lawyer landlord, after they had stalled the payment of rent for about four years. In another arrangement, James Todd at Houston, who nearly lost his holding because of arrears of rent, acquired a renewal of his lease for two years on formally renouncing his holding in his landlord's hands and signing a bond by which he promised to pay the arrears.[21] This document can be construed to show the initiative of either the landlord or the tenant but at least it shows that removal first of all required renunciation by the tenant of his right, after which on this occasion at least Todd received some reprieve.

Thomas Lyle, the grieve at Houston, was paid 40 merks a year (£26–13s–4d), John Matthew, the hind, who was in charge of the other labourers, the equivalent of two chalders of oats. John Knowles, the notary, who probably acted as clerk of the estate books, kept Shairp in touch with his affairs in the country. In May 1603 he sent a note of those tenants who were in arrears of payment. Some of the notary's facts were gleaned from Shairp's wife, Margaret Collace: 'the ladie hyrself knawis quha hes payit their dutie of the crop of 1602'. He concluded his letter to Edinburgh reassuringly, 'our folks ar all bissie at the peittis [peats] and the gardiner is bissie in the yaird'.[22] There is not enough continuous information to help us determine how much income was derived from the rents of Houston during Shairp's lifetime. The earliest surviving rentals date from 1617-18 and are incomplete. However, in 1618 the grain rents were sold for over £1,000 Scots alone.[23] The money rents, judging by other contemporary examples, may have been in the region of 20% of the whole, bringing the total rents in the lifetime of Shairp's son to somewhere around £1,500 while the feu-duty payable to the crown amounted to £40.

In 1583 the tenants became involved in the landlord's affairs in dubious circumstances.[24] The trouble began when John Lindsay of Covington, for whom Shairp had recently pleaded at the bar, took offence at the advocate's accepting a brief from Hamilton of Stanehouse, Lindsay's 'partie adversar'. Lindsay's cause had concerned tenants from whom Stanehouse was also demanding rent, so that he now vowed revenge on Shairp, refusing the latter's written explanation that Stanehouse had asked him to act for him 'generallie . . . eftir the deceis of Mr Clement Litill quha wes his advocat befoir'. Such were the hazards of the profession. Lindsay sent his son and some servants to Houston where, in collusion with a local man they set fire to the laird's corn. After court action by Shairp Lindsay was forced to grant a bond of reconciliation under penalty of 1,000 merks.

The household divided its time between Houston and Edinburgh, the master probably spending most of his time in the latter. By the later years of Shairp's career the family was certainly comfortably off, with gold and silverwork worth more than £2,000 and much jewellery, some of it given to the daughters on their marriages. Shairp's library was valued at £200 and his household goods at 2,000 merks, that is, over £500.[25] In 1604 when Shairp went to London as a commissioner about the Union, he took 3,500 merks 'spending siller' with him, leaving 23 or 24,000 merks at home in the keeping of his wife, the gold locked in 'steill boxis'.[26] Money was certainly spent on luxuries; as early as 1575 Shairp ordered some goldsmith's work from France through George Kerr in Dieppe, who lost the order and had to write for a repeat description of the desired articles, 'quhairfor I have left in suspence, quhill I knaw yor mynd, and send yow ane doubill gylt [presumably, cup] quhilk is coverit, weyand two merk ane unce, and ye sall resave the samyn furth of Johne Dawsonis schip, God willing'.[27]

There is no surviving portrait of Sir John, as he became in 1604, and we cannot help wondering what kind of man he was. There are no contemporary comments apart from that of John Knox, which implies that he had an eye to the main chance. He once reminded a friend, 'It is not sua that I suld be suittand', meaning 'it is not for me to be on the asking end'.[28] His remarks about his sons-in-law, as he set down the details of his daughters' settlements in 1604, are forthright: William Little, husband of Anna, his first-born, he described as 'a man bayth godlie and civill', while in Mr William Hume, his daughter Agnes's second husband, he is 'somewhat disappointit'. He was reasonable enough, however, to accept his daughter Isobel's love-match; 'quhais affectioun in hir marriage with Robert Dunbar of Burgie I wes contrainit to follow in respect of the treuth and honestie of the gentilman. I hope giff thai leiff togidder for ane happie success'. Robert Dunbar belonged to Moray and was a nephew of Shairp's second mother-in-law, Helen Reid.

Maybe Sir John was the kind of man whom one tends to approach through an intermediary when things go wrong – a little testy, perhaps, in later life. On one occasion one of his friends, Mr Thomas Marjoribanks, wrote to Mr Thomas Scroggie, Shairp's secretary, to decline an invitation to himself, his wife and daughter to attend a Shairp family wedding.[29] His excuses are timeless: 'my wyfe will on naiwayis gang nethyr to brydell nor na uthyr banket [banquet] . . . and hyr dochter, ye knaw scho is naywayis meit [fit] nethyr be hir self nor be hyr apparell to be ther . . . For myself, to com now upoun this suddand advertisement I can of na wayis be abill to satisfie his desyr . . . mak my excus in sic fasoun as yow think guid'. Perhaps the Marjoribanks family, having been asked at the last minute, were offended. Since the clerk register refers at the beginning of the letter to 'the gudeman' having recently behaved 'crabitlie' when his servant had failed to find Marjoribanks, perhaps professional relations were not then at their best. Shairp's wife kept Mr Scroggie acquainted with the affairs and expenses of the household at Houston. There is an agitated letter to him from her in April 1603 in which she asks his advice on how much drink-silver to give the masons at Houston, 'quha ar cravand ther morning and efternoons', and telling him that the cook is complaining loudly that the chimney is using far too much coal and what should she do about that?[30]

There survive a few tradesmen's accounts, from Thomas Hislop, an Edinburgh armourer, Robert Rankin and John Boyd, two Glasgow masons who worked at Houston house in 1600, William Ramsay, baxter in Linlithgow, Francis Robertson, Edinburgh merchant, and two tailors, John Nimmo in Leith and William Edgar in Edinburgh. A list of Sir John's clothes suggests that he dressed fashionably when not in his advocate's gown: cloaks of grogram taffeta, velvet and serge, trimmed with pasments (lace or embroidered braid trimmings), a velvet sleeveless coat, satin doublet and breeks 'cuttit out upone red taffetie' and pasmented with two rows of trimming 'on all partis, black and red', worth 80 merks (£53-6s-8d) which, incidentally, was more than Shairp paid annually in feu-duty to the crown for the lands of Houston.

In the midst of success there were family tragedies. Mr Alexander 'my greittest hoip of all my children', died at Poitiers in 1604 while studying in France. A year earlier his tutor had written glowingly to Shairp of his son's progress: 'worthy of yor self, als sober, wyse, modest and diligent in his studies as ony that cam out of Scotland thir fyftie yeis bygane . . .'.[34] Even more tragic was the case of the eldest son, Mr James, who became unfit to administer his own affairs and did not inherit Houston, which passed to the second son, Mr John. Sir John referred to James in his will as 'my eldest son quhome God hes viseit [visited] and punist with infirmitie of mynd and bodie' and desired the other sons to have pity on his affliction and see to it that he was 'honestlie sustenit'. James was given property in Edinburgh including his grandfather's old lodging in Borthwick's Close, recently renovated, where he may have lived. James had also studied in France. In 1585 he had written home from Paris to his friend John MacCalzean, like himself an advocate's son, sending greetings to the circle of friends and a copy of Virgil for his younger brother, Patrick, who was than a student at the new university of Edinburgh and was soon to become minister of Uphall, 'I menit not [I did not explain] in my letters to my father, quherin [wherein] I wrett of the Jesuites diligence, of ony disputes of theologie, as it appeiris ye understand, but onlie of disputes in philosophy. In the quhilk, nevertheless, I sall satisfie yor desyr at the next occasione'.[32] One wonders whether James showed an interest in the Jesuits at this time, as a number of his contemporaries who travelled abroad did, and if this may have led to strained relations between him and his father; Sir John's expression with regard to his eldest son, that God had punished him with his affliction, suggests that James had displeased his father in some way.

Sir John succumbed to his last illness at Houston in September 1607 and died there on 10 October.[33] He was attended by Dr Liddell who gave instructions to the apothecary, John Lawtie of Edinburgh, whose account survives:[34]

16 September — 'send to the gudman, thrie unce syrup of lemonis, 12s
— oil of vitriol in a glass, 10s
— thrie uncis concerve of berberie, 4s

21 September — Thrie medecinis for thrie dosis and a dayis compost with rhubarb, and other refresching medecinis, £6 18s

— ane refresching and cuiling compost for thrie
sindrie drinkis to be taken at thrie sindrie tymes,
price of the drink and dose, 9s

1 October   myrrh electuary, 8s

The apothecary eventually supplied the 'greit quantitie' of spices, perfumes, and powders for the embalming, which cost £16 10s, the 'myrrh and aloes and costlie mixturies', a box of 'senseor candillis' at 30s, the powders to burn 'to mak the hous weill favorit', and three musk balls. He ended his account, 'as for my painis and diligence that I usit and tuik in wirking sindry nightis lait at evin, I refer thame to be considerat by yor awin discretiounnis'. Sir John's sons, John and William, paid the account promptly and gave the apothecary £10 for his pains.

Sir John left an endowment to the poor's hospital of Edinburgh and a bursary of 500 merks to a student of philosophy in the new 'tounis college', his sons and their heirs to be patrons of it. He left the faithful Mr Thomas Scroggie 1,000 merks, asking him to 'deliver all my evidentis and writs, alsweill quhilk ar my awin as sic as pertenis to my clientis', to his executors. John Knowles the notary received 200 merks, Hugh Adamson, the writer, £40. Before the year was out the family paid Duncan Gib, a Linlithgow mason, 100 merks for building the first stage of 'ane yle in the kirk of Strathbrok about and abone the buriall place of umquhyll Sir Jhone Shairp of Houstoun thair fader'.[35] In the spring of 1608 Gib received another £40 'for augmentatioun of the hicht of the syd wallis of the Iyle' and in the winter of 1609 two Glasgow masons, one of whom, Robert Rankin, had earlier worked at Houston for Sir John himself, were paid the last instalment of 163 merks 'for thaiking [thatching], pamenting [paving] and compleiting of the Yle'.[36] A happier monument to Sir John is Houston House which he built for his family and which still stands.

JOHN SHAIRP

NOTES

1 Sir F.J. Grant, *The Faculty of Advocates in Scotland, 1532-1943* (S.R.S.)

2 J. Knox, *History of the Reformation in Scotland*, ed. W.C. Dickinson (1949), II, 47

3 G. Donaldson, 'The Legal profession in Scottish society in the sixteenth and seventeenth centuries', *Juridical Review* (1976), 1-19

4 *Ibid.*

5 Register of Acts and Decreets, xxv, fo 141

6 *Extracts from the Burgh Records of Edinburgh*, III, 142, 150; IV, 37, 57, 294, (For later service to the burgh.)

7 Shairp of Houston Muniments (S.R.O.), GD30/1653

8 *Ibid.*, GD30/1638

9 *Ibid* ., GD30/1613

10 *Register of the Great Seal*, IV, 2467, 2776

11 Shairp of Houston Muniments, GD30/1611

12 *Ibid.*, 1612
13 *Ibid.*, GD30/610 (Isle of Whithorn);
    GD30/1635, 1640 (Ballindoch)
14 *Ibid.*, GD30/46
15 *Ibid.*, GD30/811 (Agnes Moffet); GD30/
    785, 786 (will)
16 *Ibid.*, GD30/766
17 *Register of the Great Seal, III,* 381
18 Shairp of Houston Muniments, GD 30/
    155
19 *Ibid.*, GD30/145, 161
20 *Ibid.*, GD30/162
21 *Ibid.*, GD30/149
22 *Ibid.*, GD30/1675
23 *Ibid.*, GD30/611
24 *Ibid.*, GD30/2187, 2188
25 *Ibid.*, GD30/785
26 *Ibid.*
27 *Ibid.*, GD30/1624
28 *Ibid.*, GD30/1662
29 *Ibid.*, GD30/1665
30 *Ibid.*, GD30/1673
31 *Ibid.*, GD30/1672
32 *Ibid.*, GD30/1632
33 *Ibid.*, GD30/786
24 *Ibid.*, GD30/1536
35 *Ibid.*, GD30/1994/1
36 *Ibid.*, GD30/1994/3

JANE GORDON
Countess of Sutherland
1545-1629

JANE GORDON'S fate was intimately bound up with that of the Queen of Scots in the year 1566-67, the most dramatic of Mary's reign, when both women were successively wife to James Hepburn, 4th Earl of Bothwell. Jane, who suffered family tragedy and public humiliation before she was twenty-two, survived her experiences to outlive the Queen by forty-two years and Bothwell by just over half a century. Not only did she keep lifelong possession of the property that came to her by her political first marriage, but after having managed the estates of her second husband, the earl of Sutherland, she had the opportunity at the age of fifty-four to marry the suitor of her girlhood. Perhaps it is appropriate that in this 400th anniversary year of Queen Mary's tragedy the facts of Jane's story should be drawn together.

As a daughter of George, 4th Earl of Huntly, Jane grew up in a large family of nine brothers and two sisters at the heart of a patriarchal society presided over by her father.[1] His territorial possessions and influence in the north-east were enormous, with lands in Aberdeenshire, Banffshire and Angus and a string of castles which included Strathbogie, Bog of Gight, Aboyne, Ruthven in Badenoch and Drummin in Glenlivet. Through marriage alliances and bonds of manrent, his family had connections with scores of landholding families who provided political and military support when required. Huntly in turn gave his support to public authority in the north-east. He was commissioned by Cardinal Beaton in the early 1540s to assist with inquisitions in Aberdeenshire which were aimed at the detection and punishment of heretics. He was bailie of the lands of the bishopric of Aberdeen for his uncle, Bishop William Gordon, and as sheriff of Aberdeen his influence was felt in the affairs of the burgh itself. As sheriff of Inverness, his authority extended to the north and west of that burgh, including the keepership of Inverness and Inverlochy castles for the crown, reinforced by the fact that his cousin was Earl of Sutherland and that he himself became lieutenant in the north for the Queen Regent in the later 1550s. He was also involved in the affairs of central government, was chosen one of the regents for Queen Mary in 1543 immediately after her father's death, and in 1546 on the assassination of the Cardinal he became chancellor of the realm as his great-grandfather had once been and as his own son was later to be. From an early age he had had a place at the royal court. He was the grandson, through his mother, of King James IV and, since his own father had died when he was a child, had been brought up with King James V. From 1549 he held the revenues of the earldoms of Moray and Mar, the former having been previously held by the King's half-brother.

Taken prisoner at the battle of Pinkie in 1547, Huntly was released after having 'used policy with England' and, although he was identified with the French party who in 1548 sent Queen Mary to France to be brought up, he was sufficiently suspect to be imprisoned by the Queen Regent in 1555. Two years later, however, he was again in her service and in 1559 was one of her negotiators with the Lords of the Congregation as the Reformation-rebellion reached its height. During 1560 while events began to favour the Congregation, Huntly sat on the fence, probably influenced by both genuine attachment to the old religion and fear of reprisals should the rebels fall foul of the government. His temporising caused John Knox to call him a 'by-lyer' and his ability to look after his own interests provoked Randolph, the English ambassador, to remark that 'no man would trust him in word or deed'. After great hesitation and after the assurance that the insurgents were not aiming at political revolution, he signed the Last Band of Leith in April 1560, by which time the Congregation was sure of English help. In excusing his reluctance to co-operate he insisted that solidarity of conservative opinion in the north hampered his participation and even threatened his dominion there. He did not attend the parliament of August 1560 which ratified the reformed Confession of Faith, abolished the jurisdiction of the Pope in Scotland, and made the saying of mass, or attendance at it, a punishable offence. He knew about the meeting of Catholics which took place at Dunbar in December 1560 by which time it was said that he had set up the mass again in his home country. According to some reports Huntly appeared to look upon Queen Mary's return to Scotland in August 1561, after the death of her husband Francis II of France, as an opportunity for a conservative reaction to the Reformation-settlement. It was even claimed that he had offered to set up the mass again in three sheriffdoms if she would land in the north and accept his support. There is nothing to suggest that Huntly was planning to unite conservative forces in the north. In any case, the Queen's policy at the beginning of her personal reign, formed out of a combination of her own prudence and the influence of her half-brother, Lord James Stewart, was aimed at maintaining good relations with the Reformed church in Scotland, in return for which Lord James and the politicians condoned her private Catholic chapel at Holyrood.

Huntly was nevertheless clearly and openly the Queen's most powerful Catholic subject. The signs of power and material comfort which surrounded his immediate family and even extended to many of his dependants must have been reassuring facts of life to Jane Gordon and her brothers and sisters. Huntly's living was once estimated at over £660 a year. His rents included huge quantites of grain, animals, and dairy produce which were consumed by the large, peripatetic household. The family's chief home, Strathbogie castle, which he had rebuilt in the early 1550s was well-appointed in its time.[2] In the modern part of the building the beds were furnished with silk, velvet and gold-embroidered coverings, and yellow, crimson, blue, green and violet curtains. Since people then ate and talked as well as slept in the bedchambers, those of Strathbogie were provided with 'burdis' or tables, covered with velvet 'burd claithis' trimmed to match the beds. The hall, where Huntly received his guests like a king, was suitably equipped with 'a claith of state' of crimson satin embroidered with gold, ironically sent to Lochleven for the imprisoned Queen's use a few years later. There were also many-coloured velvet cushions for the seating, and hangings for the walls, one of which was of gilt leather and another, a tapestry, in five pieces 'maid in the figure of birdis and greit leiffis of treis'. Jane's mother, Elizabeth Keith, was a strong-minded, resourceful woman who remained a Catholic, although her brother, the earl Marischal, favoured Protestantism at an early stage and had publicly supported Mr George Wishart, the preacher burnt for heresy in 1546, the year after Jane was born. Jane herself was to remain a faithful Catholic for the whole of her long life.

The family's way of life was shattered in the autumn of 1562 when Queen Mary, with a force commanded by Lord James Stewart, came north to punish Jane's brother, Sir John Gordon, for certain misdemeanors; in June of that year he had seriously wounded Lord Ogilvy in a street fight in Edinburgh and was also suspected, with good reason, of being in a plot to abduct the Queen. Huntly for his part resented the knowledge that early in the year Mary had granted her half brother the title of earl of Moray, of which the lands were still in Huntly's hands, and he gathered a force for a confrontation. Sir John Gordon, having broken out of his prison, harassed the Queen's army on its northern march. Mary reached Aberdeen on 27 August to be met not by the earl himself but by his wife who, surrounded by a court of attendants, pleaded unsuccessfully for her son, Sir John. If, as is likely, her younger unmarried daughter was with her this was probably the first meeting of Jane and the Queen of Scots. Fearing an abduction *coup* by the Gordons, Mary by-passed Strathbogie on her way to Inverness, stopping at Darnaway castle where she made public the gift of an earldom of Moray to Lord James and issued an order to Sir John Gordon to surrender. A snub was delivered by the Gordons when the keeper of the royal castle at Inverness refused her the keys, an act of treason for which he was hanged after Huntly sent an order to him to admit her. Back in Aberdeen, on 22 September, the Queen issued a command to Huntly to surrender. Meantime, a force under William Kirkcaldy of Grange attempted to catch him at Strathbogie, but he escaped and the Queen's soldiers were received by the countess of Huntly at the castle, where the chapel was in readiness for the celebration of the Queen's mass. The earl and Sir John, now denounced rebels, lay low in Badenoch. Elizabeth Keith, having been refused another audience with the Queen, urged her husband to take the offensive. His forces were confined to those of his family, dependants, and local lairds, and their composition certainly did not suggest support on religious grounds. One estimate put their numbers at only about 500 men, and after a brief engagement at Corrichie, Huntly and his sons, Sir John and the seventeen-year-old Adam were captured. Huntly, ageing, overweight, and worn out with the recent exertions, collapsed and died on the field.

The earl's oldest surviving son and heir George, Lord Gordon, Sir John, and his cousin the earl of Sutherland were all condemned to death. Only Sir John, however, was executed, in Aberdeen on 2 November in presence of the Queen who fainted during the proceedings. She spared the life of the heir Lord Gordon who had been in the south while the rebellion had run its course seeking advice from his father-in-law, the Duke of Chatelherault. No mercy was shown, however, to the late arch-rebel, Huntly, whose embalmed corpse was brought to parliament in May 1563 to be solemnly 'tried', forfeited, and attained. The fortunes of the family were now in hands of the Queen to withhold or restore and, whatever their feelings about the late happenings, the break-up of their home and the loss of their possessions, any hope of restitution or forgiveness rested on their willingness to serve Queen Mary.

By 1565 Lord Gordon, his mother and youngest sister were at court where Jane and the countess of Huntly were among the Queen's ladies, the latter being on particularly intimate terms with Mary. George Gordon, who was rapidly rising in royal favour was restored to the earldom of Huntly in that year although the forfeiture of his lands was not cancelled until two years later. He came to associate with James Hepburn, earl of Bothwell, who after two periods of political disgrace was back in Scotland in 1565 and was now Mary's loyal servant.[3] Bothwell's influence in south-east Scotland, both as a landholder and as sheriff of Edinburgh and Haddington, resembled the Gordons' recent power in the north, if on a lesser scale. Under Bothwell's influence Huntly adopted a Protestant stance, refusing, with Bothwell, Fleming, Livingston, and Lindsay, to attend the Queen's mass and the Catholic baptism of Prince James in December 1566. It was Mary's idea to unite her two prominent supporters by the means of a marriage alliance, the marriage of Bothwell to Lady Jane. It was in the interests of the Gordon family to fall in with her plans and from Bothwell's point of view the match had at least one important advantage in that his prospective brother-in-law, forfeited though he was, was financially better off than himself; a good tocher might help to reduce at least some of his considerable debts for which he had had to wadset his lands of Crichton and others. Jane had perforce to accept this step in the rebuilding of her family's fortunes, although not, so it was said, without regrets for Alexander Ogilvy, the laird of Boyne in Banffshire, for whom she had earlier formed a deep attachment.

Catholic scruples, presumably on the part of the Queen and the countess of

Huntly, required the purchase from the Pope of a dispensation for the marriage of Jane and Bothwell who were related within the degrees forbidden by canon law, since Jane's great-aunt, Margaret Gordon, had married Patrick, 1st earl of Bothwell, and it was not until 1567 that the Scottish parliament enacted the decision of the Reformed church that 'marriage . . . be as free as the law of God permits', recognising marriage between those related from the second degree (first cousins) outwards and declaring lawful all such marriages dating from 8 March 1558 onwards. The dispensation was granted by the Catholic former archbishop of St Andrews, John Hamilton, on 17 February 1566.[4] Already, on 9 February, Huntly and Bothwell had settled the business side of the arrangement in a marriage contract drawn up 'with advis and expres counsale of our souverane ladie, Marie quene of Scotland'. By this Bothwell agreed to marry Jane by 1 March and to put her in legal possession for her lifetime of the Mains and castle of Crichton and other lands. Because these were in the hands of the earl's creditors, some of whom were Edinburgh merchants, it was agreed that 11,000 merks of Jane's tocher of 12,000 merks (£8,000 Scots) should be used to redeem the property, to be paid in three instalments the last of which would be due at Whitsunday 1567. The other 1,000 merks was to be handed over to Bothwell himself whenever he asked for it. It was intended, once the lands had been redeemed, that the Queen would grant the couple a new charter in conjunct fee, which would perpetuate Jane's liferent right to them. The Queen was first to subscribe the contract, followed by Huntly, Bothwell, the countess of Huntly, who could not write herself but had her hand 'led on the pen' by her brother-in-law, Alexander Gordon, Bishop of Galloway, Jane herself, and Lords Seton, Home, Drummond, and Oliphant.

Lindsay of Pitscottie records that on 22 February 1566 'the earle of Bothwell was married upoune the earle of Huntlies sister. The King and Queen maid the banqueitt the first day, quhilk continewed fyve dayis with justing and tournamentis . . .'. The Queen also gave Jane 12 ells of cloth of silver lined with taffeta for her wedding dress. Bothwell refused to have a Catholic ceremony, which the Queen had wanted, and the marriage took place a short distance from the royal chapel in that part of Holyrood abbey used by the Protestant congregation of the Canongate parish, where the ceremony was performed by Jane's uncle the bishop of Galloway. At the time of her marriage Jane was described, favourably if prosaically, as 'a good, modest, virtuous woman', and 'an excellent, noble lady'. Time and her later career showed her to be a self-possessed, somewhat straight-laced, clear-headed woman. The wedding miniatures of her and her husband show her as a pale-skinned, sandy-haired young woman wearing fashionable, though not elaborate, dress. Bothwell, with the uncomfortable look of hyper-active people when they are asked to sit still, is painted wearing a gold doublet.

Jane remained one of the Queen's friends in the months following her marriage, her name being included in the list of Mary's bequests which she drew up in June while awaiting the birth of her child in Edinburgh castle; ' a Madame de Boduel, une couiffe [headdress] garnye de rubiz, perles et grenatz [garnets]'.[5]

Papers believed by some historians to refer to Jane's married life suggest that it was not happy.[6] The honeymoon was spent at Seton where her husband was said to have been aware of her preoccupation with thoughts of her lost suitor, who in 1566 married Mary Beaton, one of the Queen's ladies. In March came Rizzio's murder and the Queen's escape from Holyrood, assisted by the countess of Huntly who used the opportunity of attendance on the Queen to collect a note from her which she passed to Bothwell who, with Huntly, met Mary near Seton and went with her to Dunbar castle. Bothwell's support and resourcefulness in this crisis convinced the Queen of his trustworthiness, and from then onwards it was reported that 'the earl of Bothwell had now of all men greatest access and familiarity with the Queen so that nothing of importance was done without him'. After the Rizzio affair Bothwell and Jane went to live at Crichton castle where began her first experience of running an independent household. To domestic responsibility was added the personal strain of living with an unfaithful husband. Bothwell's reputation as a philanderer included the charge of having a few years before abandoned a woman to whom he had been betrothed, Anna Thronsden, daughter of a Norwegian admiral than living in Denmark. In the spring of 1566 he began a liaison with his wife's sewing-maid, Bessie Crawford, daughter of a Haddington smith. Wives of sixteenth-century noblemen and lairds who had been married for financial or dynastic reasons could not easily abandon their husbands, even for the adultery which is often revealed by the mention of natural children in testaments. Jane, like other women in her situation, was obliged to make the best of it, although that does not mean that she did not feel humiliated and angry. Neither does the mollifying gift from her husband in June 1566 of the liferent of the lands and house of Nether Hailes nor the fact that, according to the testimony of a servant, she and the Earl appeared to live 'friendly and quietly together, like a man and wife as the saying is', necessarily mean that she was contented, but rather that she was able to put a face on things, keeping her part of the bargain. Their domestic affairs were to reach a crisis not on account of their personal relations but through a change in Bothwell's relationship with the Queen.

The subject of Mary's relations with Bothwell in the last months of 1566, after she had become estranged from her husband, have been endlessly discussed. There is no need to dwell on it here except to say that the suspicions and allegations of contemporaries at court that the Queen and Bothwell became committed to each other sometime during the winter of 1566-67 cannot be dismissed, although the illustrations of Mary's indiscretions which they later gave in order to prove their case against her are probably inventions. It is beyond reasonable doubt that Mary and the earl had established an intimate relationship before the death of Darnley, and it is almost certain that Bothwell, although formally acquitted, was deeply implicated in the crime at Kirk o' Field. Many contemporaries continued to regard him as guilty although a number of them, perhaps in the hope of trapping him and Mary at the same time, signed a bond on 19 April 1567 in which they supported his plans to marry the Queen.

Jane Gordon must have been aware as early as anyone of her husband's growing attachment to the Queen, whenever it developed. Perhaps Jane was with him in Stirling for the baptism of the Prince in December 1566, from which point some people dated the liaison, when Bothwell played a prominent role, receiving the ambassadors but standing outside the chapel door with Huntly, Moray, and the English duke of Bedford during the Catholic ceremony. Jane was seriously ill throughout the month of February towards the end of which her husband and her brother, Huntly, played golf and took part in archery matches with the recently-widowed Queen at Seton, a circumstance which must have intensified, if it did not partly cause, her distress. At the end of March, long before Bothwell presented the lords with his bond in Ainslie's tavern, rumours were going around that he intended to divorce his wife, some said in order to marry the Queen. This implies that Jane and he had already come to an understanding about the dissolution of their marriage and had said all there was to be said about the reasons for this state of affairs.

Two separate legal proceedings were used to dissolve the marriage of the earl and countess, one Protestant and one Catholic. On 24 April, two days before the stage-managed 'abduction' of the Queen to Dunbar, after which Bothwell obtained her 'consent' to their marriage, Jane Gordon brought an action before Edinburgh commissary court for divorce from her husband on the grounds of his adultery with her sewing-maid a year before. On 3 May, after Bothwell's lawyers had formally denied the charge and witnesses had been called, judgement was given in the countess's favour. She was pronounced divorced from the earl and free to marry again if she chose. The Catholic process was made possible by the restoration of Archbishop John Hamilton's consistorial jurisdiction which he had been granted when a possible annulment of the Queen's marriage to Darnley had been discussed at the end of 1566. Now, Bothwell raised an action in the archbishop's consistory court for the annulment of his marriage, for which purpose a commission was granted by the archbiship to six clerics on 27 April. The commissioners seem to have been reluctant to act and judgement eventually rested in the hands of one of them, Mr John Manderston, canon of Dunbar collegiate church, who may have been under pressure from Bothwell. On 7 May Manderston gave sentence in the earl's favour; his marriage to Jane Gordon was annulled on the grounds that the couple were related within the forbidden degrees of consanguinity and that they had married without a dispensation. But, as we already saw, there had been a dispensation, issued only a year before by the archbishop who now gave his authority to the sentence of annulment.

The whole case was handled with cynicism and with the collusion of the parties concerned, who agreed to suppress the dispensation; it is inconceivable that Mary herself was not aware of this document which, had it been produced, would have prevented her marriage to Bothwell; he himself cared little for laws that got in the way of his ambition; Huntly, whose forfeiture was reversed at the same time as his brother-in-law was acquitted of Darnley's murder, was obliged to facilitate the divorce, as the 'Book of Articles' prepared by Moray for the indictment of Mary at Westminster in 1568 claimed. Jane's collusion in the suppression of the dispensation is not the least important aspect of the whole affair, especially as it was she who took charge of the document itself and carefully kept it among her family's papers for the rest of her life. Perhaps the incentive to agree to the suppression of the dispensation, evidence in Catholic eyes that her marriage to Bothwell was indissoluble, was of a deeper and more personal nature and not simply that she was reminded of her duty to her family's fortunes. Probably she was glad to be separated from Bothwell. On her way back to Strathbogie from Crichton in the summer of 1567, by which time her ex-husband had taken to piracy and the Queen was imprisoned in Lochleven castle, Jane vowed in conversation with her cousin, Agnes Keith, wife of the earl of Moray, that she would 'never live with the Earl of Bothwell, nor take him for her husband'. The allegation that they were in correspondence soon after Bothwell's marriage to Queen Mary may, if it is true, refer to some necessary communication of a business nature. Nevertheless, Jane must for some time have been haunted by the knowledge that, in Catholic terms, she was still legally Bothwell's wife; she had obtained a Protestant divorce for Bothwell's convenience, and he had applied for a Catholic annulment to please the Queen, at the expense of his first wife's conscience. At the time of Jane's second marriage in 1573 she may well have believed a rumour that came to Scotland that year of his death in Denmark. By then she had safely stowed away the dispensation where it remained forgotten until found again in the 19th century among the Sutherland charters.

On 22 August 1567 Sir Nicholas Throckmorton, the English ambassador in Edinburgh, wrote to Queen Elizabeth, 'the Lady Bothwell, sister to the earl of Huntly, passed through the town within these two days, and is gone to her mother and brother in the northern parts'. Only a few weeks previously her former husband had stopped briefly at Strathbogie on his flight northwards after the battle of Carberry where, according to Throckmorton, he asked Huntly for help 'to levye force and make some styrre'. Huntly, by now reinstated in his possessions, had lost a motive for his earlier support of Bothwell; 'he fyndynge Bodwell so Lytle favored in all quarters', the ambassador wrote, 'wyll not adventure muche for hym. And now I heare saye the sayd earle can be contented that Bodwell shoulde myscarye, to ryd the quene and hys suster of so wicked a husbande'.[7] Soon after Jane's return home, the north-east became her brother's recruiting ground for the Queen's party in the civil war between the Queen's men and King's men. Although he attended the Regent Moray's parliament in December Huntly was among the Marians who found courage on the Queen's escape from Lochleven castle the following May, and he was said to have had at one time between 2 – 5000 men in the field in Fife and Angus, let alone in his own territories. He was with the Queen at Hamilton after her escape and, although he was one of those who surrendered to Moray on 14 May, the day after the battle of Langside, he continued to act as her lieutenant in the north, capturing Dingwall castle from

Moray's supporters in October 1568 and receiving widespread support from families such as the Leslies, Cheynes, Barclays, and Abercrombies in the north-east.[8] After the murder of Moray in January 1570 Mary's party felt even stronger although by now the government was campaigning against her supporters, including Huntly. He attended a parliament held by the Marians in June 1571, a few months before his younger brother Adam of Auchindoun, 'Edom o' Gordon' of the ballads, destroyed a force led by the Master of Forbes, the King's lieutenant, with whom the Gordons had their own feud. In February 1573, however, Huntly was one of those who agreed to accept the authority of James VI, at the 'Pacification of Perth'.

Meantime, the castle of Strathbogie had received another refugee, Alexander, 11th earl of Sutherland, then aged eighteen.[9] In the summer of 1567 his father, John 10th earl, and stepmother, Marion Seton, had died of poison administered to them in a meal at Helmsdale castle by Isobel Sinclair, wife of Earl John's uncle, Gordon of Gartly. The deed was part of a conspiracy by members of the earl of Caithness's family, including himself and his brother, Sir William Sinclair of Dunbeath, to eliminate the heirs to the earldom of Sutherland. The Sinclairs resented the recent territorial expansion of the earl of Sutherland, particularly through charters of church land from the bishop of Caithness, from the barony of Skibo in the south to Dounreay in the north where Sinclair of Dunbeath was actually the earl's tenant. Unfortunately for Isobel and her accomplices, her own son, John, next male heir to the earldom, took some of the food and died whereas the young Alexander, arriving late from the hunt when the meal was over, survived. On his father's death Alexander, then only fifteen, found himself in the clutches of the earl of Caithness who took possession of Skibo and Dunrobin castles, harassed the tenants and eventually acquired the ward of Alexander himself. He was forced to marry Caithness's thirty-two year-old daughter, Barbara Sinclair, who throughout their short married life carried on a notorious relationship with one of the McKays. In 1569 the earl was 'rescued' from the Sinclairs by Huntly and his friends.

The earl of Sutherland lived at Strathbogie until his minority expired in 1573. He supported Huntly in Queen Mary's cause, being with him at Hamilton where he signed the Bond in her defence, and took part in the Gordon's struggle against John, Master of Forbes, which culminated in the battle of Crabstane in 1572. He attended meetings of the privy council held by the Regent Mar in May and June of that year. In 1573, after a legal battle, he eventually got himself served heir to his father and sent a messenger into Sutherland to warn the Sinclairs off his lands; the messenger was killed in Caithness territory. At the same time he began an action for divorce from Barbara Sinclair, to whom he had been married while he was under age, but she died before the case was completed. Jane Gordon and he had lived under the same roof for almost four years. Although she was about seven years his senior, their mutual concern for the welfare of the Gordon family in its various branches and their shared experience of having been a pawn in someone else's game, and of having had to endure the humiliation of a notorious spouse, probably drew them together. In any case the restoration of Alexander's fortunes under the protection of the head of the surname, Huntly himself, must have made a match between the earl and Jane seem a suitable arrangement. They were married at Strathbogie on 13 December 1573 and returned to Dunrobin soon afterwards. Although the earl had given a good account of himself so far in his attempts to unshackle himself and his possessions from the Sinclairs' interference, it is known that his physical strength did not match his resolution. It fell to his wife to take on the practical management of their affairs, something which they settled early in their married life, for in less than two years after their marriage she was acting as his factor.[10] 'Schoe wes in a manner constrayned and forced to tak upoun her the manageing of all the effaris of that hous, a good whyle, which schoe did performe with greate care, to her owne credit and the weill of that familie; all being committed to her charge by reassoun of the singular affectioun which schoe did carie to the preservatioun of that hous, as lykwise for her dexteritie in manage-ing of business'.[11]

Even the small quantity of surviving estate papers that date from Jane's lifetime give some idea of the variety of business in which she became involved.[12] Accounts for 1580 and for 1583-5, drawn up when her husband was alive, show her concerned with the day to day affairs of the estates; feu duties were paid to her directly, she authorised payment to one of the earl's creditors, John Mason, 'in compts and rekoning betwix him and the erle accordyng to his tikat', she issued a written precept for the purchase of oxen and the payment of merchants' bills, incurred expenses of £23 5s when she was at Culmaily, a property near Golspie which the bishop of Caithness had granted to the earl's father, and was present with her husband when the accounts of Alexander Ewinson, the chamberlain, were rendered at Dunrobin castle. The accounts for the years 1616-22 are really those of her son, Sir Robert Gordon of Gordonstoun, as tutor for her grandson and his nephew the young earl.[13] Sir Robert, however, lived in England at the court of King James, making only an occasional, difficult journey to Sutherland to attend to business. The information contained in the accounts relates to the daily running of the estates by Jane herself, assisted by her son, Sir Alexander Gordon of Navisdale. Between his visits she kept Sir Robert informed by letter of affairs at home, although she would sometimes hold back the details until he came; 'Sonne, havand the commoditie be this berer [bearer] I have wretin this letir, albeit this lang tyme past I have hard [heard] na word fra you. I mynd not to troubill yow with the cuntra affaris for I suspec ye sal find facherie at lenth quhen God sendis yow weill hame'.[14] From the early years of their marriage the countess had written business letters on her husband's behalf, such as the one she wrote from Elgin in May 1576 to her cousin, Agnes Keith, now the widow of the earl of Moray and wife of the earl of Argyll, asking her, as superior of the lands of Kintessock, to seal and sign an authorisation of the earl of Sutherland's right to receive possession of them: 'and sen [since] my lordis desyr is resonable, doutis nocht bot your ladischip will seill and subscryve the said precept . . . wyth plessour and gude will, and syklyke will caus my lord your husband do the samyn . . .'. She ended, 'I have been the mair hammelie [have taken the liberty] to put your ladischip to this charge that I have evir fund your ladischipis gud favour in all my turnis . . .'.[15]

On paper at least the earldom rents were substantial. The money rent alone amounted to £1,702–0s–4d and the rents in kind to £2,588–0s–4d. However, £800 of the money came from the countess's rents from Crichton, Thornydykes, Borthwick, and Vogrie which were hers in liferent since her marriage to Bothwell – 'which apertenis to the earldom during my auld Ladye Suthirlandis lyftyme'. Moreover, as Sir Alexander Gordon lamented to his brother, 'there is na monie gettable in this cuntray' and in 1616 suggested that 'the puir tenentis' should be asked for only ten merks or 5 firlots of grain, or 'the land will go ley [fallow]'.[16] Expenditure was high, including the paying off of the late earl's debts of nearly £2,000 which left the chamberlain, and Sir Robert as tutor to his nephew, over £9,000 'superexpendit'. The expense of serving the earl heir to his father when the time came was considerable, including £20 to be distributed among the clerks and officers of Andrew Fraser, sheriff clerk at Inverness and £100 given to Fraser himself 'for his pains in taking sasine to my lord and performing his service, for the sasine ox, for a pair of gilt spurris'; the serving of the heir was both a legal necessity and a family celebration.

In addition to the scarcity of money and heavy expenditure were the varied effects of periodic bad harvests. In the spring of 1615 there was famine on parts of the Sutherland estates. In 1623 Jane Gordon advised her son, Sir Robert, then on his way north, that 'horss meit is varay schars [scarce] in this parte, thairfor ye sall do weill to come frome Murray be sie [sea]'.[17] Relations with tenants were not always happy; perhaps the disability of Jane's husband and the later minorities of their son and grandson encouraged independent action among the tenantry and even estate officials, or perhaps Jane was better at the management of the family's affairs, for which her son commended her, than public relations. In 1619 an action in the commissary court at Dornoch 'anent some disorderis committit be the erles tennentis against him' cost £17.[18] At the same time a decreet of the commissaries and 'the custom of the cuntray' obliged the landlord to compensate one of the evicted tenants, John McAlister McHuchone, for the house he had built, to the value of £30.[19] Occasionally the tenants refused to perform their carriage service, an unpopular duty which deprived them of the use of their own haulage animals. In 1616 even the chamberlain, William Innes, supported them in their refusal to transport the teind grain, causing Sir Alexander to write angrily to his brother, telling him that he had had to borrow horses for the job; 'I pray God the earle of Suthirlandis gud turn be never lippinit [trusted] to manie in this cuntray, for I think give [if] thay sawe his bake at the wall in ane gryt mater thay wald stres thame selffis litill to relief him, quhen thai maid scrupill in sik ane triffill'.[20]

The bulky grain rent was not always taken in its entirety to Dunrobin but was stored in granaries; £61 was once spent on 'girnillis at the place of Dornoch' for storing the grain rent of Strathbrora. When it had to be moved around the coastal territories or taken to some town for sale, this involved the expense of ship hire; £5 was paid to the chamberlain and his servants in freighting crears [small trading vessels] in 1619. Labourers were paid to dig peats and transport them overland. The rents in kind included large quantities of tallow, of which 13 stones were handed over 'to my auld ladye' in 1616, from which she sent some for use in the alehouse of Scrabster where the local grain crop was malted. In addition to the basic rent in money and kind, there were custom payments of lambs and kids, due as part of their jointure to Jane Gordon and her daughter-in-law, and poultry and capons, of which Jane herself was due 47½ dozen, used partly in her household and perhaps sold to defray her personal expenses. Fishing was an important part of the northern economy and a considerable element in the estate revenues. The salmon from Brora and Helmsdale were sold to merchants from Inverness, Elgin, or Aberdeen, who sent their servants over to conduct the purchases. There was a stone-built corf-house or salmon-curing shed at Helmsdale, which was repaired in 1617 at a cost of £16.[21] The cruives or fish-traps at Helmsdale and Brora cost £100 to repair two years later, 'being taken away be the speattes of the watteris'. Jane Gordon revived plans by the tenth earl of Sutherland to develop a seam of coal found at Brora in order to supply the saltpan which she had built there. In 1616 the Edinburgh merchant, Alexander Watson, was in London with a hired ship selling salt on behalf of her son, the 12th earl, but two years later a reference to £666-13s-4d got from the sale of 'the iron of the saltpannis of Broray' suggests either that the scale of operations had been reduced or had come to an end altogether.[22]

Circumstances brought the countess continuing responsibilities on behalf of her children and grandchildren. She and the earl of Sutherland had seven children including two sons, Alexander and Adam, who died in infancy. As early as 1580, no doubt because of his poor health, the earl took the precaution of transferring the right to the earldom and its lands to his oldest surviving son, John, reserving his own liferent, a common safety device which was meant to ensure the safe transfer of the property to the next generation when the time came. John, who was still under age when his father died in 1594, spent two years in France, returning to Scotland in 1600. While he was abroad, his mother sent her two younger sons, Robert and a second Alexander, to university 'to be instructed in learning and vertue', first to St Andrews and then Edinburgh. The two daughters were Jane, born on 1 November 1574, who married Hugh McKay of Farr, son of the first Lord Reay, and Mary, born on 14 August 1582, who married David Ross of Balnagowan. In 1599, as her sons were preparing to take over their own affairs, Jane married 'for the utilitie and profit of her children', as her son put it, Alexander Ogilvy of Boyne, the suitor of her girlhood and fellow-survivor of the intrigues of Queen Mary's court, whose wife, Mary Beaton, was now also dead. Their marriage contract, drawn up at Elgin on 10 December that year, provided that Jane should retain 'in her awin hand' her liferent income from both the earldoms of Sutherland and Bothwell. In any case, the laird of Boyne is unlikely to have had ambitions with regard to his wife's income. Having defeated the political and dynastic odds of thirty-three years they enjoyed only a few years together, and after Alexander Ogilvy's death Jane remained a widow for over twenty years.

Her daughter Mary, the lady of Balnagowan, died in 1605. In the years 1615-17 tragedy struck the family of her eldest son, John, 12th earl of Sutherland. In 1615 his youngest child died; 'Whair ye desyir to know of my youngest dochteris name, it wes Marie,' he replied to his brother, Sir Robert in England, 'my lady Mar wes hir godmother. She died twentie dayis since'. The earl himself died in 1616 and his wife a year later; 'a ladie of good inclination, of a meik dispositioun and very provident', as her brother-in-law described her, daughter of Lord Elphinstone. From then onwards Jane Gordon was responsible for the upbringing of her grandson, John, 13th earl of Sutherland, and for the management of his affairs, helped by her son, Sir Alexander Gordon of Navisdale who kept his brother, Sir Robert, the earl's tutor in law, informed of their business by letter. The earl's provision and board at school in Dornoch cost £67–13s–4d a year, paid to the schoolmaster, with £12 for bows, arrows, golf clubs, balls, books, paper, 'and uthir necessaires for his exercises'.[23] Recreation was taken on the links at Dornoch which the earl's uncle and tutor once described as 'the fairest and largest linkes or green feildis of any pairt of Scotland, fitt for archery, goffing, ryding and all uthir exercise, they doe surpasse the feildis of Montrose or St Andrews'. The payment of three bolls of victual to 'the woman that dressed and cured my lordis heid' may refer to some mishap during exercises.

Jane and her recently widowed daughter-in-law did not agree about the earl's schooling, only one reason for their unhappy relations in the last year of the younger countess's life. The latter had wanted to send her son to her father, Lord Elphinstone, although Sir Robert Gordon, as his tutor, had the right to decide. Jane explained this to him in a letter from Dunrobin on 24 September 1616;

> 'I put your brotheris sonne to Master Jhone Gray to lerne sum mair
> vertes [virtue] nor he culd sie athir with hir or me. I was advertist
> that scho myndit to have sent him to hir father, and there eftir to
> have purchest your gud will. Gif [if] ye be burthenist thairwith,
> advyis quha sall furneis him, for my moyen [means] is not meit
> [sufficient] for sic voyagis, and I beleve thay sall be sweir [loath] to
> wair [spend] on him thameselvis . . .'.[24]

The earl's sisters, Elizabeth and Anne, were brought up by their grandmother; their clothes cost over £131 in 1617, the year of their mother's death. When Elizabeth was married to Crichton of Frendraught in 1619 Sir Robert Gordon, who was then at home, travelled to Strathbogie and Frendraught to arrange the marriage contract and paid out £10–13s–4d in sending word about it to Lord Elphinstone, Elizabeth's maternal grandfather.[25] The two girls also came into the patronage of the Marchioness of Huntly, who took Elizabeth to Elgin to buy her wedding garments; one gown, the materials for which were bought from the Elgin merchant, John Bonnieman, cost £82, and two others, with 'uther necessaires by my Ladye Marquiss of Huntleyes advyse', cost £266-13s-4d.[26] In August 1621, when a 'tryst' was arranged at Elgin among members of the family, including Hugh McKay of Farr, Jane, then aged seventy-six, travelled with her grand-children. Sir Robert Gordon recorded their expenses of £80 in his tutor's account book, for 'ther voyage to Elgin and bak againe in August 1621 yeris, haveing gone thither with my ladye ther grandmother to meit with my Lord Elphinstone when MacKye should have trysted in Elgin. . . with the accountant [Sir Robert himself] and some of the earl of Sutherllandis freindis, which tryst did not hold'.[27] Lady Anne at least got some new clothes out of the occasion; '£89–14s–10d for ane ryd-ing goun to Lady Anne. . . when she cam to Elgin to meit hir guidschire my lord Elphinstone in companye with hir brothir and grandmothir'. For a year or two Anne went to live at Strathbogie with the Marchioness of Huntly. In the spring of 1623 Jane asked Sir Robert to bring 'Any' with him when he called at Strathbogie on his way north; 'I have wretin dyvers tymes to hir gudbrothir for hir, bot he wald nevir grant to lat hir cum to your hame cuming. Now he hes na excuis'.[28]

In her letters to her son, Sir Robert, it is in speaking her mind in family quarrels or local developments likely to threaten the Sutherland interest that Jane Gordon's matriarchal tone comes over most clearly. In the autumn of 1616 she wrote to him about who was likely to be the new bishop of Caithness now that Bishop Alexander Forbes was about to be translated to Aberdeen:[29]

> '. . . ye have caus to tak attendance that ane onfreind [unfriend] cum not in this contray, for gif thai do it sall be na small hurt to your broderis hous. Freindis hes travailit with Mr Jhone Gray quha is varay sweir to ascept sic office, seing that leving is not abill to plant [provide ministers for] the kirkis. Thairfor gif his Majestie wald taik ane ordour with Catnes [the earl of Caithness] that the bischopis landis thair mycht be restorit to the kirk, I think freindis suld move Master Jhone to ascep of it. . . .'.

If someone takes office for gain rather than good conscience, she warns him,

> 'Remember, that I advertis you that your hous will repent it for sic resouns as I will not wreit'.

At the same time she wrote to him 'with greif of hart' of how her grandson, Y McKay, had abducted a sister of the earl of Crawford by which he had lost many of his allies and friends 'and (that quhilk is warst) hurt of contience'. She believed he had now lost any hope of raising an action for divorce against his wife:

> 'Gif he mycht have proven in any caus of partesing [divorce] aganis his wyif (as I am in doubt of it) this beastlie course hes takin that away, and I heir hir freindis thinkis to intend partesing aganis him, and sua to caus hir bruk [keep] hir lyferent. He is not cum to this cuntray sen his cumming frome Ingland, nathir resavit your brothir

> nor I ony advertissment from him excep at his first landing that he
> wes cum hame. I pray God send him ane bettir advysement nor I
> heir he is of.[30]

About a year later she got a letter from her shameless grandson denying Sir
Robert's accusation that he had been working against the earl of Sutherland: 'the
warld knawis that I am ane imp off that same stock thatt him selff is off, and itt
may be thatt my will is mair than my witt'.

In another case of abduction Jane actually interfered to rescue the victim,
Jane Chisholm, the daughter of a relative, whom the young laird of Golspietower
and some accomplices had carried off.[31]

> 'I wes not obeyit', Jane told Sir Robert, 'until my lord of Catnes
> cam to Skelbo [Skibo], at quhat tyme I thretned gif thai wald not
> put the damisell to libertie I suld taik him be the hand to revenge
> it. Then wes scho brocht to me, quhen scho declarit that quhat wes
> done wes against hir will, and to gif pruif thairof scho remains
> sensyne with hir fathir and mothir, and will nevir heir to marie that
> man albeit thair hes bene offiris maid to hir'.

Sir Robert Gordon came home in 1617 in the entourage of King James VI
who was making his only return visit to his northern kingdom. Once the family
knew he was planning to travel, both his brother, Alexander of Navisdale, and his
mother wrote to him in November 1616.[32] Alexander asked to be told as soon as
possible when he expected to arrive in Edinburgh so that lodgings could be taken
for him, 'for all the best ludgeingis ar taikin alreaddy'. He enclosed a note from
their mother about some linen that Sir Robert had asked for, in which she reminded him that there was still time for him to write to her before he came north: 'I
have sein na letter of your hand sen Lambes [Lammas]. I pray, as occasioun of
berreris offiris, lat me knaw of your helth. Be not sweir, for ye knaw not quhow
lang ye will have me to wreit to, and perhapis may wiss to have me quhen ye will
not gett me'. As it turned out, Sir Robert was in Scotland for almost two years at
this time, attending to the earl his nephew's affairs. During that time his sister-in-
law, the earl's mother, died on 18 September 1617, and at the end of the same
month he stood godfather to the son of his brother, Sir Alexander Gordon of
Navisdale. In 1618 he went to Edinburgh to attend a meeting of the 'Commissioners for the plantation of kirks' – the appointment of parish ministers – and
returned to England on the death of his father-in-law the following year.

The family's principal house was Dunrobin castle where, in 1541, the 10th
earl had completed the great tower, his wife acting as 'a very diligent overseer of
the work' while he was in the south. Dunrobin was designed for defence; even the
well in the courtyard was built of good ashlar work and was completed before the
buildings that surrounded it. In 1616 the shortage of money prevented the tenants
from paying enough 'strength silver' to pay the guards at the castle, so the tenants
had to perform this duty themselves.[33] Jane Gordon appears to have preferred to
live at Crackaig, a house which she is said to have built, on the coast between

Brora and Helmsdale. Perhaps from here she could keep an eye on the mining and salt-making operations and the fishing. The house was also used by her daughter-in-law, who died there in 1617. Repairs were carried out at Crackaig after that, including £136 for 'lofting and lathing' and workmanship. More expensive repairs in 1619 included payment for iron work to the smiths, and to Andrew Thomson, master mason, for 'beamfilling and filling the harts of chimnays in the house of Crackok, and slapping and dountakking of that pairt of the hous quhilk wes biggit before with clay, and wes now crackit, bigging it up agane with lime'.[34] There are also references in the accounts to 'the place of Dornoch'. The expense of maintaining three houses in 1600 amounted to £155–13s–4d.

Members of the family were often in Elgin, a stopping place on the way to Strathbogie, Aberdeen or further south, where goods were bought, including clothes, from merchants called John Bonnieman and William Campbell. Jane herself was in Edinburgh, probably on legal business, in 1595, the year after her husband's death, and there were also longstanding contacts with some Edinburgh merchants: John Hunter, a merchant-tailor, to whom the 12th earl left a legacy, Clement Cor, who stood surety for Jane and her husband the 11th earl in their undertaking to repay a creditor, and Alexander Watson, who supplied the Sutherlands with merchandise, taking bonds in security for payment, and acted as the earl's factor selling salt for him in London. Craftsmen were naturally from nearer home, such as the smiths and masons who worked on the buildings, and Sanders Leith, saddler in Dornoch, who made the young earl a saddle and horse 'furnishings', costing £16. In spite of considerable rents in kind, supplies had to be bought for the household in a bad year or when stocks ran low. In 1619 over £53 was spent on 'marts', animals slaughtered at Martinmas for the household's winter food, and two firkins of butter for the house of Dornoch were bought in Thurso in March 1585, costing £12–5s – including carriage. It was useful to have Sir Robert Gordon and his wife in fashionable London, from whom special items might be bespoke. In May 1617 Jane was anxious about the fact that the young earl, her grandson, lacked suitable clothes; 'my guddochtir is disappointit of cleis scho promeisit to hir sonne, thairfot my barne [bairn] wantis, and I have na reddie silvir: thairfor I will desyr you to caus bring hame ane stand of hailiedayis clois to him with the furnising, cloik, doubillet, coit, breekis and schankis'[35]. At other times Sir Robert himself asked for things from home, once for strong Scottish linen: 'If ony lynning haid bene gettable in this cuntray my wyiff haid bene glaid to have obeyed your letter', but the earl explained to him from Dunrobin, 'that is not gettable heir for lynning is maid in the north, and how soon scho goeth north Robin [Sir Robert's servant] sall not returne emptie'[36].

References to less serious business are found in the letters. 'Now I have made answer to all the heidis of your letter', the earl wrote to his brother in February 1615, 'excep anent [about] my tobaco I wreit for'. Sir Robert seems to have shared King James's attitude to this novelty for his brother continued, 'Ye sall not feir that evir I mynd to use the same. I assur you it is to give away, for good tobaco is in more estimatione heir away than any bettir gift. So, excep ye send me of the fynest sort and of the best that can be haid, I will have nane, for I have promiset it to a freind'[37]. As a postcript a few weeks later he asked, 'I will entreat you, brother, to send me ane pair of the fynnest dowle [double] virginallis ye can get for money, seeing ye knaw I cannot want the lyik out of my hous in Dornoch. I lippin ye will not faill to do this, as ye wald have me cairfull to do your turnes heireftir, seeing my bairnis [Elizabeth and Anne] ar learning to play and sing. Luik that ye caus sum skilful weall [choose] thame, and to send thame in sum suir crear that cumis to Scotland, and caus delyver thame to Alexander Watsone or [before] Lombes'[38]. We can understand why Jane Gordon missed the company of her granddaughters when they left home.

For the earl's own outdoor sport he asked his brother, 'Luik that ye send me ane fyne spying glas with my tobaco if ye wald have anything sent back', and reminded him a few weeks later, 'I wreit unto you befor to send me ane spying glas, quhilk I lippin ye will send with this berair again, that be good'. He was at that time encouraging his brother to buy the house of 'Cadell Maynis Parke', then for sale; 'it is ane commodious pairt to yow to dwell into, It have both the libertie of the hillis and the sea'. Sir Robert himself described the district between Durness and Cape Wrath, called 'The Parph', as an excellent hunting ground 'where they hunt the reid deir in abundance', and it was also described in Blaeu's *Atlas* as having 'verie plenti of wolfes'. These were not always killed for sport, however; £6–13s–4d to Thomas Gordoun for killing ane wolf and that conforme to the actis of the cuntray'.

A few servants are mentioned by name, one of whom Elspeth Leslie, went to Strathbogie on Jane's behalf in 1623 and returned with Sir Robert Gordon who was then on his way north. While he was at home his mother asked him to help her retain a servant of longstanding, Barbara Low, who had gone home to her relatives: 'scho tellis me scho hes bein oft send for be thame'. The details of the letter suggest that even at the end of her life Jane was still helping people to cope with a broken marriage, in this case probably partly for her own convenience;

> 'Gif thay war desyrous of hir, I think hir fathir mycht have wretin
> to me, seing my hous wes lipnit [entrusted] to hir serveis. It is
> trowth I lyik hir serveis; and honest and faithfull servandis ar hard
> to be fund . . . I will ernestlie desyir you to travell with hir fathir
> to sie quhat help he will maik hir with Adame Smith, . . . It is mair
> my weill to have thame togidder nor to have sindre [single] servan-
> dis in thair place . . . This I remit to your awin discretioun, for I
> essuir you I can have na wining [work done] be oft cheingin
> [changing] of servandis'.[39]

The garden at Dunrobin was in the hands of James Rynd who, in 1616, was paid £22 13s 4d a year and supplied with working clothes. The year after Jane's death the garden was described as 'planted with all kynd of fruits, hearbs and flowres used in this kingdome, and good store of safron, tobacco and rosemarie'.

Jane and her family lived in a small world centred on the shores of the Dornoch and Moray Firths and their hinterland, with well-used lines of communication stretching northwards to the more exposed shores of Caithness and southwards through Moray and Aberdeenshire to Strathbogie, the headquarters of the Gordon hegemony. Sums of money were regularly paid to 'posts' to carry letters and even money;[40] to take money to Hugh Gordon of Cults to pass on to creditors in Aberdeen; to carry letters to Lord Elphinstone at Kildrummy; to go to Edinburgh and then to Aberdeen to get extracts from the legal registers of the earl's grandfather's 'service' to the earldom, so that Sir Robert Gordon could get his facts right when applying for his nephew's retour when he succeeded to the estates; to Edinburgh to get letters of lawburrows [protection] against the Sinclairs, thus ensuring that they would not interfere in the earl's territories. An agent in Edinburgh, at one time Alexander Linton, was paid to attend to legal business there. Letters from further afield took a long time to reach Dunrobin, although when Sir Robert Gordon sent his letters from London in the charge of his own diligent servant, Robin, they arrived in just over a month, and when the earl was in Edinburgh they reached him there, by the usual 'post', in about the same time.

Jane Gordon was a stickler for pointing out how long it had taken the letters to come from England, and pinning the blame for their delay and sometimes disappearance on particular bearers. She usually did so in order to explain her own delay in replying or failure to answer Sir Robert's questions; 'The xv of this instant November I resavit ane letter of youris daitit at Salisberie the 16 June'. In this Sir Robert asked why she had not replied to a previous letter, which she had not then received but which he said had been sent with 'Adam Sittharis sonne'. 'I mervell', she replied, '. . . he has owersein himself sa far that nathir brocht it wyth himself nor advertisit that he had left it in Edinburgh'. In fact, the missing letters arrived soon afterwards, delivered by 'McYis boy' who had got it from the wife of the Edinburgh merchant, Alexander Watson[41]. It was in these precarious circumstances that sixteenth-century correspondents tended to reserve the most important news to be delivered 'by the bearer' by word of mouth, and did not readily commit their thoughts to paper.

Jane's second husband, the 11th earl of Sutherland, and their eldest son, John, 12th earl, shared her Roman Catholic faith. In the investigation into the extent of Catholic practice which was carried out for the General Assembly of the church in 1587 it was noted that 'the Erle of Sutherland, with his Ladie and freindis were vehementlie suspectit laitlie to have had mess, and to be contemners of the Word and Sacrament'[42]. In 1597, Jane with the countess of Huntly and countess of Caithness were ordered to subscribe to the Confession of faith under pain of excommunication, but the sentence was not carried out at this time although they did not comply. In her latter years Jane continued to be in trouble with the church authorities over her own non-conformity and for giving hospitality and assistance to members of the Jesuit mission and other priests from abroad in their work in the north of Scotland. The Jesuits included her own brother, James Gordon, who died in Paris in 1626, and William Murdoch who was tried in Edinburgh in 1607 for saying mass in the chapels of private houses in the north including Dunrobin. In 1615 her oldest son, the 12th earl, went to St Andrews and then Edinburgh to make his peace, outwardly at least, with the kirk. 'I have done beyond all those of my professione in Scotlande' to please the authorities, he assured his brother, Sir Robert. The fact that the latter was 'of a contrarie opinion with hir in religion' never impaired the affection between him and his mother or lessened his respect for her, although her non-conformity occasionally put him to a good deal of trouble. In 1616 she was summoned before the High Commission in Edinburgh, but when Sir Robert appeared on her behalf 'he purchased unto her from his Majestie an oversight and tolleration of her religion dureing the rest of hir dayis . . . provyding that shoe wold not harbor nor recept any Jesuits'. At the age of seventy-one, they probably thought she did not have long to live. In 1627, when she was in her eighty-second year, she was excommunicated from the pulpit at Golspie by the minister, Alexander Duff. On 19 October that year, however, Sir Robert became her surety, on her being absolved, that she would 'outterlie forbeir and absteine from recepting [resetting] of preists and Jesuiteis and from heiring of mass in tyme cuming'[43]. One of the signatories of the absolution was Mr John Gray, minister at Dornoch, whom she had once supported for the vacant bishopric of Caithness and who had taught her grandson.

In the autumn of 1628 Sir Alexander Gordon of Navisdale wrote to his brother in England of their mother's serious illness; 'My Lady our Mother hes bein heavilie diseassit and verie weak continuallie thir sex olkis [weeks] bygane, and nothing expectit of hir ladyschip bot deathe. I pray God send hir a happie ending'. He was anxious about what to do about the proposal of some local lairds that 'it war necessar, quhenever God callis hir, to give hir ane honorabill buriall, and have sum of hir ladyschipis most honorabill freindis thairat'.[44] He did not know whether she herself had given any directions about her burial since she had not said anything to him about it. The main problem was the considerable expense involved. He asked Sir Robert's advice and urged him to reply as soon as possible 'for it may be scho dryve off [linger] quhill [until] the fall of the leaff, and if God callis hir ladyschip befoir that I will do my best to give hir ladyschipis buriall all the honour I can within the cuntray, conform to our awin accustomit form, and not els'. Jane lived on into the following spring and died at Dunrobin on 14 May 1629 in her eighty-fourth year. Sir Robert arrived in Sutherland shortly before and 'wes so happie as to receave her last blissing befor her death'. She was buried in Dornoch cathedral beside her second husband, with the full honours usually accorded to an earl of Sutherland.

As early as 1615 Sir Robert Gordon of Gordonstoun had begun to compile a history of the earls of Sutherland. In a reply to him in February of that year, his brother the earl apologised for being unable to answer his questions about their 'genelogie' but said that he had passed these on to Sir Alexander Gordon of Navisdale, their younger brother, and was waiting for his reply. Jane Gordon must have approved the project if she knew about it. Sir Robert gave her a prominent place in the history of the House:[45]

> '. . . a vertuous and comelie lady, judicious, of excellent memorie, and of great understanding above the capacitie of her sex; in this much to be commended that during the continual changes and particular factions of the Court in the reign of Queen Mary and in the minoritie of King James Sixt (which were many) schoe alwise managed her effaris with so great prudence and foresight that the enemeis of her family culd nevir prevaile against her. . . Further, shoe hath by her great care and diligence brought to a prosperous end many hard and difficult bussiness, of great consequence appertenyng to the house of Sutherland. . . Shoe wes dureing her dayes a great ornament to that familie: . . . and as shoe lived with great credit and reputation so shoe dyed happilie and wes (according to her own command) buried by her sones Sir Robert and Sir Alexander (now onlie alyve of all her children) in the cathedrall of Dornogh in the sepulchre of the earls of Sutherland'.

JANE GORDON

NOTES

1 J.B. Paul, *The Scots Peerage*, IV, 534-6

2 J. Robertson, *The Inventories of Mary, Queen of Scots* (Bannatyne Club) 49

3 R. Gore-Browne, *Lord Bothwell* (1937), for narrative of Bothwell's career

4 J. Stuart, *A Lost Chapter in the History of Mary, Queen of Scots Recovered* (1874), 5

5 *Ibid.*, 7

6 Gore-Brown, *Lord Bothwell*, 252

7 J. Stuart, *Lost Chapter*, 22

8 G. Donaldson, *All The Queen's Men* (1983), 110-11

9 W. Fraser, *The Sutherland Book* (1892), I, for biographical details of the earls of Sutherland

10 Register of Deeds (S.R.O.), xiv, fo 269

11 W. Fraser, *The Sutherland Book*, I, 168

12 Sutherland Muniments (N.L.S.), Deposit 313/910 (1580), 1592(1583-5), 1593(1589-90), 3323(1600)

13 *Ibid.*, Deposit 313/1597 (1616-22)

14 W. Fraser, *The Sutherland Book*, I, 131

15 *Ibid.*, II, 112

16 *Ibid.*, II, 129

17 *Ibid.*, II, 142

18 Sutherland Muniments, Deposit 313/1597(1619)

19 *Ibid.*,

20 W. Fraser, *The Sutherland Book*, II, 127

21 Sutherland Muniments, Deposit 313/1597(1617)

22 *Ibid.*, 1597(1619)

23 *Ibid.*, 1597(1617)

24 W. Fraser, *The Sutherland Book*, II, 123

25 Sutherland Muniments, Deposit 313/ 1597(1619)

26 *Ibid.*, 1597(1619)

27 *Ibid.*, 1597(1621)

28 W. Fraser, *The Sutherland Book*, II, 142

29 *Ibid.*, II, 123

30 *Ibid.*, II, 124

31 *Ibid.*, II, 131

32 *Ibid.*, II, 124-5

33 *Ibid.*, II, 128

34 Sutherland Muniments, Deposit 3132/1597 (1617, 1619)

35 W. Fraser, *The Sutherland Book*, II, 132

36 *Ibid.*, II, 116

37 *Ibid.*, II, 116

38 *Ibid.*, II, 121

39 J. Stuart, *Lost Chapter*, 60-1

40 Sutherland Muniments, Deposit 313/ 1597(1616)

41 W. Fraser, *The Sutherland Book*, II, 125

42 J. Stuart, *Lost Chapter*, 56-7

43 *Ibid.*, 58

44 W. Fraser, *The Sutherland Book*, II, 151

45 *Ibid.*, I, 168

SIR WILLIAM DOUGLAS

Laird of Lochleven, Earl of Morton

c.1540 – 1606

For those who have heard of him William Douglas's name is usually associated with the ten months during which Mary, Queen of Scots was imprisoned in his island castle of Lochleven in Kinross-shire, following her deposition in July 1567. Yet he lived to the then respectable old age of his mid-sixties, while he and his wife, Agnes Leslie, had a married life of over forty years. Whereas Sir John Shairp of Houston has left behind an exceptionally large collection of letters, William Douglas of Lochleven has left not only letters but an unusual quantity for the sixteenth century of estate records and personal accounts that throw a vivid light on his way of life and that of the tenants on his widespread lands[1].

A kinsman once said of William Douglas's father, Sir Robert Douglas of Lochleven, 'he is both energetic and manly and will keep whatever he promises'. Not every laird merited both recommendations. Of his mother Margaret, daughter of John, 5th Lord Erskine, William himself wrote that he fully expected his children to find in her 'that favour . . . that I have found all my days'[2]. The laird of Lochleven and his wife who thus inspired trust and respect in their family circle must nevertheless have begun their married life under personal strain. They were married in 1527 and only a few years later Margaret became a mistress of the ill-guided young King, James V, to whom in 1531 she bore a son, James, later earl of Moray and Regent of Scotland. It is believed that at one stage the King contemplated marrying Margaret, if her marriage to Robert Douglas could be annulled, but the alternative plan for a politically-important royal marriage alliance with France took precedence over personal preference. William Douglas always looked upon the half-brother whom he shared with the Queen of Scots with respect; no matter how the relationship had been established, the influence of the earl of Moray was to be important to the Douglases.

Margaret Erskine became knowledgeable about the running of her husband's estates, and when the laird was killed at the battle of Pinkie in 1547 she took over their management on behalf of the seven-year-old heir William, as well as the care of their five other children, Robert, George, Euphemia. Janet and Katherine. She did not remarry and lived until 1572, a central figure in the household until the end of her life. William, who was allowed to spend some time in France after his father's death, grew up a serious, almost introspective, physically-weak young man. For much of his life he appears to have suffered from some kind of chest complaint for which he received a regular supply of medicines. Later in life he had the attendance of a nurse who lived in the household and the use of a 'chair', or litter, in which he was sometimes transported.

The decade of William's teens, the 1550s, saw the public progress of the movement for religious reform accompanied by alignment of the reform party with England. Events culminated in the confrontation between the Lords of the Congregation and the French-backed forces of the Queen Regent, Mary of Guise, in 1559-60, followed by the official ratification of the reformed religion by the Scottish parliament in August 1560. Writing later about these years William recalled having heard John Knox preach in the early days of his ministry, probably in 1555 when William would be about fifteen years old, and related that after Knox had fled to Europe 'in place of himself they did burne his picture'. William was clearly impressed by the preacher, 'the instroment off the setting forthe off thay [thy] glory and the plucking away off all that quhilk wes contrar to thay word . . .'. The previous year he had been contracted to marry Agnes Leslie, daughter of George, 4th earl of Rothes, a family that had long associations with both Protestantism and anglophile politics. Agnes's oldest brother, Norman, and her uncle, John Leslie of Parkhill, had taken part in the murder of Cardinal Beaton in 1546, her father had joined the assassins in St Andrews castle soon afterwards and her brother, Andrew, who became earl of Rothes in 1558, strongly supported the Reformation-settlement.

These associations, and contact with James Stewart, his half-brother, who became a prominent leader in the revolution of 1559-60, confirmed William Douglas in his adherence to the cause. He belonged to the age-group that grew up with the Reformation, a little older than those who, like James VI, had never known a world in which Protestantism was not the established religion. His associations with Catholicism must have been those of childhood, and the first occasion on which he bore arms may have been in support of the Lords of the Congregation. In August 1568, after Queen Mary had escaped from his custody, he made his will, possibly during an illness and therefore in an unusually pious frame of mind, and appended to it an account of his experience in the form of a confession of faith-cum-prayer of thanksgiving. It was written with the benefit of hindsight and the easy belief in the righteousness of a successful cause; 'thy kyrk . . . quilk wes begun and plantit by thy onlie mercie as the same may evidentlie appeir be the success of the same'. 'Surely it may be called thy wark for it wes thy hand that wrocht the same, for we wer na cumpany'. Perhaps in the family circle he would be aware of the greater difficulty experienced by the older generation in accepting the changes. He himself could speak for those who had had to make the mental transition to acceptance of alliance with the English, the 'auld enemy', in the interests of a united Protestant front. His admission of English assistance retained a grudging overtone; 'Thee, Lord, . . . did provyd the remeid be the few number of schippis of Ingland, that wer of lait our enemeis, quhilk wes a begynning of the reconciliatoun amang us and that the hairtis of thaim quhilkis wer in malice aganis thaim throw the want of thair predecessouris in battaill wes begun to be slokinit, as I knaw be experience in my selff for the want of my fader at the field of Pinky, quhilk wes the first occasioun that I did remit the sam with my hairt . . .'.

During Queen Mary's short personal reign William believed 'the kyrk' to be under threat from her Catholic councillors and servants, and in particular he saw their attention directed towards his half-brother, James Stewart. He believed that the rebellion of the earl of Huntly in 1562 had been 'an enterprise' against those of the Queen's council who were 'off the religioun', so that Huntly's defeat and death at the battle of Corrichie at the end of a campaign led by James Stewart was seen as 'a deliverance' of 'the best hert of thy kyrk and nobilitie of Scotland fra that most abomynabil tressoun'. Like other Scots, so he claimed, William was pleased when the Queen chose a Scotsman and a Stewart to be her second husband, 'quhill [until] the Quene muffit him to pas to the mes with hir'. In his account he is ambivalent about his own attitude to Darnley, against whose marriage to the Queen the earl of Moray rebelled and was forfeited. In 1566 William was among those who were escheated for association with the murder of Rizzio, the Queen's Italian secretary; his self-exoneration, although written in the form of a prayer, was obviously meant for human eyes. He refers to the Italian simply as 'ane wekit man quha wes greitest in credit with the Quene', saying that none of the nobles could speak to the Queen 'by', or apart, from him and that he was involved in a plot to have some of them forfeited. William himself had approached Rizzio with the offer of £1,000 if he would 'stai the erll of Murrayis forfaltour', but 'hes answer wes 20 thowsand'. Thereafter William joined those who pointed out to the King how the secretary's influence with the Queen was a humiliation to him and some of them planned how to bring Rizzio to justice. 'Bot men proponit and God disponit uderwayis be sum extraordynare menis'. William swore that he never consented to deal with Rizzio outwith the processes of justice, 'nather wes it in ony nobill man his mynd', he insisted. He did not indict Darnley himself. William, meantime, went off to Argyll 'ane quhill in quiet maner'.

The birth of Prince James in 1566, begotten by a Scottish nobleman and borne by 'our native princesse' he remembered as an occasion for rejoicing and the Prince's preservation, in spite of the 'variance' between his parents, as a matter for thanksgiving, not least because the Queen had had the good sense to give him into the safekeeping of William's uncle, the earl of Mar, and his wife. There was little mystery, to his mind, about what happened after that; the Queen 'schortlie efter his baptisme did turne in famyliaritie with the Erle of Bothwill and the said erle did crually put doun his fadir in ane maist abominabil maner in Edinburt . . .'.

William maintained that after the Queen's surrender to the Lords at Carberry he had had no power to agree or disagree with the decision to put her in Lochleven castle. He tried to remain as detached as possible from the implications of this move, to the extent that some people afterwards inferred that he had turned a blind eye to her attempts to escape from his custody. In his own account of the affair he maintained that he had asked Ruthven and Lindsay to remain with him so that they might take joint responsibility for the Queen's safekeeping. Of her deposition, or demission of the crown, he maintained, 'I knaw not quhill the same wes doune'. Corroboration of his claim lies in a notarial instrument, dated at Lochleven on 28 July 1567, four days after the deposition, recording his protest in the Queen's presence that she had signed the letters of demission during his absence and without his knowledge, which the Queen then 'allowed'[3]. She also agreed that, unaware of her demission of the crown but having heard that the Lords planned to crown her son at Stirling, he offered to convey her to the coronation, which she declined. 'In respect thereof the said William protestit that hir majestie suld not be comptit [accounted] heireftir as captive or in presoun with hym, Quhilk protestatioun hir majestie allowit and admittit'.

'I desyrit at that tyme that [the] nobilatie wald haiff relevit me off my burden befoir the coronatioun of the king, quhilk I culd not gett', he recorded, protesting that the Queen's escape in May 1568 'wes ane of the greitest displesing to me'. Although he is less likely to have been moved by pity for Mary's predicament than by consideration for his family's position in this unprecedented political situation, William Douglas was not entirely the truculent gaoler portrayed by Mary's partisans, by herself in retrospect, and by those historians who choose to see her mainly as the victim of her circumstances. He had welcomed her to Lochleven in happier times: she occasionally used the castle as a centre while hunting, and in April 1563 had had a long discussion with John Knox in the castle hall before supper and on the following day while hawking near Kinross. In 1565, during the rebellion of Moray and other nobles who opposed the Darnley marriage, the Queen sent a herald to demand the surrender of the castle with its ammunition, some of which belonged to Moray. The herald found the family in trouble – William was ill, 'in perill of his life', and his sister-in-law who was with them was about to give birth to a child – so that the laird was given a royal licence to retain the castle provided he sheltered none of the rebels[4]. The first few traumatic weeks of the Queen's detention, when she was in a state of mental and physical collapse and then had a miscarriage, must have forged personal contacts, at least with the women of the household[5]. Agnes Leslie, who was herself pregnant during the Queen's stay with the family, slept in Mary's room. In fact, the Queen made friends with the members of the household, from the oldest to the youngest, something which Sir William did nothing to prevent so long as it did not appear to constitute a threat to security.

The story of how he was once easily distracted from finding out what a young relative, whom he had glimpsed through the window, was doing with the castle boats, may suggest not so much that he was slow on the uptake but that he was not in the habit of panicking at every suspicious circumstance. His wife was the Queen's constant companion, one of his daughters and a niece hero-worshipped Mary while even his mother, Margaret Erskine, whatever the truth of her alleged resentment of the legitimate Stewart in their midst, walked with the Queen in the castle garden. The laird himself, who joined her in at least on boating trip, marred by a practical joke on the part of her servants who pretended that she had escaped, once told the earl of Morton that he believed there was no vice in her.

The laird's brother, George, who also lived in the household, became infatuated with Mary and, in co-operation with William, 'the little Douglas', an orphaned relative who had grown up with the family and was also the Queen's slave, worked out the plans for her deliverance. It was not until the spring of 1568, by which time George Douglas's sympathy for the captive was giving rise to the rumour that he hoped to marry her and that he had plans for her escape, that the laird and his brother quarrelled and George was banished from the island. Ironically, this gave him a better opportunity to set forward his plans. The escape was effected on 2 May, at the end of a day of May Day celebrations organised by the resourceful William the Orphan in order to put the family in a relaxed mood and allay suspicion of his movements which were necessary in the final preparations. Perhaps William Douglas's understandable horror at being found wanting in his political responsibility was mixed with relief at the end to the dislocation in his family life and household arrangments. The young members of the family may well have missed the Queen's presence for some time, and both George Douglas and William the Orphan fled with her, the latter to remain in her service in England.

In the 1570s the laird of Lochleven, by now in his thirties, took a prominent part in public affairs, and King James, as he grew older, frequently called on his services, asking him to join in the royal lieutenant's visits to the Borders in the interest of law and order, to escort the King himself on his journeys across Fife to the Queensferry or to provide him with overnight hospitality in his castle during a royal progress to the north of Scotland. Such a request would send the household into an orgy of preparations as did the King's letter to the lady of Lochleven, in her husband's absence, asking for a loan of pallions, or large tents, for the King's use during a punitive expedition to the west march; ' . . . the schortnes of the tyme not serving that new palzeonis may be maid reddy to oure selff we have thocht gude to burdynge yow, That we may have the use of youris during this veiage [journey]. And in that respect is contentit to spair the personall service of the men, tennentis and servandis of the laird your husband dwelland on his propir landis, Except sik horssis and men as sall cary the palzeonis and twenty ma [more] careage horssis for oure awne use. Desiring yow therfoir effectuuslie That ye faill nocht to have the said palzoun sufficientlie orderit with cordis, pynnis and all uther furnitor belangand thairto . . .'[6].

Occasionally a petition to the King from one of the laird's dependants or tenants resulted in a royal letter asking his co-operation, a quicker way of putting pressure on him than through a lengthy and expensive court case. In June 1582 the King wrote a letter to him on behalf of James Stewart, son of the late John, earl of Buchan, whose ward had been granted to Douglas. Its tone suggests that Douglas could be tight-fisted. The young man, according to the King's information, was 'in greit and extreme necessitie . . . in all thingis pertening to ane honest mannis estait'. Lacking the means to assist him at present the King asked Douglas to let him have 'some reasonabil pairt of that ward' and to give him in the meantime 'some present sowme of money to helpe him to his honest necessaires quhairof it is unsemelie to sie him disappointit . . . '. About the same time the King appealed to him on behalf of a tenant in the earldom of Buchan, Henry Mowtray, whom Douglas was trying to remove from his holding although the man objected that he had a tack which had still a few terms to run and that in any case a tenant's heir expected to be given the holding after him. The King, as ultimate owner of the land as well as head of state in the political sense, was in a position to remind landholders that they must obey the rules of landholding upon which all depended. 'For our cause', the King wrote on this occasion, 'and for the kyndlie love ye awe and bearis baith to the bairne and house [i.e. of Buchan] ye will suffer him peaceablie to ryn out the termes and title forsaid without troubill or interruptioun, ather be law or besydis it . . . . Swa, luiking for some gude effect heirof, We commit yow to God, from Ruthven . . . .'. Another royal command to the same effect arrived a week later; William may well have smiled at the fifteen-year old King's postcript – 'mak me quite [quit] of this sillie auld manis cummer [bother]'.

A few weeks later the laird of Lochleven was among those members of the ultra-protestant party known as the 'Ruthven Raiders' who seized the person of the King in an attempt to remove him from the influence of his French cousin, Esme Stuart, seigneur d'Aubigny, and those who inclined towards a foreign alliance and the possibility of Queen Mary's restoration to the throne. When the King regained his freedom the following summer the leader of the *coup*, the earl of Gowrie, was executed and others, including William Douglas, were banished. During his exile he found a refuge in the French protestant stronghold of La Rochelle, from which he kept in touch with his family by letters and sent them news of the French Wars of Religion:

> 'Best belovit', he wrote to his wife in May 1585, 'efter maist
> hairtlie commendatioun, This present sall adverties you that at the
> wretting heirof I am in guid health praysit be God And desyris the
> lyk of yow and all my bairnis, freindis and servandis that ar on
> lyve. As towart the estait of this cuntrey, The King of France hes
> renuncit in the parliament of Paris all appoyntmentis and
> pacificatioun maid at ony tyme in favouris of the Religioun
> reformit in this countrey And hes commandit be his edict that all
> Ministeris avoyd thame selffis out of this cuntrey within ane

moneth undir the paine of death, And nobill and gentill men within sex monethis . . . . Swa he and thay of the Papis Legie [League] thinkis to exterminat the word of God out of this cuntrey and all partis of Europe gif God permit thame, quhilk I traist in his guidnes he will nocht bot will disppoynt all thair interprysis, althocht to the warld thay may mak thame nevir swa apperand, In respect the greit ressoun is aganis his kyrk, quhilk he will preserve as the Apill of his Ee and confound all his Ennemeis . . . . The pest is very grait in this toun presentlie, God send bettir quhen he plesis. Youris only Lochlevyn'[7].

In April 1586 he was in London on his way home and by autumn of that year was again involved in local affairs, trying to sort out a dispute over fishing between the lairds of Wemyss and Balmuto. The year 1588 brought an important change in his circumstances when, on the death of Archibald, earl of Angus and Morton, the Morton titles and estates devolved upon him and he became the 6th earl, at the age of almost fifty.

His lands were now spread through ten sheriffdoms – Kinross, Fife, Angus, Perth, Edinburgh (Midlothian), Lanark, Peebles, Berwick, Roxburgh and Dumfries, centred on the baronies of Kinross, Aberdour, Keillour (Perth), Auchterhouse (Angus), Dalkeith, Newlands and Linton (Peebles) and Caldercleir, or East Calder, with many outlying territories. His officers continually rode between the more distant properties, the countess travelled from Lochleven up into Angus to Auchterhouse, which seems to have been her special responsibility even in their earlier days, while the earl himself moved between Lochleven, Edinburgh and Dalkeith and as far as Keillour, where he often presided personally in the barony court, and his Peeblesshire baronies where he stayed at the forbidding Drochil castle built by the Regent Morton.

Travelling and transport, although difficult, were an unavoidable part of life. Lochleven's vital fleet of boats, leased to tenants in return for 'boit maill' (rent) and the duty of ferrying, were a constant upkeep: a new boat cost £20, about double the price of a horse, the normal form of transport, and there were frequent purchases of wood for boat repairs. Then there was the continual cost of going, or coming, 'owr the wattir' at the busy Queensferry: the freight of man and horses, the alms to the poor who habitually gathered at the landing-places, not to speak of the additional expense of being storm-bound at the ferry: 'gevin to yor L. lychting at the Quenisferie for a drink to yor L. and yor cumpany, 24s, ... for your L. supper, thair being a greit wind, 50s, to the gudwyfes dochtir at yor L. command, 10s, to the boitmen for your L. fraught and the hors, being in twa boitis, £3'. The tenants owed carriage service within the barony and for a certain distance but long-carriage had sometimes to be paid for, as when the 'careage men of Bischopschire', in Fife, carried fish across to Dalkeith. Carts and wains were used to transport heavier commodities, sometimes those of the tenants being requisitioned at short notice; 'It will pleis yor L. that I have bene this Mununday to Dundie', Agnes Leslie wrote to her husband from Auchterhouse in May 1591, 'and hes bocht ane tune of wyne, sevin scoir sextein pundis ($£156$) the tune and hes gevin my obligatioun to pay it the xv day of August . . . . yor L. will send to Jhone Hutsone to caus him bring owt of the barony of Kinross four kairties with sufficient horsis and men to draw the wyne. Thai suld cum to the pow of Lendoris and at thai faill nocht to be at the appointit plaice and Jhone Hutsone with thaim this tuysday at two eftir none'[8]. People turned naturally to the seaways in the sixteenth century and the Tay ferry-crossing was the quickest way to the barony of Auchterhouse. On one occasion, when Agnes went north to supervise both agricultural and building operations, the clerk noted cryptically in his account book, 'to fraucht of my ladie and deallis, 16s–8d'.

Letters and other messages were sent with foot-runners who, together with the liveried messengers-at-arms, were among the most common sights to be met with on the sixteenth-century roads. Some of these 'boys', as they were called no matter how old they were, were used to travelling enormous distances. Many of them flit anonymously through the pages of the Douglas accounts but one of them, Stenie Banks, based in Dalkeith, ran regularly for the earl of Morton down into Lanarkshire and Dumfriesshire. In 1599 he received 40s to go down into Eskdale on 3 July, and by 12 July had returned and set off again for Dumfries on another errand.

Each barony was an individual entity, 'set' to the tenants according to the custom of the barony and administered by its financial officer, or chamberlain, who was accountable to the landlord for receipt of the rents and all expenditure from them. Two generations of Hudsons, Andrew and John, served as officers in the barony of Kinross itself under the chamberlain, John Douglas of Kinnesstoun; Michael Shaw was chamberlain at Dalkeith, Robert Hepburn at Langnewtoun in Roxburghshire, and Andrew Hepburn at Linton and Newlands in Peeblesshire, Laurence Dempstartoun and John Forsyth did duty at Keillour, and Thomas Forster at both Keillour and Kinross. These men, who usually belonged to the district themselves, had an intimate local knowledge of the land, of how it was occupied and of the practical business of cultivation and stock-rearing. They had local contacts among the tenants, workmen, and rural craftsmen, and had to keep track of all expenditure however small, from the purchase of eight oxen for the plough, costing over $£100$, to a pair of boots for the earl, costing $£3$ from a Linton cordiner, or of a few pennies at a time to the poor. The officers themselves need not have been able to write as they would have the services of clerks who kept memoranda and eventually compiled their many daily transactions into the final estate accounts, although at least the two Hepburns and Laurence Dempstartoun could sign their own accounts.

William Douglas and his wife were both regularly present when the estate accounts were rendered, usually at Lochleven or Dalkeith. The 'hearing' of the accounts was still a live business in the presence of the 'auditors', with the laird and the lady, later earl and countess, personally 'allowing' those expenditures which they had authorised either by word of mouth or by written precept. Like the gathering-in of the rents at Whitsunday and Martinmas, the hearing of the accounts was an occasion for 'halding house' wherever the business took place and, invariably, for even greater household expenditure; 'for wyne and breid to yor L. chamber extraordinarily, 11s . . . . gevin for a pynt of wyne drunk in the foirchamber, 8s'. Lord and lady were also thoroughly familiar with the farming process and, in the days when the 'beir stack' might be built in the castle court-yard, were never far away from it. In the pre-industrial era lord and tenant were keenly aware of their mutual dependence and on the ultimate dependence of both on the land, the source of their livelihood. The earl crossed over to Dalkeith in 1595 'to thresche the teindis', as the chamberlain put it. His wife held house at Auchterhouse for a month 'in mucking tyme' and even lent her own 'nag' for the harrowing.

Income from the land came in the form of both money-rent and rent in kind. Although at the end of the century the latter was still the major proportion, the practice of selling the grain rents to the tenants added to the amount of money paid over. In fact, in this period of rising prices landlords were using different means to raise cash from their estates. It is interesting that the tenants had the money to pay, suggesting that they were raising cash-crops, such as wheat, and were finding ways of earning money. Full estate accounts show a charge (credit) side and a discharge (debit) side. The officers always took into account the arrears, known as the rests, in some accounts even 'the auld restis', or as we would call them, bad debts, and any authorised deductions, or defalcations. Losses by weather, bad harvest, vermin or accident were noted, being referred to as the inlaik. Occasionally an account would be drawn for a specific purpose : 'The particulare ressait [receipt] of William Oliphantis restis of the crop fourscoir four-tene yeiris [1594] fra sindry tennentis'; 'Compt of money spent in supplying the place of Dalkieth . . . .'; 'Compt of Andrew Hopburne of his intromissiounis with the teind victual of the parishes of Lintoun and Newlandis'; 'Compt of the fermes of Brakolie of 1597 and restis of 1596'; 'Ressait of the beir of Mugdrom', in which the firlot measure of Mugdrum was used in calculating the tenants' grain rent. The account books rarely balanced, with sometimes a little balance on hand but more often the officer was 'superexpendit'. Fragmentary though these are, these work-ing papers have preserved a picture of the life of the countryside. An account for the 1590s for parts of the baronies of Kinross and Keillour is arranged in such a way as to show the charge and discharge of each farmtoun and of each holding within the toun, with the tenant's name, rent paid, arrears due and details of how the rent had been disposed of[9].

'The account of the fermes of Brackolie, 1597 and rests of 1596. Made at Newhouse, 6 April 1598'

Charge: Robert Low charges himself with 23⅓ bolls meal, 4 bolls 2 firlots 2⅓ pecks beir, 4 bolls 2 firlots 2⅓ pecks horse corn ferme of 1597, and 4 bolls

3½ & ⅓ pecks meal for the rests of 1596.

Discharge: Paid to the place (of Lochleven) and received by the steward, 21 bolls 2
firlots 1 peck. Received by the lady herself, 6 bolls in complete payment
(due as part of her jointure); and delivered to William Steedman at the lady's
command, 4 bolls 11⅓ pecks beir; and paid to the place 4 bolls 10⅓ pecks
horse corn.

When making his will in 1568, prematurely as it turned out, William
Douglas assured his brother Robert, earl of Buchan, that 'the gratest cair that I
ever haid wes that justice suld be ministrat amangis my tenants without parsialitie
of ony'. Records were kept for the benefit of both lord of the ground and farmer.
One clerk noted in the margin of his account for the barony of Keillour that
Thomas Paton, a tenant of 6 Oxgangs in Easter Keillour who was accused of being
badly in arrears of rent, 'allegeit him to have had in [i.e. into the granary] 3 bolls
meal for the yeir 1599, quhilk is admittit to the girnell compt'. Much has been
written about overbearing landlords but pressure could also come from the
tenants' side, while arrangements must often have been the result of mutual agreement, however difficult this may have been to arrive at. Writing to her husband
from Auchterhouse in 1591 while arranging to sell the grain-crop to the tenants,
Agnes Leslie complained, 'I have causit convein the tenantis of Auchterhous and
hes causit the guidman of Kinnestoun deal with thaim to sei quhat prices thai will
give for thair fermes, thai will offer bot four merkis for meill and beir for na prig-
ging [haggling] that Jhone Douglas and I can mak, and mony of thaim I can gett na
thing fra tham . . . '[10].

Estate rentals give the names of the settlements that clustered on the best
arable land throughout the estates. One of the fullest is that of the barony of Kinross for the year 1540, during the lifetime of Sir Robert Douglas of Lochleven[11].
The place names are still to be found on the modern map around Lochleven: Kinross, Classlochie, Brackley, Gairneybridge, Annacroich, Carsegour, Maw,
Tillyochie, Thomanean, Dalqueich, Drumgarland, Touchie, Athron, Lothries,
Orwell, Fossoway and the Bowtoun. The most densely-cultivated settlement was
that of Kinross itself, with 37 named tenants, besides Henry Dempstartoun at the
mill of Kinross and a priest, sir David Ballingall, chaplain of St Leonard's chapel.
Ten of these tenants were women, just over a quarter of the total, either widows
with the liferent use of their husbands' holdings or women who held land in their
own right.

In addition there would be subtenants and cottars to add to this number,
whose names are not on the rental. The theory was that cottars worked for the
main tenant, usually called the husbandman, in return for which they had a house
and enough land on which to grow their own food. However, some cottars were
more substantial, holding more than the nominal cotland they were supposed to
possess, and some held their cultivation-patches directly from the landlord himself
so that they may be thought of as tenants. At Dalkeith, for example, forty-eight
cotlands were divided among fifty cottars who paid their rents of between 3s–4d

and 6s–8d directly to the earl of Morton himself. There was nothing static about landholding patterns, so that the resources of tenants within the same barony or of people within the same category of tenant might vary. There were steilbow holdings, where the tenant received seed with the land, for which he had to render a certain return of grain to the landlord once a year. There were also what were known as bowtouns, held by bowmen, stock-rearing farms where the tenant had to make an annual reckoning of the animals in his charge, usually at Beltane, and supply the landlord's household with their produce. In 1545 'Beltane wes maid' on 8 June with Robert Kyd, a bowman at Fossoway, when he had in his keeping 11 newly-calved cows, of which 5 had calved for the first time, 2 'mart ky', earmaked for slaughter at Martinmas when meat was salted down for the winter, 5 cows not in calf, a bull, 6 stirks, 142 milk ewes, 35 ewes past lambing and 4 rams. At the same time 143 sheep were transferred to Kyd's keeping from another bowman[12]. Holdings of this kind supplied animals, milk, cheese, and butter for the laird's kitchen, and skins that could be sold.

The tenants held their holdings by tack, or lease, for a stated number of years. Although these tacks had to be periodically renewed as they expired or when the tenant died, it was customary for them to be renewed to the tenant or, on his death, to his nearest of kin. In this way many tenant families enjoyed their holdings for generations. They called their claim to inherit by custom their *kindness* to the holding[13]. In the barony court landlord and tenants met to hear disputes, see justice administered, and sort out the problems of the local community. A part of the court book of Keillour in Perthshire survives, covering the years 1553-75[14]. William Douglas as baron presided over the court on six of the ten recorded occasions, once in company with his bailie, Robert Crawford. In a real sense the tenants *were* the court, taking their turn at sitting on the assize, acting as officers of the court, as measurers of disputed holdings and as 'sworn men' who looked into the background circumstances of complaints. they were very knowledgeable about the law or, as they called it, 'the lovable custom' of the barony, which governed their lives. The professionals on hand were the clerk who kept the record of the court's business, and the local notary who prepared records of agreements and other transactions, known as notarial instruments, which he engrossed in his little register, or protocol book, making an extract from it for the individual concerned.

Most disputes at Keillour, as elsewhere, concerned the land itself and the all-important matter of keeping one's boundaries, or the boundaries of each farmtoun – keeping 'guid nychtbourheid'. Those who failed to do so were accused of being 'unlawful nychtbouris'; 'quhilk day it is statut be the juge that everilk tennent of barony keip nytborheid in bigging of their dykis'. There were surreptitious attempts to take in bits of another's holding; 'the tenentis of Bordland finds upone Archibald Craufurd that wrangoslie and agane the law hes telit ther land and sawyn the samyn to ther damnage and skaith'. The boundary dykes, made of turf, did not always guarantee freedom from interference; the tenants of Craigend accused two men that 'castis doune their diks and maks fulze [compost] therof'. John Smith's complaint on the tenants at Craigend, that they had 'distroyit ane croft ryg till hym' within the ploughing area was even more serious, and tenants at Easter Keillour discovered that some from Craigend were actually digging up and removing their soil. Read as it stands these incidents sound like mere unruly behaviour and provocation but they were probably part of long-running disputes. Only the lost depositions of witnesses could have provided us with the context. The marginal note 'of nane avale' beside some of these cases suggests that on examination they had proved to be cases of disputed possession in which the person bringing the complaint had for some reason failed to prove his case.

In a situation where tenants pastured their stock together on the common in charge of the common herd, there were often disputes about animals and their ownership. The frequent lending and buying and selling of goods and animals among the farmers also led to quarrels. People got most concerned when this involved plough animals, probably their most valuable possessions, which even the law could not distrain for debt in the 'season of labor'. 'Quhilk day Jhon Murdoch, admittit and sworn as witnes in the actioun and caus dependand betwix Jhon Murdoch and Lucas Gray, concerning the selling of ane ox, and being admittit and sworne be baith parteis deponis that the ox was lauchfullie coft and sauld be the said Jhon Murdoch to the said Lucas Gray for the sowme of 7 merkis and 40d'. Murdoch was also accused of having taken an ox that did not belong to him; 'Jhon Murdoch sall gif and deliver to Jonet Jonissoun the sown of 6 merkis and 10s or ellis hir ox agane als gude as he wes the tyme he wes tane fra hyr'. It is impossible now to say whether the alleged killing of animals was by accident or design; one Keillour tenant, John Farquhar, accused John George that 'his wyfe slew ane stott of his of ane yeir auld to his heavie dampnage and skaith'; William White accused Robert Andrew that he 'slew ane kow of Williams and the said Robert sone slew tua lamis of his'.

The barony court enforced the payment of debts, including servants' fees and the handing over of goods left in legacy. Crops destroyed or eaten by straying animals had to be compensated for. Tenants who failed to cultivate their holdings were liable to eviction. From the baron's point of view the most important thing was that the land should be continually occupied and the continuity of tenancy preserved in order to ensure the harvesting of the crops and payment of rent. Tenants were continually reminded that he had the power to enforce his rights in the land, after due process of law in court; they must perform their labour-services on the mains of the barony (the home farm in modern terminology) which he farmed directly for the provision of his own household or, where labour-services had been commuted for money, pay their 'dayswork silver'. They commonly resented the time spent labouring for the baron and tried to avoid it. The landlord put the growing wood of the barony strictly out-of-bounds and fines were imposed for cutting it. Defiance of the officers of the court, such as the serjeant who saw to it that its decisions were carried out and who confiscated stock and grain, or the barony herd, who was looked upon as a public servant, were punished with a fine or confiscation of goods.

The tenants resisted servicing the barony mill, 'bringing hame millstones' or helping with repairs, since the miller was an unpopular figure in the rural community; many of his neighbours, believing that he was lining his own pockets, felt that he could fend for himself well enough without the use of their valuable time. They were accused at times of hand-grinding their own grain and thus depriving him of work and his perquisites. In the 1550s the tenants of Keillour were ordered to 'bring the stuf to the miln before Fasterse'en [Shrove Tuesday] that it may be laborit in dew time quhen the miln has watir'. Although in the last analysis the land was the laird's to give, it was the assize of tenants who, having examined the case, gave their verdict on its rightful possession, so that the laird could then use his authority. In 1564 after a case of disputed possession, an assize of thirteen local men found that the holding disputed by John George and presently occupied by Janet Johnston 'pertenis to the laird and that na man can clame ryt thereto nor kyndness therto wythout his speciall gift and kyndness therof'. They may have been his mouthpiece, but the fact that the whole business was examined in court gave tenants the opportunity to object.

The increasing tendency to commute labour-services to money-payments meant that landlords had cash with which to pay hired labour, which in turn may have slowly changed the pattern of agricultural employment as people took work outwith their own immediate neighbourhood, although tenants would themselves be among those paid workers. The Douglas accounts show agricultural labourers being employed for a variety of purposes, mostly on the mains of the different baronies under the supervision of the chamberlain and officers, but also for tasks which one might have thought could have been given to permanently 'feed' or retained servants. Details of their work remind us that jobs were much more specialised even in early modern times than is sometimes thought, and that the picture of everyone doing everything for himself is an over-simplification. Men like the ploughmen and threshers, who presumably did other work out of season, were nevertheless retained year after year for their specialist skills; the ploughmen were paid their 'bolls' in beir and oats, the threshers, or 'barnmen', their 'lots' in oats or pease. Others paid for particular tasks included the harrower, muckmen, herds, the watchcorne, or bird-scarer, and dyke builders.

There was a major dykebuilding operation in Kinross barony in 1541, not only with turf but stones, these being obtained from a neighbour, the laird of Kirkness, for which the dyke builders were paid in cash, and men were paid separately for winning and leading the stones. Mowing hay and harvesting needed more hands; the chamberlain at Drochil in 1600 paid £18 for 20 dargs [the day's labour of a man] and bought 2,000 herring, which 'cam furth of Glasgo' by the carriage men. He also gave £4 'to ane pyper to play to the scheraris [shearers] in hervest'. This, and the purchase of a new ox-yoke on St Luke's Day, 18 October, 1580, at Auchterhouse is a reminder of the communal jollifications that sometimes accompanied agricultural labour. At Dalkeith, a woman, Criste Dowie, who had come 'owr the wattir' specially for the purpose, was paid for clipping the sheep.

A good deal of money was spent on the acquisition and maintenance of farm equipment. At Auchterhouse, in 1580, Laurence Dempstertoun bought or had made 2 plough beams at 9s, 7 ox bows, 6s–8d, 2 plough sheets, 1s–8d, 1 plough head, 1s, 1 plough sheath, 10d, 3 riddles, 5s, 1 sieve, 2s, 4 haiks [fodder racks] for the stable, 14s. At Kinross in 1572 'twa naigs and ane ox to the pleuch' cost £19–6s–8d, iron for the plough-irons, £7-3s-4d, with £2-6s-4d to the smith 'for werking of it'. Smaller items were purchased by Andrew Hepburn at Drochil, such as barrows, six rakes for the hay, two shovels, and three sleds, all of which came to £4 10s. A plough complete with yokes, bows, culter and sok was bought for Wester Cowden, Dalkeith, for £10, with 5 gallons of tar for marking the sheep at £7. Smith's work on servicing the Drochil plough, between Michaelmas 1599 and Beltane 1600 had cost £10, the price of another plough. The earl himself took a particular interest in the affairs of Linton and Newlands baronies, often riding down there from Dalkeith.

> '22 September, yor L. oy [grandson] and servandis ane nyt in
> Drochellis, £20; 30 September, half ane galloun of acquavitie to
> yor L.; 11 November, your L. rade owt of Dalkeith to Kilbocho to
> fie the millar, yor expensis ane nycht in Drochell and yor cumpany,
> £15; deliverit to your L. in yor chamber, £40; to yor L. to put in
> yor napkin, £4–16s–8d'.[15]

After the earl had gone the chamberlain carried on with ordering a harrow and building 'nolt fauldis'. The byres at Auchterhouse were built of turf, including the faill or heavy roofing turfs, but that at Kinross was built partly of wood.[16] There are one or two references to the coalheuchs on the Lochleven estates, but not to those of Kelty which William Douglas feued from the abbey of Dunfermline in 1572. The actual expenses are charged on the rents of Keillour, but there is no indication whether the coal workings in question were in that barony or near Kinross, although the latter is more likely:

> 'For ale at the coalheuch, 2 dayis, 12d; to Alexander
> Beverage to pay the colliers, 10s'.

The houses most used by the family were 'the Newhouse' of Lochleven and the Morton castle of Dalkeith. The island castle of Lochleven itself was out-of-date as a residence even by the middle of the sixteenth century, with its living quarters cramped even by contemporary standards, and lack of modern fortifications, such as gun-loops. Sir Robert Douglas and Margaret Erskine did something to remedy these shortcomings by building a new great hall and kitchen in the courtyard, and in the south-east and north-west corners of the barmkin erected two towers well-provided with gun-loops, of which one, the Glassin Tower, remains. It is believed that the family used the new accommodation in the courtyard building while Queen Mary was imprisoned in the tower.[17] However, the family papers show that from the lifetime of Sir Robert himself a 'Newhouse' was being built on the shores of the loch, where the stables, apparently, were already sited. In 1552 Margaret Erskine, as her husband's executrix, paid John Steedman £44-17s-4d for 'furnishing his placis of Lochlevyn and Newhous', showing that the latter was not a dower-house for Margaret but had been begun by Sir Robert himself. Margaret's executry accounts also refer to 'a greit load of gray wark [stone] sett in the Newhous wyth uthir expensis maid therupoun', £6 for an iron window frame 'to the inner chamber of the Newhous', £11-5s for 'glass and glassbandis and mending the windowis of the Newhous and the place of Lochlevyn' and 3 dozen deals for the Newhouse. Although building was obviously still in progress the house was used to some extent; in 1546 Sir Robert himself had 'maid Beltane' there with some of his bowmen. Margaret Erskine also paid at this time for 4,000 slates for the new hall of Lochleven castle. In 1569 she made a contract with a Dunfermline smith to measure certain windows of the Newhouse and build them 'substantiously', agreeing to pay him 14s for every stone of iron worked.[18] In the 1550s much finanacial business relating to the late Sir Robert's estate was transacted there and from then onwards the estate accounts were regularly heard at the Newhouse in the presence of the laird, later earl, and his wife, and tenants were admitted to the rental there, although some of them came from the Roxburgh part of the estates. In 1616, when William Douglas's son was admitted to the lordship of Kinross, the Newhouse 'beside the lake of Lochlevyn' was designated the 'chief messuage', or property, where he formally took possession. The account of the parish of Kinross in the first *Statistical Account of Scotland* states 'the old house, for some generations the residence of the earls of Morton, situated on the north of the present [Kinross House] garden, was taken down about the year 1723, but some vestiges of the foundations are still discernible'.

The earl was often at Dalkeith, where he heard the accounts, broke his journey on visits to Drochil in Peeblesshire, and received tenants. Michael Shaw's account for 'supplying the palace of Dalkeith' in the summer and autumn of 1599 mentions various repairs: mending the brewhouse, its furnace, vats and doors, strengthening 'the eist yett' with 125 'greit naillis', making a 'band, slot and stappillis' for the wicket gate, buying 'plenschour', or flooring, nails for the bakehouse and paying two workmen for seven days' work on the drawbridge. Indoors the chamberlain paid for two 'pigs' to hold vinegar, 'gray papir' for the kitchen and bakehouse, a dozen 'prickitis and twa torchis', mending the 'chandellar', or candlestick, 'ane fillar to fill the wyne' and 'ane scuttall to draw it with', ropes to hang curtains, seventeen 'trie', or wooden, stoops, eight 'dry stuillis' and half a dozen 'wattir pottis of Inglis [English] mettill'. The furnishing of 52 vessels 'to the brydal' explains much of the preparation at Dalkeith at this time.

Although the crops from the mains of the several baronies, the produce of the bowtouns and the tenants' rents supplied the household with their basic foodstuffs, a great deal of money was spent on more appetising fare and luxury foods. The food purchased by Michael Shaw over six months of 1599 when the family often stayed at Dalkeith, including the occasion of a family wedding, included much fish and wild fowl of considerable variety: whiting, haddock, flounders, sea-trout and salmon, codlings, herring and mackerel, blackcocks, muirfowl, and solan geese. He also bought quantities of eggs, vinegar, olive oil, lard, 'a carcase of a young beef', 'a fat veal', 'a sucking pig', rabbits, Dieppe and Bordeaux 'plowmdames' (dried plums or prunes), 'callor [fresh] eggis', French wine, sack and claret, raisins, almonds, 'casnet [cane] succer', pepper, ginger, saffron, mace, cloves, cinnamon and nutmegs, two boxes of comfits, one of 'scrotchartis' and one of almonds. Over £126 was spent on sweetmeats and spices in just over a year. In 1569 Elizabeth Cook, wife of an Edinburgh merchant, James Oliphant, sent a sugar loaf weighing 21 lbs 10 oz across to the Newhouse with one of Agnes Leslie's servants, with an accompanying letter, 'ye sall ressave this succer, cannel [cinnamon], nutmeggis and saifrane [saffron] fra the boy that yor L. send the byll wyth, for gyff ther be onie... plesour or service I can do to yor L. I pray yow charge me and wyth the grace of god I sall do it.'[20] When Agnes Leslie went to Auchterhouse to supervise operations at mucking time ·in 1580, stores were laid in for her and her servants: fish from Dundee, including a turbot, or halibut, four quarts of ale, 'a leg of beef for the ladyis cuming' and 'thrie dossane menschoittis [manchets, rolls of bread of the finest flour]','togidder with 18 pieces of sweit meit'. While at Dalkeith the earl received gifts of venison from the laird of Buccleuch and 'the guidman of Carberrie', Hugh Rigg, advocate.

The large quantities of comfits and 'confections' mentioned in the Douglas accounts over the years were not all attributable to the family's 'sweet tooth', but were used for medicinal purposes. Some of the boxes of confections were bought from an Edinburgh 'sweit meit wyfe', Sarah Kerwood, whose account on one occasion came to £8, a substantial sum. Boxes of 'wat' and 'dry' confections were bought from Alexander Barclay. The comfits, made up in 'buistis', or boxes, were sugary pastilles made from seeds, spices and herbs, mixed with honey and saffron. Since Agnes Leslie also purchased quantities of the most common ingredients, such as almonds, anise, caraway, cinnamon, cloves, coriander, ginger, nutmeg and pepper, she may, like other housewives, have made her own supply. William Douglas probably used the confections as much as anyone in the household, being frequently in poor health. Michael Shaw, the Dalkeith chamberlain, once accounted for 'ane half pund of diapalma for my lordis breist', following on a purchase of sugar candy, which was also eaten as much for health as pleasure. The 'burden of herbis and chirries' carried to the Newhouse on one occasion may have been for the same purpose since cherry confections were taken for chest complaints. The presence of a nurse in the household is referred to in the later accounts; on one occasion she left Dalkeith for Kinross-shire in company with the earl. After she had been at Auchterhouse in attendence she received payment of 8 bolls of meal 'at the lairdis hamecuming'. On the journey home from Dalkeith in January 1597 the chamberlain paid 'for beiring of my lordis schyre [chair] to Leith,2s, Item, for our fraught, 6s–8d, Item, for carrying the schyre out of Bruntyland to the Newhous, 6s–8d'.

For all his serious-mindedness, William Douglas had his moments of recreation; from time to time he was handed money to play at cards, and once, at Dalkeith, ordered billiard tables to be made. At his stopping-places, such as the ferries, or when he was holding open house, he gave money to the pipers and minstrels who came to play to the company. He and his wife were often in Edinburgh where for over twenty years they rented a chamber in the foreland of the house lived in by David Somer, a merchant and leading protestant in the burgh.[21] The family did much business with Edinburgh merchants over the years. In 1541 Sir Robert Douglas redeemed a gold chain from Gilbert Lauder, merchant and money-lender, which he had pledged with him for merchandise and money. David Somer had lent him over £120, which was paid back in 1550. William Douglas himself bought cloth from William Paterson who, like Somer, has been described as a protestant activist in the municipal power-struggles of the 1560s, and had borrowed £347 from a Dundee merchant, Robert Douglas. Sometimes a relative living in Edinburgh would contact a merchant on behalf of the family; in 1569 Agnes Keith, wife of the Regent Moray, took a written order to Elizabeth Cook, wife of the merchant, James Oliphant, in which Agnes Leslie asked for 9 ells of fine black damask, 2 ells of black velvet, an ounce of black sewing silk and some yellow cambric. Lady Moray herself took the materials across to the lady of Lochleven.[22]

In Margaret Erskine's last illness medicines were bought from the Edinburgh apothecary, Robert Craig, whose account for £26 was rendered by his wife, the receipt being witnessed by Dr Alexander Preston, the King's 'medecinar'[23]. Large sums were spent on clothes; sixteenth-century materials, heavily trimmed and embroidered, were expensive, but the 'making' was usually a mere fraction of the cost and the tailor had sometimes to wait several years for his money. At her death Margaret Erskine owed a tailor, Andrew Clerk, half of a bill for £56-11s-6d for 'furneissing and werking of claithis' for the marriage of her granddaughter, Margaret Colville. In 1583 George Wauchope, an Edinburgh merchant, rendered an account for the huge sum of £534-18s for materials for clothes supplied over the previous two years and made into garments for the laird and his sons by a tailor, John Douglas[24]. The surviving account details the laird's 'thrie standis' of clothes made during these years, mainly in richly-trimmed and embroidered black materials, but including a warm gown of hunscott, a cloth made in the Low Countries, riding clothes trimmed with green Spanish taffeta and some undetailed 'nycht geir' costing £3 to make. The laird's son, Robert, had ordered a fashionable mandillion cloak with an embroidered lining, and more colourful garments than his father's, in green, grey, violet, and white.

With a considerable upkeep, including the financial support of three generations of his family and seven daughters to find tochers for – they were known as 'the seven pearls of Lochleven' – money was often in short supply. When making his will in 1568, William had reminded his brother, Robert, earl of Buchan, 'ye knaw my sonis leving will not be mekle, my Modir [being] payit and my wiffis beand deducit'. None of his own estate accounts are full enough to give an idea of his annual income but those of Margaret Erskine, as her husband's executrix, for the years 1548-53, suggest something like £330-340. If a man of £100 rent a year was reasonably 'substantious' then William Douglas should have been fairly comfortable, especially after he succeeded to the Morton estates in 1588. However, more land meant a greater upkeep. In 1599 the Roxburghshire chamberlain, Andrew Hepburn, reckoned on £982-13s-4d from the teind-silver of Newlands and Linton, but actually overspent by £455-18s. The chamberlain's own expenses over six months had amounted to £400. When he was in France in 1585 William wrote home to his wife asking for money,' gif it wer bot ane hundreth crownis, for I am neir ane end of the siller that I had already'. Meantime, he borrowed the equivalent of £750 Scots in La Rochelle. Accounts with merchants, like those with the tailors, tended to run up for years and were paid in instalments, and if a bond had been granted for payment, a safeguard that many merchants demanded, interest had to be paid as well. Nevertheless a merchant could not afford to lose a client even if he were in arrears: in 1574, two years after Margaret Erskine's death, the Dundee merchant William Kinloch wrote to Sir William, 'pleis yor M. wit, I hef resavit fra yor servand . . . ten pundis money for the rest of a debt awand be yor umquhyll [late] moder, quhome god assolze, for the quhilk I thank yor M. of yor guid remembrans, and gif [if] it be yor M. plesor to charge me as yor moder did with sic penneworthis as I wes accustomat . . . sic as wynis, claith, silkis and uder necessaires . . . I salbe at yor M. comand . . .'.[25] The money that William carried in his pockets he received from his chamberlains and clerks, sometimes large sums being handed to him after the accounts had been made up or a sale realised but at other times small amounts were given to him for minor expenses or specific purposes, such as alms to the poor; 'to the puir at Leith Wynd at yor L. onlouping [mounting], 10s'. He carried small sums in his pockets, tied in the corner of a handkerchief; 'to yor L. the 20 July to put in yor napkin neuk, 20s 8d'.

Family papers and letters record his lifelong contacts with others who were involved in public and local affairs; making 'tryst' with the Rutherfords who insisted on holding the tower of Langnewton on his own lands[26]; an attempt by the laird of Covington to drag him into his quarrel with Sir John Shairp over the burning of the latter's corn, by asking Douglas to witness Lindsay's assurance not to trouble Shairp until the business was settled[27]; an order to him from the privy council to grant an assurance in his turn for an alleged offence which he had given to Lord John Hamilton when the latter was passing through Fife, at which Douglas 'marvellit' when told by his brother[28]; a letter from the formidable Sir Duncan Campbell of Glenorchy who swore that none of *his* men had been involved in driving off the cattle of the tenants at Keillour, but promised to look into the matter[29]; giving hospitality at Auchterhouse to John Erskine of Dun, kinsman and fellow-champion of the reformed kirk, in whose company he must have been able to relax[30]; paying the stipend of the reader at Kinross, Alexander Wardlaw, the first protestant clergyman in the parish kirk, appointed at Candlemas 1561 only six months after the 'Reformation parliament'[31]. Even the political division into King's men and Queen's men during the civil war of 1568-71 could not entirely separate friends. 'Richt traist cusing', wrote Archibald, 5th earl of Argyll, supporter of Queen Mary's cause, from the west of Scotland in July 1570, evading Douglas's request for news from that part of the country because 'variance amangis us . . . suld nocht be aggreyit amangis [between] freindis in thair awin particularis [privately] . . .'. In any case, he said, Douglas's people were not inclined to believe any news 'that cumis out of this airthe [airt]. Thairfoir, I omit the samin'. If the other wished to send any of *his* news, however, Argyll would be glad to hear it. He ended, 'Commend me to my Cumar [godmother] yor wyf, I hoyp to God that schortly fryndis on this syd may recompense yow of ony kyndnes ye sawe'.[32] Personal letters often reveal what the history books obscure, that personal friendships were often stronger than political alliances.

WILLIAM DOUGLAS

NOTES

1 Morton Muniments (S.R.O.), GD 150
2 *Ibid.*, GD 150/2234, fo 10; Douglas's narrative of the Reformation and the reign of Queen Mary is contained in this same manuscript.
3 *Registrum Honoris de Morton* (Bannatyne Club), I, 26-7.
4 *Ibid.*, I, 12-13.
5 A. Fraser, *Mary Queen of Scots* (1969), Chapter 18.
6 This and the following royal letter, *Registrum Honoris de Morton*, I, 144-5, 133-4.
7 *Ibid.*, I, 143-4.
8 *Ibid.*, I, 176-7.
9 Register House Series (S.R.O.), RH 9/3/72.
10 *Registrum Honoris de Morton*, I, 176-7.
11 Register House Series, RH9/1/2.
12 *Ibid.*

13 The principal of kindly tenancy is more fully discussed in connection with 'The Farmers of Melrose'; see also, M.H.B. Sanderson, *Scottish Rural Society in the sixteenth century*, Chapter 5.
14 Register House Series, RH 11/41/1
15 Morton Muniments, GD 150/2086
16 *Ibid.*, GD 150/2080; Register House Series, RH 9/1/3.
17 Details of the buildings at Lochleven castle from *Report of the Royal Commission on the Ancient and Historical Monuments of Scotland, Fife and Kinross; Lochleven castle*, guide written by N.Q. Bodan for The Scottish Development Department, Ancient Monuments Division.
18 Morton Muniments, GD 150/2190.
19 *Ibid.*, GD 150/ 2727 (1599)
20 *Ibid.*, GD 150/2727 (1569)

21 M. Lynch, *Edinburgh and the Reformation*, 16, 90, 105-6; Morton Muniments, GD 150/2186, *passim*.

22 *Ibid.*, GD 150/2727 (1569).

23 *Ibid.*, GD 150/2190, 16 March 1574.

24 *Ibid.*, GD 150/formerly box 148 (1583).

25 *Ibid.*, GD 150/2191.

26 *Registrum Honoris de Morton*, I, 60-1.

27 *Ibid.*, I, 135-6.

28 *Ibid.*, I, 85-6.

29 *Ibid.*, I, 177-9.

30 Morton Muniments, GD 150/2080.

31 *Ibid.*, GD 150/2190, 3 August 1561.

32 *Registrum Honoris de Morton*, I, 52; the earl of Argyll although a supporter of Queen Mary was also a consistent member of the Protestant party. His wife, Jean Stewart, was a natural sister of the Queen and the earl of Moray.

PATRICK NIMMO

Tailor

PATRICK NIMMO worked in the crowded conditions of the densely-populated burgh of Edinburgh, practising one of its most prominent crafts. After the last serious outbreak of plague which occurred in 1584, the population of Edinburgh dramatically increased in the general rise which doubled the number of its inhabitants in the century after 1540. The bulk of the population was contained within something like one hundred and forty acres, concentrated in the towering 'lands' on the High Street and in the closes and wynds leading off it. In an outer half-circle lay the separate burgh of the Canongate, the suburb of the Cowgate and others such as Bristo, Potterrow and West Port, and the development 'under-the-castle-wall' near to the landward parish church of St Cuthbert. Business was guaranteed to a tailor, in supplying both the everyday needs of 'the neighbours' of the town and the demands of fashionable society and its attendant professional circle. The masters of the tailors' craft guild were not only numerous but influential and comparatively prosperous, appearing regularly among the craft representatives on the town council and high up in the scale in the burgh tax rolls.

The practice of the craft was carefully regulated and its privileges jealously protected in what was a conservatively-minded and monopolistic community, the craft guild, in a sense burgh society in miniature. Training, from apprenticeship to freedom of the craft, was made a long expensive process in order to regulate the number of masters. In 1531 the cost of a new freeman's 'upset' was £5 and 'ane honest denner to the sworne maisteris therof'; by 1586 it had risen to £19 'in contentatioun of his banquet', with £6 'to the offesar'. According to approved rules drawn up in 1584 an apprentice had to serve for five years, followed by three years 'for meat and fie', the journeyman-stage. The desire of trained men from outside the Edinburgh guild to operate within it is reflected in the concession that if a man had not served an apprenticeship with an Edinburgh freeman he might be entered provided he married a freeman's daughter. More often, unfreemen, including those from the burgh of the Canongate, simply tried to steal the Edinburgh freemen's trade: 'quha daylie cumis within the fredome of the samyn and takis furth wark, schaipin and unschaipin, pertening to the burgessis and freemen of the burgh and wirkis the samyn in thair awin fredomes, and thereftir inbringis the said wark agane to this burgh to the awner therof and takis thair pryce thairfor and thairby also grettumlie hurtis the dekyin and brether of thair commoditie and proffeit . . . '.[1]

There was also the problem of those indwellers, non-burgesses, in Edinburgh who, without burgess rights or obligations and unattached to masters, worked in private houses, lofts and chambers, wherever they could find a workspace, taking payment as if they were freemen of the craft. Their work was to be confiscated and they themselves imprisoned and fined. There were tensions within the craft structure itself for, in controlling the number of masters, the rules created a 'bulge' of trained but unfree men, allowed board and a small daily wage but with few immediate prospects of advancing themselves in their craft. Their frustration and low pay encouraged them to take part with the apprentices and servants in the craft riots that punctuated the latter part of the sixteenth century in the burgh. There is little evidence that in Scotland there were tailors' workshops of the kind that already existed in London and some of the larger English cities. With a few exceptions the Edinburgh tailors could not afford to operate on this labour-intensive basis. Yet there was a pool of skilled, unfree workmen who were unable to set up on their own account but continued to take low-paid work in the small, household-based tailors' booths. Master tailors doubtless had different ways of looking at this. Some may simply have regarded unrest among their workmen as a discipline problem, for the control of which they were accountable to the kirk session in post-Reformation times. Others must have exacerbated relations in the booth by encouraging unfreemen to use it as a base in taking work in their own names, charging them a sum of money for the liberty. In 1584 the craft council deplored the action of some of its own members who 'under colour of servandis' kept unfreemen in their booths in this way, ordaining that no workmen be received who were not bound to serve for meat and fee.[2]

However necessary the tailor's work to the personal comfort and vanity of the people, he shared the fate of all craftsmen who deal personally with the customer of being treated like a kind of retained servant. If there had been the equivalent of the music-hall in the sixteenth century, the caricature of the little, bent, under-fed 'whip-the-cat' tailor would have been one of its favourite victims, as he was later to become. While some craftsmen knocked-off with the hours of daylight, those who worked with textiles toiled on into the night to complete orders. They must have been torn between reminding customers of unpaid bills and losing their custom altogether. Today's mass-production of garments has made us forget the drudgery of turning out, at speed and by hand, the heavy, elaborate garments of earlier centuries. Although the whole burgh was theoretically the market-place, individual craftsmen, including tailors, tended to draw their regular income from a number of regular customers, and their day-to-day work came from the neighbourhood rather than the town. A picture of the normal scale of their operations, and a reminder of the fact that their work consisted as much of mending as of making clothes, is found in the articles of November 1584 which argued that the best way to squeeze out the unfreemen was for the freemen and their servants to give the neighbours as good a service as possible:

> ' . . . thairfore quha swa wirkis thair nichtbouris claythis sall at all tymes quhen he is requirit, upoun 24 houris warning appoint ane of his servandis for quhome he sall ansuer to pas to the nichtbouris dwelling hous for mending and repairing of sic ornamentis and clething as ar to be mendit of all sortis without exceptioun. And the said servand to entir to the wark at fyve houris in the morning ungangand owt without leiff quhile [until] nyne houris at evin, and to haif thairfor ilk day twelf penneis and his meit; . . .'.[3]

It must have eased conditions in a small workroom that the business operated as a sewing agency which took some of the workforce out of the booth for a day at a time. Besides sewing clothes, tailors were often asked to repair upholstery such as bed curtains and chair covers.

Patrick Nimmo was apprenticed to the Edinburgh tailor, Adam Hunter. James Nimmo, tailor in the Canongate, was a relative of the previous generation, possibly his father or an uncle. The mention in his account book of his brother, Alexander Nimmo in Bancreis, or Bancreif (location untraced but in Nimmo's case possibly in the south-west), suggests that the main stem of the family still lived to landward and that James in the Canongate was probably an uncle. Alexander's designation is that of a tenant farmer. Patrick's master, Adam Hunter, ran a comparatively small business, appearing among the lowest categories of tax-payer in the burgh tax-roll of 1583 at 5s a year, but Patrick himself was more successful. He married Marion Uddart, a daughter of Martin Uddart, Ormond pursuivant of the Lord Lyon's court and a junior member of a well-known merchant family, through whose right as a burgess's daughter he was made a burgess of Edinburgh in April 1586.[4] Two months later, on 7 June, he was made a freeman of the Edinburgh tailors' craft.[5] Marion may have had a comfortable upbringing since her father left over £200 of silver ware and household goods, although she and her sister Rebecca may have been fairly young when he died in 1568.[6] Later, she and Patrick came into possession of rents from the house in the Canongate that had belonged to James Nimmo.[7] Apart from this, Patrick's income was probably derived from the practise of his craft, from the regular custom of certain clients in and outwith the burgh. Whatever his practical training, he never learned to write, merely putting his initials to formal documents the texts of which were engrossed in his account book.

The book, kept for him by clerks – it shows several hands – is a rare survival for the period.[8] In fact it did survive only because it later became a law clerk's receipt book and found its way into legal records. It consists of 105 folios, covering the years 1597-1609, the individual accounts being crossed-out as payment was received. Here and there among the accounts are memoranda of Nimmo's own expenses and notes of business which he attended to for clients, a subsidiary service which many merchants also offered to their customers. In these additional memoranda are a few glimpses of Nimmo's way of life. An account fairly near the beginning of the book to 'Agnes Massone, landisladie' suggests that he was renting premises at that stage; details in the account are a mixture of clothing expenses and repairs to the workplace: 'for mending the glass windoes', repairing the cobbles before the building, a new band to the 'yett', 'through lock' and nails to put them on with, money for lime and sand and the cost of flooring the loft. He also made a note of 13s 'of lent silver that yor maidin borrowit'.[9] Much later, after an account dated May 1605, he noted 'quhat I have depurssit in graithing [furnishing] the buith', possibly his own premises:[10]

> 38 deals - £13-6s
> 2 little roof spars to lay the flooring on and to be 'wall plattis to the wallis'
> 2,000 and 25 flooring nails
> 3,000 plencher nails (for the floor)
> 500 door nails
> 100 'windock [window] naillis'
> 'Payit for redding of the buith of quarrell' (? rubble) and carrying it out
> To the mason for workmanship and lime
> Four 'battis' of iron to couple the wall plates to
> 'For locks and bands to the kist and overbuird'
> To the wright for workmanship
> For the sawing of twenty deals

The whole cost just over £42. The most interesting items on the list of expenses are 'the kist and overbuird', probably the cutting-out table and box beneath it into which the tailor threw the offcuts and clippings. By mid-17th century these clippings were called 'cabbage' or 'garbage', taken by the workmen as perquisites. In the woodcut in *The Book of Trades* by Amman and Sachs (1568) showing the tailor, the 'kist' can be clearly seen beneath the cutting-out table.[11] At one time Patrick paid for repairs to the house in the Canongate that had formerly belonged to John Nimmo, including the cost of posts and twenty threaves of bere straw with which to thatch it.[12]

The earliest account in the book dates from 1590, four years after Patrick became a freeman. The entries relate to clients who kept running accounts, not the day-to-day work done in the houses of the neighbourhood, and the garments in question were probably those which the tailor made himself or on which he closely supervised the work in the booth. The texts of the entries are the 'office copies' of bills sent to customers from time to time, of the kind that also turn up in family papers, although sparingly for the sixteenth century. The clients included noblemen, lairds, small proprietors, officials of various kinds, and a handful of undesignated individuals, with the wives and occasionally daughters of the men in these groups. When a tailor was made a freeman it was specifically stated whether he was free to make men's or women's clothes.[13] Although Patrick Nimmo was free 'to werk all maner of men's werk' he did make women's garments as well, a reminder that rules should not be taken literally as a guide to what was actually done. His most regular customers were a group of Hamilton lairds and their dependents and, on one occasion each, the 1st and 2nd marquis of Hamilton, perhaps a compliment to Patrick's handiwork for their relations and acquaintances. The pattern of Hamilton clients, with the earliest dates of their accounts, is:

> Sir John Hamilton of Lettrick, 1590
> John Duncan, servant to the 1st marquis of Hamilton, 1598
> David Hamilton, son of Hamilton of Bothwelhaugh, 1598
> Hamilton of Innerwick, 1599
> James Hamilton, 'servant to the advocate', c. 1600
> Hamilton of Torrence, 1601
> Sir Alexander Hamilton of Fenton, 1601
> John Hamilton, chamberlain of Kinneil, official of the 1st marquis, 1601
> Hamilton of Stanehouse, 1601
> Margaret Hamilton, former nun of Sciennes monastery, Edinburgh, 1601
> John, 1st marquis of Hamilton, 1602
> James, 2nd marquis of Hamilton, 1605
> Mr James Hamilton, commissary of Lanark, 1606

Although Patrick Nimmo had been only a child during the civil war of 1568-73, following Queen Mary's deposition, the craft in which he had been trained had felt, like any other, the effects of the contest between the King's men and Queen's men not only for control of the national government but of the town and even the crafts themselves. It has been said that on the whole the poorer crafts supported the Queen, or at least the poorer craft-members, of whom Adam Hunter, tailor, was one, and that the tailor craft was dominated by Marian partisans from 1567 onwards.[14] Patrick's master is not recorded among those who were prosecuted or became actively involved during the military conflict, but his sympathies may nevertheless have been clear-cut. Patrick received his freedom just a year after the Hamilton family, Mary's supporters, were rehabilitated, numbers of them having been forfeited as a result of the civil war, and it is possible that he may have found his earliest customers among representatives of former Marian families who had been known to his master's working household.

The other notable feature of the pattern of customers is the large number who came from the south-west of Scotland, from the neighbourhood of Kirkcud-bright and Wigtown, a part of the country with which Nimmo may have had connections: Murray of Broughton, Lindsay of Dunrod, the Gordons of Grange and Auchland, Brown of Land, Stewart of Garlies, the laird of Ernock, the lady of Barnbarroch, McCulloch of Drumorell, McLennan of Barneicht, David Vaus, Charles Maxwell, John Meikle, clerk of Kirkcudbright, Mr Robert Glendinning, minister of Kirkcudbright, and John Hannah, provost of Wigtown. This is a phenomenon which is encountered over and over again in the testaments of Edin-burgh merchants and craftsmen, reflecting the perennial tendency to give trade to a countryman or relative, partly in the hope of getting better terms or more extensive credit.

In a working record such as Patrick Nimmo's account book even the short-est sentence may hold valuable information. Reading the entries is almost like examining the garments in order to understand their construction. For the six-teenth century, from which so few garments have survived, documentary and pic-torial record must be used together and compared in order to glean the information both on the construction of the garments themselves and the tailor's business methods. In most cases the tailor supplied the cloth, lining and trimmings for garments, charging separately for the materials and the making, the latter being a very small proportion of the total cost. In 1601 the laird of Stanehouse's 'Scots claith' clothes cost £6 to make and the materials themselves cost £48-11s-7d. Since he received so little for his workmanship it paid the tailor to stock materials in quantity, becoming a merchant tailor, or to buy them wholesale from the merchant. There is evidence that Patrick Nimmo stocked materials for sale, trimmings and certain accessories such as hat strings, shoe ribbons and points, as well as supplying cloth for garments which he himself made up. In August 1601 he gave the chamberlain of Kinneil's servant, Charles Gibb, 3 quarters of London brown cloth at £9 the ell, red stemming (a woollen cloth) brown silk and silver pasments and blue sewing silk, with a hat string, a pair of woven shanks (stock-ings) and two dozen points. At other times he made clothes for the chamberlain and his family. On 22 June 1587 he helped out the merchant, Robert Joysie, for whom he also made garments, with some fustian and linen and a dozen green silk points and four dozen green silk buttons ' for his majesteis grene claithis', sending them off with a messenger-at-arms.[15] In the summer of 1602 he charged Sir John Hamilton of Lettrick for 8 ells of pasments 'send to yow with my boy'. When Thomas McLennan of Barneicht called at the booth about his own order, Nimmo 'delyverit to yorself ane mask to yor wyfe', which the laird no doubt took home as a novelty from Edinburgh.

When the customer supplied the cloth this sometimes caused problems, the most predictable of which being that there would not be enough. Nimmo fre-quently notes this in customers' accounts: to the laird of Garlies, 'half oz gray pasmentis [trimmings] mair nor William Bailie coft to yor M. claithis, pryce is 16s', or to the laird of Stanehouse, 'for thrie naillis of claith that I furneist mair nor I resavit, that wes forgot in the last compt, 30s'. In making a gown for the wife of Sir John Hamilton of Letterick, the tailor found himself short of every-thing, Spanish taffeta, burret, buckram for stiffening, pasments and even black sewing silk. It must have been difficult to remember all these details in a busy workshop and a craftsman who could not write himself must have required the constant presence of a clerk on the workforce.

The occasional reference to material used 'at yor command' and 'at comand of yor lettir' reminds us that the tailor worked to both written and verbal instruc-tions, the latter sometimes at second-hand. In the case of regular customers for whom he held patterns or strips of paper as measurements this was not a great problem, even as to fit. Contemporary with the Nimmo account book is a letter to a tailor in Edinburgh from Anna Menteith, wife of the laird of Dundas, asking him to make clothes for herself and her daughter. It is worth quoting as giving a good idea of how much was left to the tailor's judgement and discretion:

'William,
Ye sall tak aff of this gray stemming fra David Mitchell to be the ryding cloik and skirt, ye sall wirk the skirt with twa pasmentis together even doune rownd abowt, And the cloik with twa twas rownd abowt the taill, and waill [choose] the pasmentis nixt ane of the colouris therof agreand with the claith, and Spanische taffatie to lyn the lapps of the cloik as ye sall think maist conform to the rest. Item, ye sall tak off ane welicoit [petticoat] to Margaret of this skarlet stemming and put thrie twais of pasments about the taill of it as ye sall think maist agreing thairto. As concerning the sleivis to the bowret gowne to Margaret, mak thaim of sic collour of satine cowttit owt as ye sall think maist fittand. Item, as for the uther twa welicoits the berar will informe yow. And lykwayis, he will schaw yow anent the gowne neckis. And tak off velvott to be ane huid to my selff.
Yor gud freind
Annas Menteith
lady Dundas[16]

We hope the tailor got the number of pasments right and that the servant had sufficiently mastered the ladies' instructions about their new wyliecoats by the time he arrived at the tailor's booth carrying the various bundles of cloth already bought from a merchant.

As well as visits from customers or their servants the tailor was expected to call on his clients. Patrick Nimmo once charged the wife of Sir Alexander Hamilton of Fenton for his horse-hire twice to Fenton tower and once to Pin-kie.[17] His work continually brought him into contact with other craftsmen. In 1605 he paid for the dyeing of the marquis of Hamilton's 'blak castle hat', the embroidering of the marchioness's burret and shot taffeta gowns and the heavier 'goffering' of her riding cloak. Occasionally, clothes which Nimmo made were dyed to the customer's chosen colour, like Charles Maxwell's and the laird of Ernock's silk shanks, for which dyeing cost 30s a pair. Parts of garments were sent out to the embroiderers, none of whose names is given, whose charges were paid by the tailor and passed on to his customer in the account. An embroiderer was paid for 'out cutting' the breast and sleeves of the lady of Letterick's kersey gown, a skirt and sleeves of rose-coloured satin, and for 'mushing', perhaps stamping out a pattern, on the laird's black satin doublet.[18]

Payment of accounts was a long drawn-out business, nearly all bills containing arrears from previous accounts. Part payment was common. The chamberlain of Kinniel's 'first compt' of 1601 came to £30–12s–6d of which he paid £15, £3 of it arrears from a previous account, and proceeded to ask Nimmo to buy and send out to him a selection of groceries, sugar, pepper, ginger and an ounce of quicksilver which alone cost £18. On some occasions the customer paid Nimmo when the tailor called on him; Claud Hamilton younger of Torrance paid him £6 at Hamilton in the winter of 1601, at which point he was in the process of running up a fifth account, none of the others having been paid in full. The chamberlain of Kinneil's account was also paid at Hamilton the following year. It may have been worth the journey not only to get an order but to prevail on a client for some payment at the same time. Into the account book is written the mutual agreement about their reckoning by Nimmo and James McCulloch of Drumorell, 'the fyrst tyme we met in Minigof' (Minnigaff), on 27 September 1607.[19] There is one instance of payment having been made to the tailor's wife. Nimmo seems to have occasionally resorted to taking a customer's obligation, a safeguard which merchants used rather more frequently; in June 1601 he reminded Thomas McClellan of Barneicht of the £14–8s–5d that ye ar adetit to me forby yor obligation'. On the other hand he granted a bond, on 28 June 1606, to repay Alexander Nimmo in Bancreis, his brother, the sum of £150 before the following Whitsunday.

The detailed tailoring accounts have preserved a picture of how Scottish society dressed in the last decade of the sixteenth century and for a few years after King James VI and his court left for London in 1603. Men's tailored garments consisted of doublets, breeks or hose, shanks and socks, coats, jupes, cloaks, and outer gowns. For women, the tailor made gowns and their components of bodice, sleeves and skirt, waistcoats, wyliecoats, doublets, hoods and cloaks, and riding cloaks and skirts. Black was the smart colour, for best clothes and richer folk, but garments were also made for both sexes of blue, brown, green, grey, 'sad', 'lemon', yellow, olive, orange, purple, 'cramosie', red and scarlet cloth.

The man's doublet, the basic upper garment, was worn over the shirt, dipping in front and flaring into a short 'skirt' just below the waistline, standing out over the nether garments and thus concealing the points by which the latter were secured to the doublet.[20] Patrick Nimmo made men's doublets from taffeta, satin and bombazine, a mixture of wool and silk or wool with a silky finish which was used as a substitute for velvet. A grey satin doublet for Sir James Hamilton of Letterick in 1601 used 3¾ ells of material costing £27.[21] The doublet was stiffened and lined and padded out in front into the fashionable shape which at the end of the century was known as 'peascod'. Claud Hamilton's green fustian doublet, made in 1601, required 2 ells of stenting, or stiffening material, which was often poldavie canvas, half a pound of caddes, a cotton wool or flock padding which was inserted between stiffening and lining and stitched into place, and a quarter of taffeta, possibly for a small, visible area such as the lining of the collar.[22] Even when the outer material of the doublet was fine, the lining was generally serviceable, usually plaiding, linen or tweel [twill]. Three quarters of 'new stenting' for the laird of Garlies' green satin doublet suggests a repair. 'For a nail of stufe to eik your breekis' sounds more like a necessary alteration. Around the turn of the century sleeves might also be padded; James Hamilton, the advocate's servant, had a doublet made of black satin of which the sleeves were padded with caddes and made from the plaiding used to line the body of the doublet. Sleeves were often detachable and might be made of a different material from the main part of the garment. The materials for James Hamilton's black satin doublet are detailed:

6 quarters of fine stenting	12s
9 quarters of tweel to line it	22s–6d
3 ells plaiding for the sleeves and to make the lining	24s
¼ pound of caddes to pad the sleeves	5s
1 ell of black buckasie (fine buckram) to line the tails, breast and bands (a reinforced band carried the eyelet holes for the points)	13s–4d
3 oz 6 drop weight of additional pasments, over and above those supplied by the customer	£5–1s–3d
¾ oz of sewing silk	18s–9d
4 dozen and 3 buttons (32d a dozen)	11s–4d
½ ell 'round' stenting to stiffen the neck and 'burrs' (? wings on the shoulders, made of looped tags)	4s[23]

Leg wear was either breeks (breeches) worn with separate shanks (stockings) or hose consisting of breeks and long tailored stockings made as one garment. Most suits in Nimmo's account book were made with breeks and shanks, although there are a few references to hose. Late in the century the most common style of breeks for separate stockings was the Venetians, which were knee-length fastened below the knee with points or 'strings' as Patrick Nimmo called them, or buttons. Their outline was either wide at the top and gathered into the waist to give a pear-shape, with a certain amount of stuffing, or voluminous throughout with a very smooth surface. Breeks were made from velvet, russet, which was a heavy woollen homespun, freize and French cloth. The tailor lined them with plaiding and tweel and stiffened them with buckram. When they were stuffed this was done with hair, probably horse hair, and the hair was covered with harden, a coarse quality linen. Alexander Gordon of Auchland's breeks, made of 'fine French purpour [purple]' cloth, costing £15, had half a dozen 'silk and silver' buttons at each knee and silver braid. The laird of Ernock's cost £7-8s-9d (£1 for the making) and at the same time he had a pair of silk shanks to go with them dyed and soled by the tailor,[24] rather more economical than the laird of Auchland's. Hose mentioned include those made for the marquis of Hamilton from 'sad silk russet searge', for the merchant, Robert Joysie, from black worsted, and for Sir James Hamilton of Lettrick from grey London cloth, lined with tweel and plaiding and provided with buckram 'pouchis'.[25] Socks were worn as well as shanks. Although they may have served at times as linings under boots, the decoration applied to the 'soikheidis' implies that they were a fashion feature, sometimes made of red or purple stemming or taffeta and trimmed with fringes, pasments and points.

Of garments worn over the doublet, the jupe, fitted and sleeveless, may be said to have approximated to the English jerkin. It was usually made in the same material as the breeks or hose and carried a large number of buttons for both the front opening and decoration; that made for Sir John Hamilton of Letterick had 114 silk and silver buttons. The shoulders were stiffened with buckram and like the doublet had shoulder 'burrs'.[26] Mr Peter Kennoquhy had a jupe made of green worsted trimmed with grey pasments. The coat was an outer garment of jacket length, buttoned in front, strengthened on the hem with buckram, the tails lined with serge or sey, the latter a serge-like woollen cloth. The laird of Innerwick's son's coat of green London cloth had the buttonholes worked with black silk, with buckram 'to lyne the taillis and to be pouchis and to lay abowt the knees and the breistis of the said coit'. The neck was lined with taffeta.[27] Coat and breeks were, like jupe and breeks, usually made of the same material. The making of an olive-coloured cloak, coat, and breeks cost £5-10s.

The cloak, which was often the most eye-catching garment, might be elaborately decorated although made from sturdy 'Essex gray' or London cloth. The marquis of Hamilton's cloak was made of 'cullerderoy' cloth, a tawny or purple material, in 1605. Cloaks were of various styles such as Spanish, with a hood, the long French cloak which sometimes had wide sleeves. It is difficult to identify types in Nimmo's accounts because he seldom gives the amount of material used, but since he usually made cloaks as part of a suit, of cloak, coat and breeks, or cloak, coat and hose, or cloak, jupe and breeks, this probably means that here it would be the short, shoulder cloak rather than the heavier, additional garment worn out-of-doors. Charles Maxwell's cloak took 3¾ ells of London cloth, the neck was lined with velvet and the whole was trimmed with silk pasments. Sir John Hamilton of Lettrick's russet cloak had silver pasments and 3 dozen silver 'lang taillit buttonis', some of which would have been for decoration. Mr Peter Kennoquhy's riding cloak of 'scheipis cullour' was also lined in the neck with velvet and on the front with taffeta. There is an interesting reference to 'rantering' which, according to the *Concise Scots Dictionary*, meant mending or repairing. Nimmo charged Kennoquhy £2-6s-8d which was 'payit to the ranterer for rantering 7 ellis of yor blak cloke',[28] suggesting that he put out repair work to men who were not in his own workshop. One wonders how many 'stickit' journeymen took on repairs and alterations.

In Nimmo's account book, women's gowns were made of velvet, kersey, burret, which was a coarse woollen fabric, damask, grogram and taffeta. The lady of Fenton's gown was made of 'pasvelour' stemming, a velvety textured material which it is thought may have been of a purple colour. It took 6½ ells of the material to make the gown, with 3 quarters of buckram and 3 quarters of poldavie stenting for stiffening, the finer canvas being used for the bodice, an ell of linen and one of plaiding to line the sleeves and some caddes to stuff them, with an ell of taffeta to line the tail and shoulder 'burrs'. Nimmo charged for '3 unce and ane half of pasmentis mar nor yor woman coft' and paid 4s for a box with clasps in which this gown was delivered.[29] Damask and kersey gowns each cost £5 to make for the lady of Lettrick, with 13s 4d to the embroiderer for working the breast and sleeves of the kersey gown, the sleeves being of rose-coloured satin. The laird of Innerwick's daughter, Elspeth, had a gown of 'chainging', or shot, burret which needed 9 ells, at 42s an ell, the sleeves stiffened with buckram and stuffed as was the fashion late in the century. It had eight orange buttons and was embroidered on the breast and 'litill taillis'.[30] The laird of Innerwick's wife and another daughter, Jeanne, had 'winter gounis' made along with his 'stand of winter claithis' in November 1599.[31] Wyliecoats, stiffened at the hem and heavily lined with plaiding or scouringis', were made from fustian and grogram. Elizabeth Hamilton's wyliecoat was lined with both fustian and tweel, 1¼ ells of fustian being used for 'the bodeis'. In the winter of 1604 Patrick Nimmo made 'brydle claithis', wedding garments, for the daughter of his regular customer, the chamberlain of Kinneil. These included:

> a chamlet silk gown and a wyliecoat lined with linen; a velvet night bonnet (for indoor wear not bed) decorated with gold pasments, with a cambric mutch to wear under it; 2½ ells of tammy crape 'to hir craig [throat]' and a fine fringed neckerchief worn over the shoulders; a rail for her head, made of fine linen or cambric and worn like a shawl over the back of the head, or as an elaborate veil in the style of Mary, Queen of Scots; two hoods; a taffeta gown; a chamlet silk cloak; two other wyliecoats and a riding skirt and cloak.

The whole account, which included 'ane wardigaird' or receptacle for keeping clothes in, amounted to £58 8s 4d.[32]

The tailor undertook a variety of jobs besides making the basic garments. Some of these involved headwear, trimming, and lining hats to complement suits, and occasionally purchasing a hat on the customer's behalf. He even once bought 'ane felt to yor Mastership of ane hat', the makings of a hat for a particularly discriminating customer.[33] The felt is mentioned in the account of the Hamilton laird of Innerwick for whose family Nimmo made many clothes over the years. The laird's son, Alexander, who once had socks decorated with gold pasments, ordered a Spanish hat in 1599 which cost £5, a very substantial sum. For the laird himself Nimmo 'bordered' and lined two hats. A hat and hat-string were purchased for Sir John Hamilton of Lettrick and Charles Maxwell. Elaborate hat-strings might be made by an embroiderer; Lady Ogilvy once paid £40 to the King's embroiderer, William Beaton, for a hat-string to wear at her son's wedding.[34] A hat bought for Sir Alexander Hamilton of Fenton's 'man', probably his personal servant who would accompany him, cost £8 when lined with velvet. Even a less wealthy customer, Thomas McLennan of Barneicht, had a hat lined with double Spanish taffeta, with a 'poke' to keep it in.

Receptacles were occasionally purchased for clothes as well as for small items such as hats; James McCulloch's stand of clothes was sent in a 'pockmantie', or portmanteau, which cost 13s.[35] Claud Hamilton of Torrance, who ran up bill after bill without paying off any of them in full, once gave the tailor a hat in part payment, which was no doubt re-trimmed for a more thrifty customer. The widow of the laird of Dunrod, by then married to a Mr Robert Thomson, had a velvet coif made 'of the new and Inglis facion'. Occasionally the tailor lined armour. In 1597 he sent part of a sheepskin to Alexander Ford to be prepared as a lining for the tails of the young laird of Innerwick's jack, a padded leather coat worn as armour. Two years later he covered two steel bonnets for the laird himself.

The account book, with its different clerks' writing, the entries heavily crossed out, the language cryptic and work-a-day, is, like other survivals of its kind, the nearest we can come now to the atmosphere of the busy craftsman's workshop: the measuring, cutting, and endless stitching, interrupted by the coming and going of the servants of clients and other craftsmen; journeys to visit customers or, nearer home, to choose cloths and trimmings in the merchants' booths; making sense of customers' instructions as well as attending to their shopping commissions and even occasional legal business; sitting down with the clerk to take stock of the financial situation. The brief entries themselves sometimes give us the feeling of looking over the tailor's shoulder, by referring to the smallest details and processes; lining, binding, stiffening and padding, matching trimmings and the colours of the sewing silk in the dimly-lit workplace, stitching thousands of buttonholes and buttons in the year, and attaching pasments, strings, ribbons, braids and fringes.

As for the customers, the impression of their dress is of good, plain materials in fairly subdued tones with, as we might expect, more colour in the garments of the women and the younger generation of men. Apart from the marquises of Hamilton, they were mainly middling lairds and professional men and their womenfolk. In default of portraits of most of them it is interesting to have this verbal picture of what they wore:

Mungo Ross, baxter, Edinburgh – Two stands of worsted clothes.

John Meikle, clerk of Kirkcudbright – Doublet and breeks of black bombazine, trimmed with black pasments; a cloak of black English cloth with velvet at the neck; black shanks and garters; at the neck a linen 'overlay', or turned-down collar.

James Hamilton, commissary of Lanark – Doublet and breeks of black taffeta, both embroidered with cut-out work, the doublet having white taffeta at the neck and black buttons, the breeks fastened at the knee with tapes known as 'knittings'; a cloak of black serge trimmed with taffeta.

Robert Joysie, merchant, Edinburgh – Doublet of black bombazine; jupe and breeks of black corded silk, the breeks having pockets and fastened at the knee with knittings; a coat of black serge of Florence; black worsted hose; grey socks.

John Hannah, provost of Wigtown – A riding cloak and hood of Scots grey.

Mr Robert Glendinning, minister of Kirkcudbright – Coat and breeks of black 'cloth of the seill', the coat lined at the neck with taffeta, the breeks 'buffed out' and fastened at the knees with 'strings'.

Mr Peter Kennoquhy – Riding cloak of 'sheip's' colour, lined with velvet at the neck; jupe and breeks of green worsted trimmed with grey pasments; doublet of tammy fustian trimmed with grey pasments; socks of grey French stemming.
– Breeks of tammy French cloth with brown pasments; a coat of green French cloth; a cloak of Scots green.
– Doublet and breeks of black satin.
– Doublet of grey satin; breeks of grey velvet; brown socks; black cloak.

Thomas McClellan of Barneicht – Doublet of fustian, lined with tweel and with silver buttons; a taffeta jupe with silver buttons; taffeta breeks, with knittings and silver buttons at the knees; socks of tweel, fringed at the tops.

John Brown of Land – Doublet of black satin, with 3 dozen and
one buttons; breeks of black frieze, with
worsted garters at the knees.

Alexander Gordon of Auchland – Doublet of green Spanish taffeta,
with green pasments and 3½ dozen green
buttons; breeks of fine French purple cloth,
trimmed with pasments and silk looping and
silver buttons at the knees.

David Hamilton, son of the laird of Bothwelhaugh – Doublet of
green Spanish taffeta, embroidered in cut-
out work with red taffeta showing through;
breeks of grey kelt (homespun); coat of
same material as the breeks, with grey silk
buttons.

Claud Hamilton of Torrance – Doublet of green fustian; coat and
breeks of brown frieze cloth, with knittings
at the knees of the breeks; socks of dark
olive-coloured London cloth.

Alexander Hamilton, son of the laird of Innerwick – Doublet and
breeks of purple fustian; cloak of green
London cloth; socks of stemming decorated
with gold pasments; a Spanish hat
– Coat, cloak and breeks of brown London
cloth.
– A stand of purple frieze clothes.

Wife of Sir John Hamilton of Lettrick – Gowns of kersey
(embroidered on the breast and on the rose-
coloured satin sleeves), damask, grogram; a
hood, gown and skirt of figured velvet.

Wife of Sir Alexander Hamilton of Fenton – Gown, waistcoat and
skirt of purple satin; gown of 'bishop' satin;
a 'gingelein' gown with a silver lace
waistcoat and skirt; a black chamlet doublet
and skirt; a black taffeta doublet and skirt;
a black burret gown.

The Marquis of Hamilton (1605) – Doublet of raised velvet
– Doublet and breeks of green satin
– Doublet and socks of dark ('sad')
perpetuana
– suit of grey velvet
– suit of grey satin
– a black 'castle' hat
– a cloak of cullerderoy

The most cheerful, if shortest, account in the whole book must surely be that of Margaret Hamilton, an elderly ex-nun of the Dominican nunnery of St Catherine of Sienna, locally known as Sciennes, near Edinburgh. Sciennes earned a commendatory line or two from Sir David Lindsay in *Ane Satyre of the Thrie Estaitis* on account of the standard of education of the nuns and their exemplary moral conduct. In the freedom of her old age Margaret ordered from Patrick Nimmo 3 quarters of red Spanish taffeta, which he had delivered to William Hamilton of Woodhall for her, and 'ane pair of red hose'.[36]

In 1581 a clerk in chancery jotted down a ribald rhyme in the register in which he was working – as his fellow-clerks often did. It does not flatter the circumstances of the tailors' working conditions, and reads:

'Queritur'

Betwix twa tailyeoris ane lows
Betwix twa cattis ane mous
Betwix twa toddis [foxes] ane crawing cok
Betwix twa young freiris [friars] ane madin in hir smok

Quhilk of the four ar in greitest danger?
The resolutioun of the questioun

Young freiris ar furious on madis in thair smokis
And fockces are ferce or crawing cokis
And cattis are couteillis in taking of myce
Bot tailyeoris ar tirantis in killing of lyce'.[37]

PATRICK NIMMO

NOTES

1 J.D. Marwick, *Edinburgh Guilds and Crafts* (1909), 138-9

2 *Ibid.*, 139.

3 *Ibid.*, 139-40.

4 *Roll of Edinburgh Burgesses, 1406-1707* (S.R.S.).

5 Roll of Edinburgh Tailors (S.R.O.), GD1/12/63; unfoliated, under 7 June 1586, at back of book.

6 Edinburgh Commissariot Records, Register of Testaments (S.R.O.), CC8/8/2, fo 105v.

7 Canongate protocol books (S.R.O.), B22/22/28, fo 147.

8 Nimmo's account book (S.R.O.), RH 9/1/7; hereafter, Nimmo's account book.

9 *Ibid.*, fo 9.

10 *Ibid.*, fos 33, 34.

11 See plate 3

12 Nimmo's account book, fo 36v.

13 Roll of Edinburgh Tailors, GD1/12/63.

14 M. Lynch, *Edinburgh and the Reformation* (1981), 206-7.

15 Nimmo's account book, fo 7v.

16 Dundas of Dundas Muniments (S.R.O.), GD 75/577.

17 Nimmo's account book, fo 99v.

18 *Ibid.*, fo 5v.

19 *Ibid.*, fo 44v.

20 Information on the construction of garments has been drawn from Janet Arnold, *Patterns of Fashion, the cut and construction of clothes for men and women, c. 1560-1620*

(1985); C. W. and P. Cunnington, *Handbook of English Costume in the 16th century* (1970); J. Ashelford, *A Visual History of Costume, the Sixteenth Century* (1983); S. Maxwell and R. Hutchison, *Scottish Costume, 1550-1850* (1958).

21 Nimmo's account book, fo 6.
22 *Ibid.*, fo 4v.
23 *Ibid.*, fo 10v.
24 *Ibid.*, fo 12.
25 *Ibid.*, fo 6.
26 *Ibid.*, fo 6.
27 *Ibid.*, fo 12v.
28 *Ibid.*, fo 21v.
29 *Ibid.*, fo 16.
30 *Ibid.*, fo 13.
31 *Ibid.*, fo 12v.
32 *Ibid.*, fos 31-31v.
33 *Ibid.*, fo 13.
34 Airlie Muniments (S.R.O.), GD 16/32/1.
35 Nimmo's account book, fo 35.
36 *Ibid.*, fo 4.
37 Register of Signatures: E2

JANET FOCKART

Merchant and moneylender

d. 1596

JANET FOCKART, who outlived three merchant husbands and died in 1596, must have been a kenspeckle figure in 16th century Edinburgh. During her long widowhood she is found as a creditor of the government, trading in partnership with other merchants and, towards the end of her life, mainly concerned with money-lending. She was acquainted with many notables around the royal court, from some of whom she took substantial pledges for loans. Her establishment was well enough known for 'Janet Fockart's twa closis' to be mentioned in a legal document in order to locate the adjacent dwelling of another woman.[1] The fact that the woman concerned was a 'wad wyfe', or pawnbroker, may suggest that Janet's credit empire sheltered lesser offshoots. Not much is known about her first husband, John Todd; their son William outlived both parents. Through her second marriage to the merchant William Fowler, she became the mother of one poet, Mr William Fowler, friend of King James VI, and grandmother of another, William Drummond of Hawthornden, son of her daughter Susannah. In mid-17th century, however, when one of her descendants had a family tree drawn up for the purpose of obtaining a birth brieve, Janet Fockart was replaced as his great-grandmother by one 'Janet Fischer of the English family of Fischer'[2]; perhaps the family had reasons for wishing to forget about her. From time to time she quarrelled with her family who even took her to court. She once ejected from her household a boy whom she suspected of having the plague, for which the privy council later compelled her to compensate him and the family with whom he had been 'inclosit'.[3]. She may have been difficult to live with; one wonders if her third husband, James Hathoway, who committed suicide in 1579, found it too much for him.

Janet's forebears may have been the Fockarts who are found among the Edinburgh burgesses in the late 15th and early 16th centuries, perhaps related to those of their surname in the parish of Lasswade and probably descended from the Fockarts of Fockartoun in Kelso abbey's barony of Lesmahagow in

Lanarkshire.[4] She and her second husband, whom she may have married just before 1560, were established in the circle of influential merchant families which included the Uddarts, Tennants, Fishers, Todricks, Dicks, Achesons, and Littles. The Fowlers came from burgess stock with a record of civic service, an ancestry of which William, the poet, later wrote with pride:

> 'My grandfather, guidschir and father, ye, and befoir thaim thair
> progenitours on baith the sides, sa lang a thay had the usury of life,
> hes bene obedient subjectis unto thair kingis, and borne officis as
> magistrates in the toun of Edinburgh. Thair honestie and guid
> behaviour towardis all men war . . . knowin togidder with thair
> faithfulness towardis thair superiours . . .'.[5]

John Fowler, William the merchant's father, had been common clerk of the burgh from 1520. His mother, Sibilla Lindsay, had been one of a small group of committed protestants in the burgh in the early 1540s[6], and William himself was a consistent but not militant adherent of the Reformed religion. It is appropriate that his son should have coined the metaphor of usury to describe the good use made of their time by his ancestors, for profit-making was a preoccupation of the family. The Fowler children, who had an extremely comfortable upbringing, were William, who became a merchant, a second William, the poet, who attended St Leonard's college, St Andrews, his twin-brother John, Susannah, Barbara and Janet. Also in the household was William Todd, son of Janet Fockart's first marriage.

Both as a young man and after he had acquired public responsibility William Fowler tended to be chosen as a spokesman for those who had complaints to make, whether to the town council or the monarch, which may indicate that not only was he influential but determined and articulate. In 1557, not long before he married, he was one of the representatives of the 'haill young men burgessis sonnis' who objected to being asked to pay a share of the burgh tax of £1,200 which was raised to pay the town's fine for remaining away from the muster at Fala Muir, maintaining that this was against the privileges granted to the unmarried sons of burgesses.[7] They won their point. During Queen Mary's personal reign Fowler became involved in public affairs. In 1562 he was one of a long list of 'faithful brethren' who contributed to the kirk session's fund for the proposed building of a new hospital.[8] He was on the town council from 1546-47, 1569-70, and a bailie from 1565-66. He was at one time made responsible for the Queen's revenue from her French lands. In 1565 he was one of those council members who reacted angrily to Darnley's attempt to silence John Knox after the former had taken offence at one of the minister's sermons; Fowler and other council delegates had an audience with Mary and Darnley at which they objected to censure of Knox, saying that they would not 'grant that his mouth be closit'.[9] In June 1567, after Mary's abduction by Bothwell, Fowler, Edward Little, and the prominent goldsmith, Michael Gilbert, rode to Dunbar to clear the burgh from any imputation of collaboration with the Queen's opponents, the earls of Atholl,

Montrose, Morton, Mar and Glencairn, who with others had entered the capital.[10] After the Queen's deposition and flight to England Fowler, although he identified with her party, appears to have played a double game, pleading on behalf of Mary's agent, John Leslie, bishop of Ross, with Cecil and Leicester in 1571 but also acting as a source of information for the earl of Lennox and the King's party. Perhaps he was trying to keep the favour of both sides in his own interest, being at that time concerned about his merchandise which had been held in France since early in the year. He, Michael Gilbert and others took letters from Mary to Bishop Leslie in May 1571.

Involved though he was in public affairs, it was his business operations that gave him his influence in the burgh. In 1565, when a tax was levied to raise money to purchase the superiority of Leith, he was assessed at £20, putting him in the ranks of the more substantial, although not the richest, merchants.[11] These were the men who engaged in overseas or 'outland' trade, who probably represented a sizeable minority of the whole trading community. They were often related and did business through the same factors resident in France, the Low Countries and Poland. They sometimes 'ventured' goods together, shared a ship's cargo or even the ownership of the vessel. Their business was marked by the predominence in their merchandise of luxury goods such as wines and expensive cloths, by money-lending activity and the ownership of burgh property. Trading and sharing the risks together, they often stood security for one another in their business dealings and legal transactions. In February 1562 William Fowler and Alexander Uddart shared the money-lending services of Walter Cant, bailie of Leith, giving him £1,000 which he obliged himself to repay to them in francs in Paris through the treasurer of Queen Mary's uncle the marquis d'Elboeuf.[12] In 1566 Fowler and Uddart jointly stood surety for an Antwerp merchant who obliged himself to deliver a quantity of fine silk to the treasurer of Scotland in return for 6,000 bolls of mixed wheat and bere for shipment to Flanders.[13] Their circle of international contacts grew out of years of overseas trade. Much of William Fowler's trade was with France; a pack of French merchandise worth over £2,000 was awaited when he died in January 1572. Once, when a Paris merchant, Jean Builduik, gave him goods to the value of 270 francs on credit, taking an obligation for payment, a cut-throat Leith money-lender, Robert Wilson, jumped in, bought Fowler's obligation from the Paris merchant and sued him for the debt, which Fowler paid in crowns of the sun and pistolets.[14] He himself once acquired an obligation, worth 250 francs, which had been granted to another Paris merchant by Thomas Lindsay in Leith.

At home, Fowler's customers, like those of his fellow importers, would include the retailers, great and small, who probably accounted for the bulk of Edinburgh's trading community, from middling merchants, who also bought home-produced goods, down to the cramers in the luckenbooths. The testaments of a number of these shopkeepers show them buying goods, especially small-wares and perishables, from the bigger merchants.[15] In additon to the retailers the importing merchants also supplied craftsmen with their raw materials, such as timber and iron; the tailors with a wide range of cloths, the smiths with iron, the dyers with alum and potash, the clerks and printers with paper and the wrights with timber. Fowler's stock, inventoried at the time of his death, consisted mainly of fine cloth and trimmings, with a quantity of dress accessories for both sexes and of women's and children's headwear, about which Janet Fockart, who must often have been in charge of selling in her husband's absences, would no doubt be particularly knowledgeable.[16] The quality of the merchandise reflects an affluent, or extravagant, clientele, but the extraordinary quantity of goods in stock may suggest that business had not been so brisk as a result of the civil war; William Fowler died during the siege of Edinburgh when many burgesses are believed to have suffered materially. Be that as it may, the contents of the booth and warehouse make their own contribution to a picture of Edinburgh's better-off inhabitants and visitors, the goods they bought, wore and worked with and the luxury items they coveted.

The cloths included woollen fabrics such as frieze, which had a heavy nap on one side and was often used for cloaks and coats, and serge, which was twilled or worsted and was also used for outer garments, including women's riding clothes. Plain serge cost 45s an ell but the better quality serge of Florence could cost as much as £4. Druggit, at 30s an ell, bombasie (or bombazine), only 5s, camelet and stemming were all mixtures of wool and silk, camelet might even contain some cotton. The silks included the popular taffeta and satin, with quantities of velvet in many colours, greatly in demand by the fashionable in this period. Many of the fabrics had a luxury finish: 'argentie' or silvered serge, bombazine 'riggit with silk', figured and 'champit' velvet with an all-over pattern, 'paintit boutclaithis', which was a thin or open-textured fabric, and shot taffeta 'schynand yellow and blew'. The materials came in many colours: black, white, purple, violet, yellow, orange, crimson, blue, green and grey. Among the more serviceable materials were fine linen 'holland' cloth, canvas, a hempen cloth which was sometimes striped and popular for doublets, and sackcloth, which was finer than its modern equivalent and was sometimes used for outer garments.

There were a good many dress accessories, which would be sold to shopkeepers or to tailors who chose them to match their customers' garments: belts, 'bends' or sashes, collars, 'garnetouris for wemenis neckis to gownis', which were trimmed with red taffeta and silver thread, and 'overlayis' to hands and necks, that is turn-down collars and turn-up cuffs. Belts were narrow and shaped to fit the curve of the waist: velvet belts with 'hingaris' for all the small items which people carried on their belts – purses, bags, inkhorns, pomanders and mirrors – velvet belts edged with leather or embroidered in many colours, Morocco leather belts with buckles, others decorated with pearls and women's belts embroidered in gold and silver. Belts came complete with bag and 'whinger' (short sword) even for children. Sashes for women were of lawn edged with gold thread. Collars were made of crape or lawn edged or embroidered with gold or silver.

These were extremely expensive articles costing between 23s and 30s each, as much as an ell of some fabrics. White collars corded with gold, which arrived from France, cost 50s each. In the second half of the century there was a choice of neckwear between the plain turn-down collar, or overlay already mentioned, and the goffered collar or ruff, which increased in size in the late 1560s and in the next decade became a separate article of dress. Items in William Fowler's stock which are described as '17 ells schorne warkis', '5 ells of schorne warkis', '5 ells of schorne warkis for ruffis' and '7 braidis (?breadths) plane for ruffis' may be lengths of material to be goffered and made up into ruffs; Philip Stubbes, in his *Anatomie of Abuses in England* (1583), satirised the ruff as a ridiculous new item of dress 'whereof some be a quarter or a yard deep, yea some more'. The actual material might be plain linen, cambric, embroidered or open-work or even lace. The last-mentioned came into fashionable use at this time; William Fowler's stock contained no fewer than 200 ells of 'Dantellis' or narrow scalloped edged lace for ruffs.[17] He also sold sets of ruffles; 'a neck and hand with ruffis, 12s', '4 neckis and handis with ruffis, 25s', and '2 handis and neckis with ruffis, 5s', the variation in price suggesting different types of fabric. He had women's and children's coifs in quantities up to two dozen, made of fine materials such as silk, lawn and 'net' and embroidered with gold, silver or coloured thread. A 'stand' of three coifs for children, in lawn and silk embroidery, cost 30s. There were also black silk coifs of the kind worn under their hats by older men. Bonnets were made of burret, velvet and taffeta and hats were of velvet, taffeta, felt and 'velour wob', embroidered and trimmed with tassels and hat-strings.

Besides large quantities of trimmings such as were used by the tailors, there was the usual personal haberdashery: buttons, some of them made of gold and English silk, silk and worsted garters 'of the smallest sort' and 'of the mid sort', needles and thimbles in cases, one of these being fitted inside and gilt, papers of pins, points and ribbons, broad and narrow and many-coloured, including some Florence ribbons used 'to knit gentilwemenis hair'. There were items for everyday personal use: leather bags and locked velvet purses, cases of bone combs decorated with gold, mirrors, including 11 crystal mirrors, pen knives and tooth picks. These smaller items would be sold by the cramers or carried by chapmen to landward households. There were a few household articles: flasks, brass stands for use at the table, covers for tables and 'knoppis' or ornamental nobs for bed posts. Perhaps a reminder of happier times at court were the 14,000 counterfeit pearls 'for masking', presumably for masque clothes, along with a number of 'hair beirdis', more elaborate than the players wore themselves. Also for lighter moments were the hoods for hawks and merlins and the hawk bells. For more serious mood there were new testaments, psalm books, an English bible and six copies of 'the proverbis of Salomon'. The only mention of perishable goods is of three puncheons of wine that had been sold, but not yet delivered, to Elizabeth Douglas who was probably an ale-wife and tavern keeper.

As has been pointed out, William Fowler did business with people on both sides of the political divide; he was too shrewd a businessman to allow his own loyalties to stand in the way of trade. His clients, in addition to a handful of tailors, included a number of the nobility – Lady Fleming, the earl of Huntly, who owed him £120 at the time of Fowler's death, the earl of Rothes, Lord Seton, who owed him over £164, Lord Ruthven, the earl of Atholl, Lord Fleming 'surnamed with the grit baird', and the Regent Lennox – and a large number of lairds and their families. In addition to trade, he and his family drew a regular annual income from his interest in burgh property. Those who owed him rent for the Martinmas term, 1570, who are mentioned in his testament, were John Mure and John Nicholson, tailors, and John Houston and David Lyle, merchants, all for booth-maill, Andrew Abercrombie, Mr Alexander Syme, advocate, Mr James McGill, son of the clerk register, and one, John Hamilton, for lodgings, or chamber-maill, and John Davidson, merchant, John Dick, cook, and John Ochiltree, writer, for house-maill. The half-year's rents ranged from £6 to £10 for booth-maill and £4 to £10 for a house. Fowler also lifted annualrents from property in Edinburgh and Leith.

The family's own house stood in Fowler's, later Anchor, Close on the north side of the High Street. Towards the end of William's life he planned improvements to the building: a new entrance from the street which would give easier access to his 'backhoussis', one of which he leased to John Finnie, and new chimneys in two chambers against the west wall. This occasioned a contract between him and his neighbours, Thomas Dickson, furrier, and John Cooper, tailor, perhaps those known to have been members of the Queen's and King's party respectively.[18] The neighbours' gable wall was to be rebuilt with ashlar stones, while Fowler undertook to have a gutter of lead or stone made to carry off water from his house's 'eisdrope'.[19]

He died in the midst of his affairs in January 1572. On the face of things his widow was left comfortably off; apart from stock in the warehouse, debts to come in amounted to almost £3,000. In reality, however, life was difficult for Janet Fockart in the 1570s. To begin with she was left with a family of seven children to bring up; the oldest son of her second marriage must only have been about thirteen years old and William Todd may not have been much older. One of the first things she did was to abandon plans to enlarge the house, and on 14 September 1573 the burgh court handed her back the contract between William Fowler and his neighbours. It was two and a half years before his executry affairs were sufficiently in order for his testament to be recorded. During that time Janet kept the business going but, because of military operations, trade was going through a bad phase and her sales, if the account of them given in her husband's testament is correct, were not extensive. After Fowler's death a pack of French goods, worth just over £2,000, arrived, a mixture of serviceable and luxury items some of which may have been personal orders: tailors' and barbers' shears, belts and chains of jet, 2 cases of gilt knives, 6 'paintit pennaris and inkhornis', small yellow and white pins, half-a-dozen 'greit sark prenis', a dozen mirrors, worsted, silk and perfumed gloves, enamelled combs, 2 pairs of stiff lawn sleeves embroidered with red silk, lawn collars, gold and silver coifs and the usual selection of cloths.

Less welcome repercussions from her husband's French trade was an action raised before the privy council early in 1574 by the Leith money-lender, Robert Wilson, who now demanded interest on the sums Fowler had already paid him in order to clear the bond to the Paris merchant. Janet was by now married to James Hathoway who, with herself and her children, is named in the act of the privy council of 2 February 1574 by which they found in Janet's favour and ordained Wilson to drop his proceedings.[20] At the hearing before the council Wilson compeared personally in company with his forespeaker, Mr John Shairp, advocate; Hathoway and the Fowler children were represented by Mr David McGill, advocate, while Janet compeared personally on her own behalf. She maintained that her late husband had paid Wilson at the highest possible rate of interest that could be charged on goods given on credit in the first place – 'of the maist rigorous maner' – but that, nevertheless, Wilson 'for plane okker [usury] of the said sum' continued to pursue the family and intended to arrest their goods in France, notwithstanding 'that . . . the law of god nor yit the lawis and customis of the realme permittis ony okker or interest in sic caissis'. The increasingly secular approach to business dealings in the 16th century was eroding the earlier attitude of official bodies, particularly the church, to the matter of usury, and Scotland was in line with other protestant countries in accepting a reasonable level of interest as a necessary fact of business life; 10% came to be regarded as the borderline between legitimate and immoral interest-rates by the end of the century. It was into this financial world that Janet Fockart herself began to move in the 1580s, especially after the traumatic experience of James Hathoway's death. He took his own life on 31 August 1579, and this, because of the crown's rights to the goods of a suicide, put the family's livelihood at risk. Without delay Janet bought his escheat from the crown, the 'gift' being officially dated two days after his death.[21]

On 28 September 1580 she and three Edinburgh merchants, James Dalziel, John Hamilton and John Dick, in partnership, made a contract with Robert Stewart, earl of Orkney, Queen Mary's half-brother, who was newly-instated in his Orkney estates, arranging to buy from him for £1,560 thirteen lasts of butter and eighteen barrels of oil from his Orkney rents, he promising to deliver them to their factor in Kirkwall before St Andrew's Day.[22] Should he fail he was to pay £12 for every barrel of 'waist fraucht'. In addition to the foregoing arrangment the partners loaned him the large sum of £5,340 'for performeing of his lordschippis bissines and effaires' to be paid in three instalments between the date of the contract and 1 April 1581. As security for the repayment of his loan he in the meantime assigned to them 180 chalders of Orkney victual (bere and malt) and the whole 'flesche dett' of his Orkney lands, which he promised to make up to 40 lasts, using some of his household supplies to make up the amount if necessary. The flesh was to be sold in Orkney but the victual, shipped south at the earl's expense and risk, was to be sold by the partners in the markets of Leith, Dysart, Kirkcaldy and Kinghorn, 'the frie money' remaining in their hands. If all went well the partners could hope to make a good cash profit. John Dick, a wealthy merchant with Orkney connections, may have taken the initiative in the deal which to Janet Fockart may have appeared to offer a comparatively secure trading arrangement.

She was used to trading on her own, however, having taken bonds for repayment even during William Fowler's lifetime. In May 1581 she sued the chamberlain of Arbroath abbey for failing to honour his obligation of a month earlier to pay £1,021-12s-6d in name of Lord John Hamilton who, as commendator of the abbey, had granted her a bond as long ago as 1570 for merchandise which she had sold him.[23] In 1580 she successfully sued James Arbuthnot of Lentusk, who was escheated for non-payment of £310-15s according to an obligation which he had granted to William Fowler and herself.[24] In November 1581 John Pollock of that Ilk, as the assignee of Lord Maxwell who owed Janet 250 merks, obliged himself to pay her.[25] Throughout the 1580s she continued to ask bonds for the payment of bills and collect interest and expenses when the dates of payment passed, and from time to time she began proceedings for debt-recovery which when successful led to the escheat of her debtors. She achieved the escheat of the master of Eglinton whose father had owed her over £100 on two bonds.[26] She continued to hold some burgh property although the fact that her assessment dropped to £6 in 1581 and £12 in 1583 from William Fowler's £20 in 1565 may suggest that she had parted with some of it. The earl of Morton at one time owed her £194 for a combination of merchandise received and house rent.[27] George Sinclair of Mey, in Caithness, granted her a bond in 1588 for payment of his 'chamber maill' which was not paid until seven years later, by his son.[28]

From the proceeds of trade and ownership of whatever property she retained Janet apparently made enough capital to engage in straight money-lending. A series of receipts, written in her own bold hand, is to be found in the Douglas of Lochleven papers, usually granted to Agnes Leslie, the laird's wife, for the annual interest on a loan of 1,000 merks.[29] Her initiative and business success helped her financially with the upbringing of her family and ensured her sons a decent education. Her oldest son, William Todd, wrote in an accomplished italic hand. Her younger son called William, the poet, attended St Andrews university in the late 1570s and became a cultivated member of the literary circle at the young King's court. Going to England in 1582 to recover a debt due by Queen Mary to his late father, he made contact with the English court and became a spy for Walsingham. He became secretary to Queen Anne and spent some time in Italy and, possibly, France. The family became part of the circle surrounding the King's flamboyant second-cousin, Esme Stewart, lord of Aubigny, who arrived in Scotland from France in 1579 and soon became a rallying point for a mixed group of former Queen's men, francophiles, opponents of the Regent Morton, and supporters of the Lennox claim to stand next in line to the throne; theirs was a political world to which the Fowlers belonged through their late father's loyalty and service to Queen Mary. Esme Stewart lodged in Janet Fockart's house when he first arrived. Three years later, after the *coup* known as the Ruthven Raid which put an end to his ascendancy and sent him into exile, he met Janet's younger son William Fowler in London and greeted him warmly, reminding him that 'the first house which I came into in Edinburgh at my cumming to Scotland was your mother's, and it was the last lykeweyes at my departeur from hence'.[30] Contact with the court is reflected in the loans which Janet made to the government. The accounts of the royal mint in 1578 refer to sums of £24, £65, and £209 due to her on account, while the exchequer met in her house in 1593.[31]

In the 1580s there was strife in the family circle. In September 1582 Janet's elder son William Fowler, the merchant, was contracted to marry Barbara Gibson, daughter of George Gibson, a writer to the court of session. The following January he raised an action in that court against his mother for allegedly allowing the family house in Fowler's Close to deteriorate and for causing a wall to be taken down and some timberwork removed.[32] Janet's earlier abandonment of the renovations planned by her husband when the children were young may have resulted in genuine deterioration, but the removal of a wall and timberwork seems to indicate actual building alterations. No doubt the court case came at the end of a family quarrel about what should be done, and may have been precipitated by Janet's decision to go her own way. As her son pointed out, she was the liferenter but the property would be his after her death, and liferenters were obliged in law to keep heritable property in good repair. At the end of the court case she gave security to do so.

The quarrel with her son-in-law, John Drummond, son of Sir Robert Drummond of Carnock, was even more serious and complicated.[33] John was contracted to marry her daughter, Susannah, in May 1583. Provisions in the contract suggest that the young couple may have lived in Janet's household and that John became involved in her business affairs, an arrangment which not surprisingly soon broke down. In terms of the contract Janet was to pay John a tocher with her daughter of 3,000 merks, which after three years she had still not paid in full; she undertook to sustain Susannah in household with her during her lifetime, and John agreed to assist Janet to get in all her debts 'from whatever creditors'. That this led to disagreements and financial tangles is revealed by the decreet of a panel of arbiters a few months after John had taken his mother-in-law to court, who ordained that they should settle all accounts between them, 'baith of merchandise and othirwayis', and that Janet should compensate John for unspecified expenditures by making over to him her right to the laird of Lochleven's bond for 1,000 merks. Janet submitted to the registration of both the contract and the decreet arbitral, and paid the balance of tocher, only after pressure from the courts. Meantime, another William had been added to the household, William Drummond, the future poet, who was born in 1585. He and his family lived thereafter at Hawthornden which John Drummond had bought from its previous owners.

In later years Janet may have done less trading and more money-lending. She continued to live, very comfortably, in the house in Fowler's Close surrounded by household furnishing worth 1000 merks (£733-6s-8d), far more than those of many lairds who died in the second half of the century.[34] Her silverware alone was worth £300, including a mazer weighing 30 ozs. She had a substantial amount of ready money in various purses at the time of her death: £505-11s-8d in gold £5 pieces, crowns of the sun, angel nobles, testoons, gold 50s pieces, ryals, 2 merk pieces and sous. Even more spectacular was her jewellery, some of it purchased and given to her over the years and some, one suspects, unredeemed pledges: 8 pairs of gold bracelets of different designs; a ring with a pearl and one with a ruby; 7 gold chains of varying lengths, a popular ornament of the time worn either as a necklace or girdle; 4 tablets, or pendants, two of them on chains, one round in shape and one set with diamonds and rubies; a collection of jewels which may have come from settings or had been sewn on to garments, 3 sapphires, 3 diamonds, 3 emeralds, 5 rubies, an amethyst, a turquoise and an opal; 'ane jowell efter the signe of ane parokat [parrot] set with two diamonds and an emerald, worth £20, and 'ane jowell haifing the signe of the airk of Noe [Noah]', worth £14. She still possessed a cross of gold on a small chain, proscribed for wearing but kept for its intrinsic value.

Many of her clients owed money on the basis of written obligations, more likely to have been straight loans than bills for merchandise. Some of the amounts were large: Lady Gowrie, £636, Sir Walter Ogilvy and James Ogilvy of Blairock as cautioners, 2,100 merks, the cautioners of the earl of Orkney, 1,200 merks, 'the auld lady Justice Clerk', £100, John Wemyss, fiar of Logie, £320, the widow of Kerr of Ancrum, £395 10s 5d, Lord Glamis, £1,044, and the merchant, Patrick Moscrop, £600. Her son, Mr William Fowler, owed her 74 crowns, as well as 450 merks for Flemish money forwarded to him in Flanders. People could run up huge bills, however; the earl of Orkney once noted 'spendit in Janet Fockartis, tua hundrith and sevintene poundis money to my lady', and some obligations may have been given for the payment of accounts. In addition to asking for bonds or obligations Janet took substantial pledges from those who received loans – even her son, William Fowler, the merchant, and his wife pledged a chain and gold belt for 500 merks. Some of the others were Patrick Leslie, Lord Lindores, commendator of Lindores abbey, member of the Queen's party in the 1570s, who borrowed £600 for which he pledged a woman's gown of cloth of silver, two great gold pieces, some gold buttons and a jewel; George Home, not otherwise identified, who borrowed £100, pledging a chain of gold; Lady Orkney, wife of Robert Stewart, earl of Orkney, who pledged a diamond ring, a chain and a pointed diamond ring for £100; Janet Curle, a pair of 'garnessingis' [earrings] of pearl and gold for 500 merks; and Alexander Lindsay, Lord Spynie, son of the 10th earl of Crawford and Margaret Beaton, whose title came from a secular lordship created out of the lands of the bishopric of Moray, who pledged a 'tairget' of gold and seventeen diamonds for a loan of 200 merks.[36]

Janet died in May 1596 without making a will and her son, the merchant, would inherit not only the family property but the considerable proceeds of her business life. There was not much left in 'hir merchand buith' when an inventory was taken in the days following her death: a piece of dornick, a lint wheel, a piece of tapestry, a pair of plaids, a doublet, coat, breeks and, significantly, 16 'auld fassent hattis', a 'keiking glass', three crape strings, 3 gold cauls for women, 4 pieces of linen for making cushions, a length of linen to make serviettes and 4 table covers, all estimated to £90. It is almost as if the booth had become the attic instead of a place of business. It was a far cry from the well-stocked warehouse of William Fowler in 1572 which Janet herself may have helped a notary or clerk to inventory after her husband's death – when the descriptions of quality accessories for 'gentillwemen' almost have a ring of pride in them. Nevertheless, whereas William had left moveable estate of £7,900 Janet left £22,467-3s-9d after almost quarter of a century of inflation. Although she and her son the merchant may not always have agreed, he must have been glad of the fruits of her enterprise and business ability, provided he had hopes of getting in her considerable debts.

Perhaps Janet's 17th century descendants did not like to think of having a 'wad-wyfe' in their ancestry, for wad-wife she had been, if of an exalted variety. A neighbouring wad-wife on the High Street, Elspeth McNair, died five months after Janet leaving only £663.[37] The pattern of that part of their testaments relating to their debtors is the same. Elspeth's clients were writers, a baxter's wife, and the occasional laird as well as her neighbours, who borrowed comparatively small amounts for which they pledged a silver piece, a small silver belt, a gold ring, a mazar, 'a cloik of his wyffis' and 'hir black goun'. Janet left no will to tell us whether she had any generous impulses at the last moment. Elspeth left 10 merks to the town's hospital and small bequests of clothes. Only the scale of their operations separated these two women who happened to be in a position to take advantage of the material and financial difficulties of those in their social circle. The Drummonds of Hawthornden, with higher claims to fame, may have tried to cut Janet Fockart out of their family history, but it is very likely that even more of her activities have yet to come to light in the records of her time.

JANET FOCKART
NOTES

1 Justiciary court records (S.R.O.), small papers, JC 26 Box 2.

2 Genealogical information from *The Works of William Fowler* (Scottish Text Society), III; D. Masson, *Drummond of Hawthorden* (1873).

3 *Book of the Old Edinburgh Club*, XV, 43.

4 G.F. Black, *Scottish Surnames*.

5 *Works of William Fowler*; for birth brieve of John Fowler, see *Register of the Great Seal*, 1660-8, p.50.

6 M. Lynch, *Edinburgh and the Reformation*, 328-9.

7 *Extracts from the Records of the Burgh of Edinburgh*, III, 14.

8 M. Lynch, *Edinburgh and the Reformation*, 265.

9 *Extracts from the Burgh Records of Edinburgh*, III, 199.

10 *Ibid.*, III, 231.

11 M. Lynch, *Edinburgh and the Reformation*, 374.

12 Register of Deeds (S.R.O.), v, fo 53.

13 *Ibid.*, viii, fo 364.

14 Register of the Privy Council (S.R.O.), PC1/7, fo 173 (unprinted).

15 M.H.B. Sanderson, 'The Edinburgh Merchants in Society, 1570-1603; the evidence of their testaments', in I.B. Cowan and D. Shaw, *The Renaissance and Reformation in Scotland, Essays in honour of Gordon Donaldson* (1983), 183-99.

16 Following details of Fowler's stock from his testament: Edinburgh Commissariot records, Register of Testaments (S.R.O.), CC8/8/3, fo 360v.

17 P. Earnshaw, *Lace in Fashion* (1985), 13.

18 M. Lynch, *Edinburgh and the Reformation*, 324, 297.

19 Edinburgh Burgh Records, Register of Deeds (S.R.O.), B22/8/2, fos 29v-30; subsequently cancelled and returned to his widow, Janet Fockart.

20 Register of the Privy Council, PC1/7, fo 173 (unprinted).

21 *Register of the Privy Seal*, VII, 2029.

22 Register of Deeds, xviii, fo 129

23 Diligence records, Forfar (S.R.O.), DI 57/1, fo 97v

24 *Register of the Privy Seal*, VII, 2569.

25 Register of Deeds, xx, part i, fo 93.

26 Eglinton Muniments (S.R.O.), GD 3/1/207.

27 Register of Deeds, xxv, fo 264.

28 Mey Papers (S.R.O.), GD 96/253.

29 Morton Muniments, GD 150/2192.

30 *Works of William Fowler*, III.

31 *Exchequer rolls, XXII*, 309: *Treasurer's Accounts, XIII*, 245, 387, 391.

32 Register of Deeds, xxi, fo 452.

33 *Ibid.*, xxiv, fo 128, xxv, fo 72.

34 Following details from Janet Fockart's testament, Edinburgh Commissariot Records, Register of Testaments, CC8/8/29, fo 399v.

35 R. Vans Agnew, *Correspondence of Sir Patrick Waus of Barnbarroch Kt.* (1887), I, 288-9.

36 Lord Lindores was the son-in-law of the earl of Orkney, whose presence and that of several members of the Elphinstone family, the earl's servants, among Janet's debtors suggests that she maintained contact with Orkney and the earl long after the business contract of 1580.

37 Edinburgh Commissariot Records, Register of Testaments, CC8/8/29, fo 260v.

THE FARMERS OF MELROSE

Life on the Land

THE typical sixteenth-century Scot, if there was such a person, was not a towns-man but a countryman, a tenant-farmer. If he was lucky enough to live in good agricultural country it was highly likely that he would be a church tenant. The monasteries in particular had put down their roots in some of the best farmland in Scotland – in contemporary terms – east and mid Lothian, Berwickshire, the Tweed valley, the fertile crescent of north and central Ayrshire, Fife, the Carse of Gowrie, the Perthshire straths, parts of Angus, lowland Aberdeenshire and Banffshire, and the laich of Moray. The tenants of Melrose abbey had the best of one world and the worst of another, for their good arable land and wool-producing pastures lay right in the path of invading English armies. In 1544 the earl of Hertford, in retribution for the Scottish government's cancellation of an Anglo-Scottish marriage-treaty, reckoned to have destroyed 192 settlements, towers, farmsteads, fortified houses, and the protective walls within which people and stock had taken refuge, 243 larger villages and seven monasteries and friaries. There were times during that and the following years when the settlements must temporarily have looked like refugee camps. After a struggle, however, the tenants recovered, rebuilding their quickly-assembled homes and farm structures and enduring a starvation diet until the next harvest. Their landlord did not fare so well, for the fabric of the great church of Melrose and living quarters of the monks suffered badly in repeated invasions and cost more to put to rights. For the monastic community, destruction of the property was accompanied by the effects of secularising influences in the administration of the monastery, not least in the indifference of the superior to the plight of the monks themselves and the diver-sion of the funds away from maintenance towards property-speculation. Changes in the balance of the religious community's way of life over the centuries made it more and more difficult to pursue the spiritual function of the monastery in the face of its time-consuming secular responsibilities. There had also been changes over the years in the abbey's relations with the tenants who cultivated the estates,

as their forebears had done long before the abbey came to the district. To understand these changes it will be best if we start at the beginning.

The ideals of the Cistercian community, the reformed branch of the
Benedictine order of monks, are reflected in the statutes of the General Chapter
of the order held at Citeaux, the mother-abbey in France, in 1134, two years
before Melrose abbey was founded.[1] The principle, briefly, was that the monks
should not live by the labours of others but by their own efforts, not from rents
as laymen did, or tithes or the patronage of parish churches, but from the produce
of the ground, the flocks, and the herds. They were meant to be involved with
the farming process. For this reason they might possess land, stock, and fishings.
In practice, their involvement in farming was a managerial one – the medieval
monk, at least in the twelfth century and in this part of the world, may have tended his garden or kept bees but he did not follow the plough or tend sheep. A
strict daily routine of religious observance made it difficult for him to leave the
monastery precincts, unless for specific reasons and with the abbot's permission.

Farm management on the ground was in the hands of lay-brothers, known
as *conversi*, who lived communally in the abbey precincts, worshipped in their
own choir within the church, but did not take full monastic vows. These lay-
brothers could be quite numerous – it is believed that up to 200 of them may
have been accommodated at Melrose at times in quarters the foundations of
which can still be traced on the west side of the cloister.[2] They may have done
some of the actual cultivation but their role was primarily administrative, to use a
modern term; they were in charge of the labourers on the abbey's estates. The
abbot and choir monks, we might say, were the policy-makers in the business of
monastic estate-management.

The actual cultivation was mostly done by the indigenous population, some
of whom would be serfs and bondmen, belonging to 'the master of the ground',
although it is thought that these were small in number in this part of the borders.
The husbandman and cottar, although personally free, owed many labour services
to the landlord unless, as gradually happened, these services, such as harvest
work, were commuted for a money payment. At the period of the monastery's
foundation in 1136 all of these farmers held their land at the goodwill of the lord
without written rights. Initially it was possible to work the abbey lands from the
focal point of the monastery. King David's charter, granted about 1143, conveyed
to the abbey the lands of Melrose, Eildon, Darnick, and Gattonside, with fishings
in Tweed and pasture, all near at hand. However, other gifts of lands from the
Kings of Scots and other laymen soon followed until the abbey's estates spread
further and further afield, eventually throughout and beyond the parish of
Melrose itself, including Newtoun (now Newtown St Boswells), Lessudden (St
Boswells itself), Blainslie, and others.

Increasing endowments made it more difficult to go on managing the estates
from the centre and led to the creation of granges, that is outlying farms and

administrative units with intensively-cultivated areas and large concentrations of stock, both cattle and sheep, for the Tweed valley was both fertile for crops and good pastoral country. The estates were divided into blocks centred on the granges where the lay brothers and their servants lived for spells at a time, administering the complex of barns, byres, stables, sheepfolds, brewhouse and, where suitable, a mill. At Buckholm, next to Appletreeleaves and now partly built over by the town of Galashiels, which was granted to the monastery by Richard de Morville in the reign of King William 'the Lion' (1165-1214), a byre was erected which could hold 60 cows. At Whitelee de Morville granted the abbey a site on which to build a shelter for either 100 cows or 120 sheep. When Patrick, earl of Dunbar, gave Melrose pasture for 500 sheep and 140 cattle he agreed that his own stock would return to Earlston at night. In these concentrated areas of farming activity there were settlements in which the labourers lived; at Blainslie, for example, there were three settlements, the Overtoun, Middletoun, and Nethertoun, placenames of the kind which are repeated all over the map of Scotland.

Large concentrations of stock imply an efficient organisation which in turn suggests profitable farming. Since the monastery did not render payment to the crown for its property with which it was so generously endowed, other than by rendering the spiritual service of intercessory prayer, its considerable revenue was far greater than was required to sustain the convent, the lay-brothers and servants annually, even allowing for upkeep of the buildings and the hospitality they provided. The abbey was in the farming business in a big way. From time to time it was party to a property-dispute which was taken all the way to the papal court for settlement, such as that with Patrick, earl of Dunbar, at the end of which, in 1208, he granted the monastery the land on the west side of the Leader called Sorrowlessfield after the former possessor, William Soroueles.[3]

In the 12th and 13th centuries better weather conditions resulted in cultivation higher up the hillsides than today, but this pattern receded as the border monasteries and others took over arable land for sheep-farming. The wool crop from large flocks of sheep was one of the principal sources of Melrose abbey's wealth; at the end of the 13th century the flocks were said to have numbered about 12,000. As early as 1182, that is forty-six years after the abbey's foundation, Count Philip of Flanders granted the monks of Melrose the liberty of free passage through his country and an exemption from toll when they came to sell their wool. In 1225 Henry III of England gave the abbots of Melrose and Coupar Angus leave to send ships to Flanders with wool and merchandise. The ledger of an Italian merchant from the mid-13th century shows him handling wool from monasteries in Scotland and England; the 50 sacks a year from Melrose equalled those from Jervaulx, in a list of eleven abbeys, and came behind only those of Fountains (76 sacks) and Rievaulx (60 sacks).[4] There is also evidence of horse-breeding. The earl of Dunbar, on his departure for the Holy Land, sold the abbey his stud of brood mares for the then large sum of 100 merks sterling.[5]

The Wars of Independence of the 14th century reduced the wool trade. The period also saw the end of substantial territorial endowments. It also saw the beginnings of a further change in estate-management which was to accelerate in the 15th century – the practice of leasing out the lands to the tenants on formal, legal terms which by the 16th century had come to be written rights of possession. This is particularly important in relation to the status of those tenants from whom the last traces of serfdom had disappeared by the last quarter of the 14th century, earlier than in England. In addition to the possession of written rights the tenants increasingly had their labour services commuted to money payments. Although this added to the total rents due it gave an added element of independence to the tenant's outlook. Money payments, or rents of any kind for that matter, are less personal in character than the duty of labouring on the landlord's own fields and herding his stock. By the 16th century the peasant farmers may have tended to think of themselves less as a labour force and more as employers of labour, the labour of the cottars and farm workers whose small holdings meant that they had to take paid work in addition to the labour which they performed for the husbandmen in return for their 'tied' houses.

Living on rents drawn from the labourers of the ground was against the original Cistercian ideals as set out in the 1134 statutes. But monastic estate-management was becoming less paternalist and more like that of lay landlords. The system of granges was fading out by now, and the presence of the monastery's representatives in the countryside was reduced from the on-the-spot supervision of the lay-brothers to the periodic demands of the officers of the landlord's court who reminded the tenants that rent-day was coming, at Whitsunday and Martinmas. The terms of a tenant's lease, or tack, usually carried the obligation to attend that court at least three times in the year. The farmers, who held their land in return for, first, services, and later rent, continued in the era of tack-holding to guard jealously their customary rights of inheriting their family holdings. Altogether, the century between the early 1400s and early 1500s saw the marked development of tenant-continuity and assertiveness, something that has been noted by historians of contemporary England and certain European countries. It is unfortunate that for Melrose there is a dearth of records for the 15th century of the type that reflects tenancy patterns, but these developments can be clearly seen in the records of the abbey of Coupar Angus, a Cistercian house colonised from Melrose in 1168 whose estate-management was probably similar to that of the mother-house.[6]

Changes in the internal character of the monastery also had an effect on the way the lands were administered. First of all there was secularisation of the office of head of the monastic community, a change from which the monks were to suffer as much as anyone. From the early 16th century onwards the canonical practice of electing the abbot internally by the members of the convent from one of their number, gave way to the appointment of someone with royal or baronial influence behind him, nominated to the pope by the crown, who may not have been a monk at all. The commendator, as the new-style head of the abbey was called, took virtually no part in the internal, spiritual life of the community, and his interests tended to be financial and dynastic. Even although the commendator was a cleric, who had been given the minimum mark of clerical distinction, the tonsure, in youth – as in the case of Cardinal Beaton who at an early stage, as we saw, became commendator of Arbroath abbey – the effect was detrimental. Although the superior of the lands was still the abbot and convent jointly, secularising processes meant that the partners in this corporation were no longer of one mind with regard to the use of the property and its revenues.

The most notorious of the commendators of Melrose on the eve of the Reformation was James Stewart, the oldest illegitimate son of King James V (not to be confused with his younger brother, later the Regent Moray), half-brother of Queen Mary, who was made commendator when still a child, which meant that as the King administered the abbey's revenues on his behalf these simply went into the royal coffers. As an adult James Stewart had exceedingly bad relations with the monks of Melrose, refusing to use money that he had raised from feuing the land for necessary repairs to the abbey kirk, and on at least one occasion during a discussion with them 'grew crawbit' and threatened to assault the elderly subprior, the senior member of the convent.[7] Michael Balfour, the commendator in the 1560s, not only feued some of the land to his relatives rather than the tenants but also to Queen Mary's third husband, the earl of Bothwell. Bothwell received huge charters, including such settlements as Gattonside and Newtoun, but on his fall in 1567 the commendator recovered the property by buying Bothwell's escheated lands for £5,000. James Douglas, son of William Douglas of Lochleven, was the last of the commendators. He enlarged the lodging known today as 'the Commendator's house', placing the initials of himself and his wife, Mary Kerr, above the doorway as he would have done on any private residence. The Melrose property passed to the earl of Haddington at the turn of the century, and was later bought by the duchess of Buccleuch.

Another internal change in monastic life was the fact that the monks had ceased to live entirely off the common funds but had for some time been allocated 'portions', in effect salaries. This did not necessarily mean added personal security for they were dependent on the goodwill of the commendator and his chief financial officer, the chamberlain, to make sure that they got prompt payment of their allowances. They were also dependent on the goodwill of those tenants who inhabited the lands which were earmarked for their portions. Sometimes, when a monk died, the commendator would grant his portion to an outsider just like a piece of property. In 1533 commissioners arrived in Scotland from the mother-house of Citeaux to inspect the Scottish Cistercian houses. They censured the practice of monastic portions and the personal allowances for the monks' food and clothes – 'habit silver' as it was called – and ordered the convent of Melrose to return to the practice of sharing everything. The abbey sent representatives to meet the visitors in Edinburgh where they denied that they possessed property in any real sense, maintaining that they were merely allowed the 'use' of these revenues. The commissioners agreed, with certain restrictions: the yards, or gardens, of the monks must be of equal size, the produce from them must be common property, and there must be a common path running through them all. It seems that if they could get the arrangements to *look* as if they were held in common this would be acceptable. The visitors conceded that there might be portions, but no double portions – in Sir David Lindsay's *Satyre of the Thrie Estaitis* the abbot boasts:

'My prior is ane man of greit devotioun,
Tharfor daylie he gettis ane doubill portioun'.

There was little likelihood of tightening up the rules internally in 1533 when the abbot was Andrew Durie, cousin of the future Cardinal Beaton and later bishop of Galloway, who when he resigned the abbey of Melrose in favour of the King's notorious son, James Stewart, was granted a pension of 1,000 merks from the abbey revenues.[8]

These revenues were among the highest monastic incomes in Scotland by mid-16th century, probably surpassed only by those of the priory of St Andrews and, possibly, Arbroath abbey: over £1,700 in money, very large quantities of grain including 14 chalders of wheat, a cash crop which grew only in favoured arable areas in that period, over 700 capons and poultry, 105 stones of butter, 8 chalders of salt (from the saltpans at Prestonpans), 340 loads of peat and 500 'carriages' due by the tenants with their own horses and carts. Much of this revenue was handled by the succession of non-monastic commendators throughout the later 16th century. It was all a far cry from the 12th century and abbot Waltheof who, so it was claimed, had once blessed the stores of grain in a time of dearth so that miraculously there was enough to go round all the abbey's settlements while the famine lasted.

In the 16th century change also affected the abbey's tenants. The families of these people had cultivated their holdings generation after generation and there is no reason to doubt that many of them had been there since medieval times. The practice of customary inheritance (as distinct from the kind of inheritance that was guaranteed by charter), which has already been alluded to in discussing William Douglas of Lochleven's tenants, by which holdings were passed on was well-established in Scotland by this time, as it was in England and parts of Europe. The easiest way to see how the principal worked is to look at the circumstances of one or two families from the Melrose district.

The first is that of Marion Cochrane, widow of John Stoddart in Lessudden. In 1555 she made provision for her two daughters, Christian and Katherine. A marriage contract was drawn up by which Christian was to marry Robert, son of Ninian Bryden in Rutherford; Robert 'sall compleit the band of matrimonie with the said Christian and sall com to the said Marioun in househald and entyr to the stedyng quhilk the said Marioun occupiis, the said Marioun being the principal disponar of the gudis [stock] of the said stedyng'. On Marion's death it was arranged that the holding should pass to the couple. Robert would 'entyr' to the steading as the farmer, under Marion's direction, but his right to do so, spelled out in his marriage contract, came to him with his wife through her mother. The other daughter, Katherine, was to be given £40 by her sister's father-in-law, Ninian Bryden, and to be allowed 40 merks of profit from the steading annually 'quhill scho is reddie to marie'.

Marion Cochrane herself is the key figure in these arrangements. She is called the occupant of the steading which was really inherited through her, and if we knew more about her forebears we would probably find that she had inherited it in turn, by customary right, a right which she passed on to her daughter. She had what was known as the 'kindness' of the holding. Writers have often tried to define kindly tenancy as a distinct form to tenure, but kindness was not so much *how* the tenant held as *why*: by being kindly, that is kin, usually nearest of kin, to the previous occupant, in effect heir. Customary inheritance in Scotland operated on the kindly principle.[9] That is why the tenant families in many parts of the country were able to keep possession of their holdings generation after generation, passing them on from heir to heir down through the family.

The example of the Winterhope family from Elliston, south-west of Lessudden, shows a holding being inherited through the father. In March 1606 Robert Scott of Haining whose father had feued the lands of Elliston from Melrose abbey in 1568 and who was therefore the immediate landlord of the tenants there, admitted as kindly tenant Helen Winterhope, daughter of the late George Winterhope, 'to all and haill that ane half husbandland . . . of Eleistoun occupiit be the said umquhile George, quhilk half husbandland lies rinrig through the landis of Eleistoun . . . for all the dayis of hir lyfetyme . . '. Helen was not yet seventeen and her mother had remarried, her stepfather being her uncle, Thomas Winterhope. The terms of her life-lease laid down that her mother, Janet Inglis, should be her guardian until she reached the age of seventeen. Should her stepfather outlive her mother, Helen, on reaching the age of seventeen, was to compensate him for the loss of his use of the farm to the extent of £10. If she failed to do so he was to retain the use of it until she did pay him. The payment having been made he was to remove so that Helen might 'entir therto and possess the . . . land as hir kyndlie mailling [holding]' for her lifetime. In this case the kindness of the farm had passed to a daughter from her father and her stepfather had only been allowed the use of it until she became seventeen. Thereafter the use would go to Helen's husband when she married but the kindness itself – the right to inherit the holding – would pass through her to her heir.

If the kindly principle was *why* tenants retained possession of their holdings, *how* they held them depended on the terms of their written rights: life-leases, known as 'rentals', such as Helen Winterhope had, or tacks for varying numbers of years, from three to nineteen.[10] One of the most far-reaching changes affecting many country people in 16th century Scotland was the gradual but inexorable spread of the form of heritable possession known as feu-ferm, on lands belonging to the church, by which many tenants became proprietors of their holdings.[11] For various reasons ecclesiastical landlords wished to capitalise on their estates in this period and they did so by feuing the tenants' holdings, sometimes to outsiders but very often to the tenants themselves, pocketing the sizeable down-payments for the feu charters and realising, at least for a time, an increase in their income, because the feu-duty was always set higher than the previous rent.

The feuing of church land created a great wedge of new proprietors in Scottish society in many of the best farming areas, a new generation of owner-occupiers where there had previously been only tenants. It is remarkable that in spite of the unsettled conditions of the times and the fact that there were land-speculators around, 64% of all feus granted on the estates of Melrose abbey from the 1540s until the end of the century went to the sitting tenants. Very large numbers of these people lived at Newstead, Newtoun, Gattonside, Lessudden, Darnick, and Blainslie.

The lands of Newstead, in which the commendator's brother, Alexander Balfour of Denmylne, had at one time an interest, were first feued to the tenants in 1564 – about 206 Scots acres in holdings ranging from two to twelve acres each.[12] Thirty-three tenants are named in the Newstead charter. If we allow for four persons to a family, a very conservative estimate for the sixteenth century, we get a figure of 132 people. Add to these about half that number of cottars and perhaps about 20-30 labourers who lived with their employers, the husbandmen, and we arrive at something in the region of 230-250 inhabitants at Newstead, most of whom became owner-occupiers as a result of feuing.

The people of Gattonside, having briefly become the earl of Bothwell's tenants in the 1560s, returned to the abbey as their immediate landlord on his forfeiture. Then, in 1590, 47 of them received feu charters of their holdings.[13] There were more feuars at Gattonside than at Newstead but the holdings were smaller, usually of four acres or less. The feuars included several members of the Boston family who prospered thereafter and are commemorated by a memorial tablet in the abbey kirk. Lessudden was feued as early as 1529 to Arthur Sinclair whose kinsman, Henry Sinclair, dean of Glasgow cathedral, inherited the land from him in 1549. In 1556 the dean resigned the lands which were then feued among 40 inhabitants – the area feued amounted to just over 30 husbandlands, about 1,040 Scots acres.[14] If Sinclair was compensated for his resignation – which happened in similar circumstances elsewhere – the tenants would pay dearly for their charters. In 1557 Marion Cochrane took a feu of her holding in Lessudden.[15] In her charter it was laid down that her 1¾ husbandlands would be her property for her lifetime and after her death would pass to her daughter, Christian, and her husband Robert Bryden. Their son, John succeeded to the land in 1614. Blainslie was feued from the late 1540s onwards. The feuars of this northerly Melrose property undertook carriage of fish from North Berwick and salt from Prestonpans, a service which they already performed as tenants.

If times were difficult how was it that so many tenants came to feu their holdings? Were they put under pressure by the landlord or did they see advantages in it for themselves? What concerned them was security of possession for their families, something which was threatened by the appearance of middlemen, with the possibility that the holdings which their families had held for generations as kindly tenants might be feued 'over their heads' to outsiders. For the many who did obtain feus, however, feuing simply regularised the security which they had long enjoyed in practice by customary right. It is sometimes said that as a feuar the farmer had a better chance of making good than as a tenant and in some ways he did gain advantages. A feuar's charter usually gave him greater rights in the use of the land than the tenant's tack. The annual feu-duty, usually paid in money, was a fixed sum in a period of rising prices and market values, which gave him an economic advantage over his superior in the long run. If he and his neighbours who had previously held shares of the settlement's lands all took feus of their holdings they became known as feuars-portioner, or simply portioners, a designation used with pride and even carved or tombstones. Where there had been a single-tenant farm before feuing, the owner was a little more substantial than a portioner and might be called a 'bonnet laird'.

Some feuars soon found themselves in financial difficulties having paid large sums for their charters as well as for official confirmation of their titles – from the papal court before the Reformation and the Scottish crown after it – and facing the continued annual feu-duty which contained an element known as the 'augmentation', an increase on the old rent. Some feuars wadset (mortgaged) their land in return for loans. In 1575 John Gibson, feuar in Lessudden, wadset his two husbandlands to an Edinburgh advocate for a loan of £100,[16] and Andrew Darling, portioner of Appletreeleaves, drew up a contract with John Newlands, burgess of Edinburgh, by which in return for 100 merks he granted the burgess the right to uplift an annualrent of 12 merks from his feu, thus depriving himself of part of the annual returns from his farm.[17] These dealings could be the beginning of the end for some feuars, for if they failed to repay the loan and redeem their lands these might pass for good into the ownership of the creditor. The arrival of an outside feuar created a layer of interest between the abbey as superior and the cultivators of the soil. Sometimes the newcomer, who lived outside the area, would subfeu the land to the resident farmer, giving him restricted rights in the property; elsewhere the presence of a middleman simply gave the kindly tenant the character of a subtenant, in practice if not in law.

We have yet to discover what happened to the cottars and landless labourers whose wellbeing had previously depended on the kindly tenancy of the farmers above them. As times changed their position became increasingly vulnerable. In the 17th century bigger proprietors tended to buy up many of the small feus, until a century later villages like Gattonside and Lessudden were still dominated by the mansions of those proprietors who had engrossed much of the old feuartouns. In fact, it is for this reason that the title deeds and marriage contract of

Marion Cochrane's family have survived in the family papers of the Scotts of Raeburn who came to own the lands of Lessudden. As the feuars were bought out and the middle layer of rural society was gradually removed the cottars and labourers probably took the brunt of the dislocation caused by the agricultural 'improvements' of the 18th and early 19th centuries.

In the case of the Melrose lands feuing came comparatively late in the 16th century, so that during Queen Mary's reign most of the inhabitants of this part of the Tweed valley were kindly tenants of long-standing for whom the development of farming methods lagged behind that of their rights of possession. Farming operated within a vicious circle of low productivity, holdings were small compared with what we today would regard as a decent-sized family farm, and the return from the crop was generally three or fourfold, compared with the twentyfold increase which the farmer expects today. From evidence given in the 1550s about the lands of Drygrange it appears that there and elsewhere on the abbey's estates land-intake had halted and the ground was becoming over-cultivated. The size of holdings varied considerably but the general pattern seems to be that on those lands nearest to the abbey, such as Melrose itself, Newstead, Darnick and Gattonside the holdings were the smallest on the estates. These lands had been among the earliest endowments of the monastery, originally farmed directly, where the inhabitants showed most clearly the characteristics of a labour force and their holdings had been small cultivation patches from which they and their families had derived their food. Even by the 16th century the holdings in these places tended to average between two and six acres.

Further afield, on those lands which had formed granges and had been farmed at a distance, so to speak, or had been granted to a substantial tenant who might even be a laird, the land-units were bigger. At Lessudden, which was a comparatively late endowment of the 14th century, only four out of forty recorded tenants in the 16th century held less than six acres, while most of the others held at least a half-husbandland, that is 13 acres. At Newtoun the majority held 13 acres or more and 8 out of 19 tenants named in one document held a full husbandland each. At Blainslie, further away still, the holdings were even larger, as many as 39 and even 52 acres in some cases.

It has been calculated by some historians that it required a minimum of 8 to 10 acres to sustain a family of four in medieval times.[18] Since the methods of cultivation scarcely changed and the expected crop-yield was much the same in the 16th century as it had been in the medieval period, we can say that 8 acres would still be the necessary minimum. If this is so then many Melrose abbey farmers held more than the minimum, some a lot more, in this excellent arable and pastoral country. Only at Gattonside could it be said that holdings were consistently small; about two-thirds of the tenants there who received feus in 1590 held fewer than 8 acres. However, it is difficult to have a clear picture of a family's entire possessions. They sometimes held land in more than one place, but this can only be discovered where there is a run of estate rentals over a period of years showing the entry of tenants, as there is for Melrose's sister-house Coupar Angus. Besides, sometimes the very small holdings are accounted for by the fact that peasant farmers, in order to provide for various members of the family, particularly sons, occasionally practised what is known as partible inheritance. That is, the father when he became old, or in his will before he died, would bequeath his kindness to different parts of the holding to different sons who, when the tack was renewed or the parent died would ask the landlord to 'enter' them to the particular parts of the farm of which they had been left the kindness. This had the effect of splitting up the holding among the members of the family. Some tenants with the same surname who held very small portions of a settlement may in fact have been brothers, but rentals and even the 'omnibus' feu charters do not reveal relationships.

Apart from the size of his holding there were other circumstances that made life difficult for the farmer. To begin with there were the frequent bad harvests when families faced the choice of whether to eat more of what they had in order to keep up their strength throughout the winter, or save the grain for the next sowing. The methods of cultivation and the arrangements of the farming settlement limited production. It is ironic that in those centuries when all the peasant's intuitive skills and accumulated experience were at their height in coping with his environment, his unrelenting application to work brought him in such small returns. He did indeed work to eat and eat to live. The grain, as we saw, yielded only a three or fourfold return. The means of increasing the fertility of the soil was limited to the dung supplied by the farm animals. The trouble was that the farmer could not afford to keep too many cattle since there was little on which to feed them during the winter months. Most dung fell on the rough pasture land of the outfield which was ploughed only occasionally, or on the common pasture. The use of root crops and grasses to maintain a crop-rotation which would not exhaust the soil was unknown at least until the 17th century. Hay came from the natural water-meadows, and thus the fodder supply was low. Oats were fed only to the precious draught animals and riding horses; little fodder, fewer animals, less dung and low crop-yield. Nevertheless, it must be said that with all its limitations, some of which were so far outwith the powers of the farmers to remedy, the farmtoun with its components of arable, pasture, meadows and summer sheilings was ideally suited to the needs of subsistence farming.

On top of the limitations imposed by farming practices there were considerably outlays, annual and periodic, which in the later 16th century increasingly took the form of cash payments. The demand for money put pressure on the farmer to sell more of his crop, or to borrow from his neighbours, either money or replacement grain; testaments are full of the evidence of these debts between neighbours. The element of regular outlay in the peasant economy is not often stressed, beyond mention of the basic rent, but it was all-important at the time because these obligations had to be met, however little the family had left over for themselves. In practice there was little difference between the

obligations of a tenant on a secular and one on a church estate except in one respect. Lairds still continued to demand labour-services or cash commutation
towards the cultivation of the Mains of the barony – what is now called the home
farm – whereas on church land the grange system, which had drawn on most
labour in medieval times, had largely died out by the 16th century. Visual rep-
resentations of medieval life are apt to distort the picture; they tend to show
well-fed, well-clad peasants dutifully bent over the plough or the harrow, members of small, familiar, supportive communities, living in a quiet world where the
loudest mechanical sounds were those of the mill-wheel and church bell. Life was
not as safe or as simple as that.

The most important annual outlay, the rent, was paid twice in the year, at
Whitsunday and Martinmas, after a reminder by an officer of the landlord's
court. The chamberlain with his clerks and serjeants in attendance 'sat' to receive
the rents, probably on several days and at the monastery itself. The rent consisted
of three parts: the money-rent or maill, the grain-rent or ferme, and the small
custom payments in kind or kane, such as poultry or cheese. The grain rent came
from the staple crops of bere, oats, pease, and wheat. The last was not used by the
farmers for food but grown as a cash crop or as part of the rent. In addition to the
rent the farmer had to undertake two or three carriages a year, with carts, sleds,
wains or pack-horses, an irksome duty which needed not only a cart and horse
but a servant or member of the family to accompany it.

Annual outlay was not over with the payment of the rent. In the autumn and
winter the grain was ground at the landlord's mills to which the farmers were
'thirled', that is, obliged to take their crops to be ground. People were prosecuted
for evasion of this unpopular obligation, using hand-mills at home. Thirlage continued throughout the 17th and much of the 18th centuries and was greatly resented. Not only was it time-consuming to transport the grain to the mill and wait in
the queue for it to be ground, but certain payments had to be made in connection
with the process: 'multure' which was a tax on the amount of grain ground,
usually paid in grain itself, went to the landlord or the tacksman of the mill, who
might be a local laird or the miller himself; a percentage which went to the working miller and the perquisite known as the 'knaifschip' which was taken by the
miller's servant. The miller was often an unpopular local figure who was suspected of cheating. Because he operated a monopoly which his family often held for
generations he was a substantial proprietor in the neighbourhood, and generally
regarded as being on the landlord's side.

Some annual payments were due to the church by the inhabitants as
parishioners. The most substantial of these were the teinds (English, tithes), the
tenth part of all produce, crops, stock, and dairy produce, eggs, poultry, and the
young of the animals, which were set aside for the parson's deputy, the vicar. In
practice, since the revenues of Melrose parish were annexed to the abbey, who
paid a priest to serve the parishioners, the teinds went into the coffers of the
abbey chamberlain with the rents. The small teinds at Melrose accounted for 8

stones of wool, 8 stones of cheese, and 60 lambs. There was a practice of selling the teinds to the parishioners, just as there was a practice of selling them the grain rent. The collection or 'riding' of the teinds was a disruption as well as an exaction, since the grain was supposed to be left on the fields until collected.

Further complications arose when the teinds of the parish, or from particular lands within it, were not collected directly by the abbey but leased to a tacksman whose factor came round to lift them. This must have caused chaos at times; in the middle ages, if church statutes are anything to go by, the collection of the teinds led to all kinds of evasion, cheating, threatening behaviour and even assault. The payment was often stubbornly resisted; the registers of the court of session are full of actions for non-payment of teinds by parishioners – many cases quite futile. It was said in mid-16th century that Melrose abbey's teinds from the annexed parish of Ettrick had not been paid since before Flodden in 1513. At Easter there were special offerings for the parish priest, known as 'Pasche [Easter] fines', which were not always given cheerfully.

Within his own household the farmer had to pay his servants' fees, at Whitsunday and Martinmas, with an extra 'bounteth' and perhaps a pair of shoes or working apron of harden or linen. If testaments are an indication servants' fees were very often in arrears. Many servants were young or dependent relatives who lived with the family. Others were those with special skills, such as ploughman, shepherd, herd, thresher, builders of dykes and sawyers of wood.

Then there were occasional payments, occasional only in the sense that they occurred at irregular intervals for some of them would happen frequently. When the tack of the holding fell due to be renewed a payment known as grassum was charged, usually in cash and equivalent to several years' rent. A further payment, called entry-silver, was made at the term from which the new tack was formally said to run. Feuars paid double their feu-duty when an heir succeeded and their feu charters usually stipulated periodic grassums (every three or five years). The farmer regularly laid out money to rural craftsmen such as the weaver and waulker who wove and finished cloth made from yarn spun at home by his womenfolk, and sometimes a tailor and shoemaker. A wright was paid to make wheels and other parts of carts and wains, or to mend them. The best-paid craftsman was the smith, who both shod horses and made and repaired ironwork, such as the parts of the plough.

A peasant farmer faced an outlay in seeing his sons and daughters married and settled with a piece of land. Tochers, paid in instalments, were often in arrears like servants' fees. When the head of the family or remaining parent died there were more exactions, in the midst of the family's natural distress. There was the payment to the notary who arrived within nine days of the death to make an inventory of the farm stock aand value the household goods. There was the 'quot' charged on the value of the net estate after the person's testament had been recorded in the commissary court. In the middle of this legal business and what we would now call bureaucracy there was the payment to the landlord of the

'herezeld', an animal taken as death-duty from the husbandman class, the back-
bone of the rural tenantry. The parish priest sent along his clerk to demand the
'corsepresent' (corpse-present), another animal, and the 'umaist claith' or best
cover from the bed, and to ask for payment for the burial service.

The testaments of a handful of Melrose tenants survive. These seem to have
been middle-of-the-way in substance for tenant-farmers and small feuars, leaving
an average net estate of around £300 Scots. Their aim, of course, had been suf-
ficiency rather than surplus and they had few luxuries. There was a lot of
borrowing among them of money, animals and grain. Their main crop on their
holdings was bere, the four-rowed barley common in Scotland, and other crops
included oats, wheat, rye and pease. Most people had at least one horse, or mare,
used both for riding and haulage. George Blackie in Gallowbridge, in 1588, had
'four young nags', while the fact that someone owed him £6 each for two mares
suggests that he may have been breeding horses. He was rather better-off than the
others whose testaments survive, leaving over £600 Scots, and had loaned a man
in Westhouses £32 'of reddie gold'.[19] Everyone had a few cattle, of which the
ages and types are given, cows with calves, in or not in milk, quoys, stots; a cow
was worth £3 to £6. There were always far more sheep than cattle, something
which is characteristic of many parts of Scotland, not only this wool-producing
area. William Linlithgow of Drygrange sold wool in Edinburgh.[20] Edward
Romanes in Blainslie, who had 100 'slaughter scheip skinnis' worth £60, John
Darling in Appletreeleaves, with his 80 ewes, and Robert Ramsay in Colmeslie,
with 140 sheep and 68 lambs, had the biggest flocks.[21] Romanes was possibly also
selling to a merchant. Oxen, valued at £6 to £8, were the farmer's most valuable
possession, which were used for ploughing and haulage, sometimes contributed to
the communal plough-team and at other times used by substantial farmers with
their own ploughs. Edward Romanes left his son 4 oxen with the plough and corn
to sow the ground, 'incais he lieve to bring up my bairnis'. Thomas Letham in
Newtoun had 8 oxen, William Spottiswood in Whitelee 9, and William
Linlithgow in Drygrange, a feuar, 10 oxen.

Among the most interesting parts of the testaments are the provisions for
families. According to the letter of the law as it stood at that time only moveables
could be conveyed in a will, yet we find tenant-farmers leaving their kindness to
the holdings to sons, or to their widows for their lifetimes. John Maben in
Melrose left 'my rowme [holding] and stedyng to my spous Janet Mureheid and
to Robert Maben my son'.[22] Robert Wallace, also in Melrose, left to his son,
William, 'my akir of land quhilk wes coft [bought] fra Thomas Lauder'.[23] John
Hall in Threepwood bequeathed all his gear to his wife, Elspeth Thomson, to be
disponed by her as she thought fit, also 'the possessioun of my rowme in Threep-
wode induring [during] hir wedowheid, and gif scho mareis to leif the samyn'.[24]
This last proviso was added by many husbands of the period in an effort to prevent a stepfather from meddling with the children's inheritance. Money was
sometimes set aside to be 'laid out upone land' for members of the family, and

sums were left for daughters' tochers when they came to be married. James Nicol, a merchant in Melrose who died in 1593, left £90 and £100 respectively to his two daughters. Robert Ramsay in Colmeslie left his wife and daughters 1,000 merks, 200 merks to each of the daughters when she came of age. Wives were commonly made executors and tutors to their children under age. James Nicol ordained that his wife, Isobel Dryden, 'be maister of all sa lang as she levis . . .'.[25] William Hay in Gattonside left to a son William 'the crop of the orchard land yearly quhill [until] the profeit thereof mak hym £120'. Bequests sometimes consisted of animals and grain. Robert Ramsay left his mother a cow and 10 sheep. John Hall in Threepwood left to his father 'my best ryding geir, with ane claything of my best claithis, ane meit almerie [cupboard] and ane stot in Blainslie'.

Many people pastured stock with neighbours who thus earned a little money. John Garvie in Hilslope, Melrose parish, had cows and calves 'in pasturing and foddering' with tenants in Brintaburn, Brownwood, Brighaugh, Whitesland and Housebyre. He also owed a neighbour half a boll of bere 'for ane ox hyre'.[26] Others loaned money at interest on the basis of bonds drawn up for them by the ubiquitous notaries or by a writer in Lauder. George Blackie in Gallowbrig was due £32 of ready gold from Bartholemew Darling as well as £14 'of auld comptis [accounts]'. Lists of debtors and creditors preserve the names of local tradespeople: David Hoppringle, apothecary, Thomas Bower, smith, John Wallace, lorimer, Alexander Thomson, waulker fuller, Thomas Wood, wright, and Bessie and Tibbie Letham, alewives, all in and around Melrose itself.

The perishable homes of these people have vanished. They were usually one or two-roomed, wooden or cruck-framed structures in which two tree trunks were tied together at the top to form an inverted V shape that was the cruck, one at either end of the house and others in between. They were low-walled and thatched, the windows unglazed, with sometimes an animal skin to cover the doorway, although there are references to the upright woodwork that carried more substantial doors. Cooking, eating, and much indoor work was done by the central fireplace, the smoke from which escaped through a hole in the roof. There were not many hours of daylight in such a house so that the family probably went to bed early, especially in winter. The beds in the poorest houses would be straw-filled pallets, with wooden 'stand' or permanently-erected beds in more commodious dwellings. All age-groups shared the same living and sleeping quarters and the major experiences of life, birth, illness and death, took place in this everyday environment. The animals shared the same roof, in their stalls behind a partition or wall, and the poultry usually roosted in the beams of the living space. Substantial tenant-farmers and feuars would have their own barns, byres, and stables, with a turf dyke around the close and perhaps a lockable yett. Those with smaller holdings on jointly-cultivated farms would share the barn, barnyard and other premises. Feuars also lived in peel-houses which were partly built of stone, which in times of danger might afford shelter to their more vulnerable neighbours and could provide separate living and sleeping quarters and had more substantial furniture.

Household goods are not often detailed in testaments but are usually valued as a whole; accumulatively worth between £4 and £66-13s4d in the surviving testaments of Melrose people. Occasionally there is a list; Janet Bouston and her husband Thomas Letham in Newtoun had household plenishings valued at £52-14s, consisting of 2 aumbries or cupboards, 2 kists, 3 pots, 4 pewter plates, 4 pewter trenchers, 2 cauldrons (alone worth £10), 2 furnished beds, 4 bed coverings, 2 long curtains probably for a bed, 8 pairs of sheets, 12 ells of kersey and 4 of frieze cloth. They owed money to a weaver and a waulker.[27] Details in a court action before the sheriff of Roxburgh in 1539 suggest the interior of a peel-house, although there were not many feuars on the Melrose estates at that time and the house concerned may have belonged to a husbandman. The family concerned, called Grahamslaw, lived at Newtoun. They possessed a 'meat board' or table and the trestles on which it was set up when in use; there was not enough space in these houses to leave large pieces of furniture sitting around. The table had a cover, forms for the family to sit on and one chair, probably for the head of the household. The 'chandler' or candlestick would have been moved around to wherever it was needed. There was a 'stand bed' made of wood with a feather-filled bed, sheets, blankets, a covering, bolster, and 'coddis' or pillows. For cooking there was a cauldron, brewing vat, barrel, crook, spit, and tongs, a pot, pan, pewter dish, meal kist and salt vat and a ladle. The quart and pint stoups were made of wood, not pewter. In the yard was a plough with its 'irons', a harrow, ox-yoke, two oxen and two horses, suggesting a mixed plough-team as well as haulage animals.[28] Sometimes an inventory includes cloth woven from the family's own wool or flax; a smith's wife at Gattonside had 6 ells of white cloth and 6 of linen, the latter still 'at the wobsters', and Katherine Watson in Melrose had 20 ells each of linen and harden.

Marion Cochrane in Lessudden, whose family retained their property until 1672, died at her dwelling there in November 1559 only two years after she had taken it in feu. According to the details in a court case involving her son-in-law, Robert Bryden, the house was a peel-house.[29] Although Marion's net estate was valued at only £16, just about three times what she paid annually to the abbey for her 1¾ husbandlands and garden, she left her family 4 plough oxen, 2 horses, 3 cows and a few sheep, wheat in the barn to be sold and pease and oats in the barnyard to be threshed. Among the witnesses of her will was dene John Turnbull, one of the monks of Melrose.[30] Her family enjoyed considerable status in the community at Lessudden yet she did not leave many of this world's goods behind her. Towards the end of her life, however, she had seen her family gain written, legal recognition of their customary rights to their holding; her feu charter survives to prove it, signed by the 'crawbit' commendator, James Stewart and ten members of the monastic community. The increased security of those small feuars who were her neighbours, and of the two or three generations who followed them, was the result not only of a revolution in estate-management on the part of their landlord but of the farmers' tenacious hold on their customary rights of possession over previous centuries. As the country mouse in Robert Henryson's poem said to the town mouse:

'Greit aboundance and blind prosperitie
Oftymes makis ane evill conclusioun;
The sweitest lyf, thairfor, in this cuntrie
Is sickerness [security] with small possessioun'.

THE FARMERS OF MELROSE

NOTES

1 Background to the management of the abbey estates in the middle ages from *Liber de S. Marie de Mailros* (Bannatyne Club, 1837), Introduction.

2 J.S. Richardson and M. Wood, *Melrose Abbey*, Official Guide, 20-1.

3 C.S. Romanes, *Records of the Regality of Melrose* (S.H.S.), III, xlvii.

4 T.B. Franklin, *A History of Scottish Farming* (1952), 80.

5 J.A. Symon, *Scottish Farming* (1959), 58.

6 M.H.B. Sanderson, *Scottish Rural Society in the Sixteenth Century*, 46-8.

7 *Melrose Regality Records*, III, 155-7.

8 Vatican Archives, Register of Supplications: 2538, fos 90v-91; microfilm in the Department of Scottish History, University of Glasgow.

9 M.H.B. Sanderson, *Scottish Rural Society in the Sixteenth Century*, Chapter 5; Stoddart marriage contract, Scott of Raeburn Muniments (S.R.O.), GD 104/3

10 *Scottish Rural Society, Chapter 4*.

11 *Ibid*, Chapters 6-11.

12 *Melrose Regality Records*, III, 357-63.

13 *Ibid*., III, 384-7.

14 *Ibid*., III, 232-7.

15 Scott of Raeburn Muniments, GD 104/5.

16 Register of Deeds (S.R.O.), xiv, fo 130.

17 *Ibid*., xiv, fo 140v.

18 C. Lis and H. Soly, *Poverty and Capitalism in pre-industrial Europe* (1982), 3; others have put it at 10-13½ acres: J.F.C. Harrison, *The Common People* (1984), 46-7.

19 Edinburgh Commissariot Records, Register of Testaments, CC8/8/19, fo 178.

20 *Ibid*., CC8/8/3, fo 155v.

21 *Ibid*., CC8/8/24, fo 30v; CC8/8/3, fo 187v; CC8/8/23, fo 289.

22 *Ibid*., CC8/8/6, fo 149.

23 *Ibid*., CC8/8/3, fo 156v.

24 *Ibid*., CC8/8/23, fo 357.

25 *Ibid*., CC8/8/26, fo 281.

26 *Ibid*., CC8/8/21, fo 202.

27 *Ibid*., CC8/8/1, fo 163v.

28 Roxburgh Sheriff Court Records, Court Book, (S.R.O.), SC62/2/2, 23 July 1539.

29 Scott of Raeburn Muniments, GD 104/48/1.

30 Lauder Commissariot Records, Register of Testaments, CC15/5/1, fo 22

WALTER MORTON

Shipmaster

MANY sixteenth-century Scots were very conscious of being Europeans. A steady stream of them made their way to France, the Low Countries, Poland and Scandinavia as traders, travellers, students and teachers, diplomats, soldiers and pilgrims. There they made contact with fellow-countrymen, some of whom were expatriate relatives, in the immigrant Scots communities of such towns as Dieppe, Rouen, Veere and Danzig. The factors of Scottish-based merchants travelled with the cargoes, doing business on their behalf in the thronging markets of France and the Netherlands. Other factors were resident, the most important of whom was the Conservator of Scottish trading privileges at Veere who acted as both a consul for the Convention of Royal Burghs and a commercial agent for the merchants, and at the same time ran a social centre for visiting Scots at the Conciergery House.[1] Many Scots who never went abroad frequently bought and used imported foodstuffs, fine cloths, craft materials and luxury items, and some of them treasured books from the European printing presses. As a small country on the northern fringe of Europe, Scotland had to be outward-looking for economic reasons. She shared a cultural heritage with Europe, whether Catholic or Protestant. Whatever has been said of political alliances such as the 'auld alliance' between Scotland and France, it was in the ordinary, everyday contact made by travelling Scots that many of the lasting links were forged and maintained.

Walter Morton, from one of the Fife ports, possibly Burntisland, was typical of the kind of Scot through whom these contacts were made. In the last decade of the century he regularly sailed his ship the *Antelope* across the North Sea, round the Baltic, into the northern French ports and the wine ports of the Bay of Biscay, sometimes calling on the outward or homeward journey at the English ports of Plymouth, Dover, Yarmouth and London. His memorandum book of expenses – he had a clerk to keep the proper accounts – gives a more personal and lively picture of his life as a working shipmaster than any formal record could have done.[2] If asked he would have given his occupation as skipper. That was his special skill. He was in complete charge of the vessel, her fitting-out, provisioning and maintenance, the hiring of her crew, the payment of all seagoing dues and the necessary negotiations with officials. Like many people in his day, and since, however, his activities spilled over into related areas. He acted as factor for a number of men and women at home, for whom he sold goods, mainly cloth, and made a variety of purchases with their 'free money' realised from the sales. Not unnaturally the merchant guilds frowned on men who were essentially seamen doing such business, and the Dundee guild, for example, ordained that 'no merchand presume to mak any mariner or skipper factor to his gear . . . in respect the greit skaith [damage] of making ther mariners and skippers factoris who have no perfectioun of knowledge to doe the same'.[3] Needless to say, the practice went on. Walter Morton's reasonable standard of writing and familiarity with business detail shows that he had had considerable experience of factoring. Not only so but, like other factors, he broke into the merchants' province by doing a little trading on his own account and even occasionally handled goods for a foreign merchant. His varied interests are characteristic of the trading world in which he operated.

Since he often refers to the *Antelope* as 'our ship' he presumably shared ownership. When transporting his own goods, as distinct from those of merchants, he shared the ownership of the cargo with one James Cooper. Walter's identity may be gathered from a receipt, the text of which he copied into his book, complete with date and signature, and which he prefixed with the words 'the sum of all that *I* receivit'. The list of crew hired for each voyage usually includes the name 'Walter Morton', sometimes designated 'skipper', which may have been his way of denoting how much was due to himself in his capacity of shipmaster. It is noticeable that when he uses the phrase, 'the names of them that came *with me* . . .', Walter Morton's name is omitted, so that it seems safe to infer that this was the skipper himself.

It is difficult to say what kind of ship the *Antelope* was. The 'crear', or crayer, a slightly old-fashioned, low-built vessel of between 30 and 40 tons, is sometimes mentioned in Scottish customs accounts of the period, as are the 'hoy', which was the Dutch 'heu', a single-decked, sloop-rigged ship, and, occasionally, the more up-to-date 'flie-boat', the Dutch 'fluitship'.[4] Since her skipper sometimes mentions payment of 'cabar fie', the charge for the service of a lighter in loading, it suggests that she was one of the three-masted, square-rigged ships that sometimes found it difficult to negotiate the inner waters of the German and Netherlands coasts and had to be loaded from lighters that plied between the ships and the ports. This operation added to the time spent at ports and to the expense of the voyage. These bigger vessels also needed a crew of about fourteen, the *Antelope's* being sometimes as many as twenty-one, whereas there was a new lightweight 'boyer' which could be handled by a crew of five or six, making it one of the cheapest ships to sail at the end of the century. The *Antelope* probably had a burden of between forty and seventy tons, since on three occasions she left France loaded with 42, 48 and 62 tuns of wine. She did have some modern features, including a separate top-mast of the kind said to have been invented by a Dutch seaman about 1570 and commended by Sir Walter Raleigh as 'a wonderful ease to great ships', in that it was capable of being separately struck.[5] She was of caravel construction which had come in about mid-15th century, in which the method of laying the ship's timbers flush against one another had replaced the older clinker-built vessels in which the timbers overlapped; Walter paid for 'carvel nails', pitch and tar in Danzig on one occasion, with 'trees to our main mast and sawing of thaim . . . '. We do not know how much the *Antelope* cost to build, but Morton and his partner had a new ship built in Norway at a price of just over £700 (about £63 sterling) and also bought a second-hand one, 'John Gersounis auld schip . . . from William Hegee', for £500 (about £41 sterling).[6] This represented a considerably investment in a vital piece of equipment which, like the modern motor car, depreciated fairly quickly and needed constant repairs.

One reason for the slow turn-round on voyages was the congestion at ports, due to the limited sailing season, mainly between May and November, with long queues at the toll in the Sound of Elsinore which led to the Baltic. In 1598 the *Antelope* left Dieppe on 15 March and arrived at Danzig on 8 April. Having reached the roads there extra food had to be bought while she waited to be taken into the harbour: 'for flesche abord to keep the schip in the raidis, 30s', and eventually the hefty sum of £3-15s 'for the guiders denners quhen thay brocht in the schip'. Perhaps in order to avoid what the Dundee council called the 'tyme of thrang' when no ship was allowed to lie with 'hir braid side' to the quay, braver skippers may have sailed earlier in the year. In some years Morton was in the Baltic in April and in Dieppe as early as February. Before setting out on the latter voyage, in February 1597, he prudently renewed the ship's ropes and lanterns and paid for a new compass 'and mending of our auld'.

Getting clear of the home harbour could also be slow. In 1595 the *Antelope* was freighted to Dieppe as late as 16 November but the bill of lading, that is the certificate of loading and undertaking by the master to deliver the cargo safely, was not completed for another nine days. One hold-up involved 'my expensis owr the watter [the Forth ferry] twyce seking of ane kebell [cable]'. On 12 August 1597 Walter began noting his outlay 'boune to Spane' but it was not until 7 September that he 'sallet out of Scotland', part of the time having been taken up in business dealings with those whose cloth he was taking with him to sell in return for Spanish wine. As his book is not entered in strictly chronological order and the year-dates are not often given, we cannot follow the complete pattern of the ship's voyages but, considering the number of ports and other towns mentioned, in most cases several times, she probably did the three annual round trips which historians think to have been the norm.

Ports and towns visited	Dates of voyages, if given
Konigsberg (modern Kaliningrad, Lithuania)	2 undated

Danzig (modern Gdansk, Poland)	April 1589; May and July 1597; 4 undated
Elsinore	April 1589; May and July 1597; 4 undated
Norway (ports unspecified)	3 undated
Bruges	1 undated
Flanders (ports unspecified)	2 undated
Fecamp	January 1594
Dieppe	November 1595; February and May 1597; 1598; May 1599; 6 undated
Honfleur	January 1594
Rouen	January 1594; 3 undated
Kelboyse (?)	1 undated
Corbeil	December 1594
Crotoye (?)	December 1594
Conferteine (?)	January 1594
St Martins	January 1595
La Rochelle	January 1594 and 1595
Bordeaux	September 1589; September 1594; January 1595; 5 undated
Lisbon	March 1589; July 1600; 3 undated
Spain (? Cadiz)	September 1597; October 1598; 1599
Plymouth	(?1594)
Dover	March 1589; February 1597
London	1599 (? coming from Spain); October 1599 (? going to Spain); 1 undated
Yarmouth	(?) 1595; (?) 1599

The timespan of the voyages and visits to towns covers 1589 to 1600, although it is obviously not a complete record and the years 1590-3 and 1596 are not referred to. A large number of voyages are undated. The places visited range from Spain in the south to Norway in the north. The French ports were visited most years, taking into account the undated voyages, and perhaps the *Antelope* wintered in France in 1593-4 and 1594-5. In January of both years Walter was waiting in the north of France to return to the great wine and salt port of Bordeaux. In 1595 he hired a mixed crew of Scots and French seamen, which cost him 160 francs and a free entertainment, or 'freelacht', in a tavern after the hiring. He travelled overland on his way to La Rochelle to pick up his ship. The charter-party, or trading agreement, was drawn up at St Martins on the Channel coast, which suggests that he was engaged to carry goods for a French merchant;

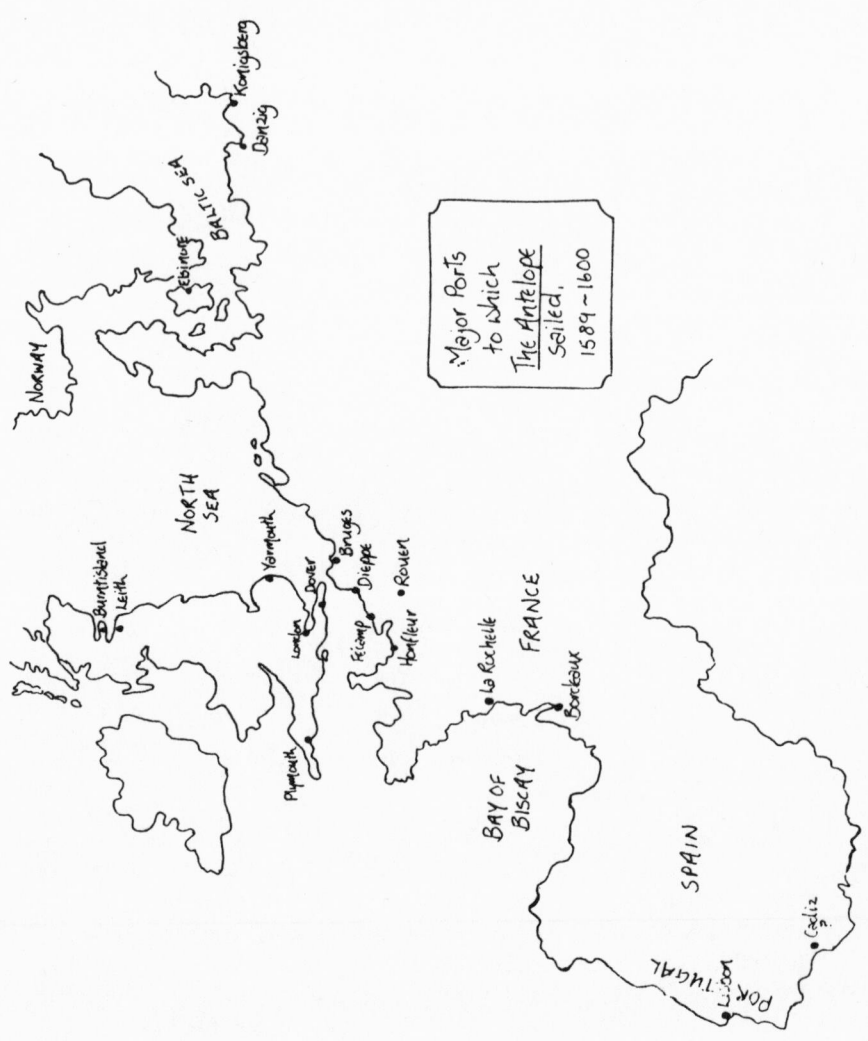

Map showing ports visited by Walter Morton's ship, the
Antelope, **1589-1600**

this was not unusual, many Scottish ships being used in the international carrying-trade around the coasts of northern Europe. In 1594 he had a dispute with a French merchant, when he had spent 7 francs in going 'to the Rochell ine protestanne aganis the marchand'. In St Martins he bought a barrel of meal for the ship's cook and some linen for a new St Andrew's cross for the ship's flag, paying 5s-10d for the making of it. In the winter of 1594 the ship had been at Rouen, when a pilot was hired to take her down the river and a boat hired to take the skipper round to Honfleur.

At regular intervals Morton and John Ramsay, the clerk, who seems to have travelled with him, 'made compt and rekening' of how much had been spent in the last port of call and worked out the balance of sales and purchases, a complicated business involving different currencies. It would have been good to have had the clerk's orderly account book and the bundles of bills and receipts that must have gone with it. But there is something very human about the cryptic sentences in the skipper's notebook which carry the atmosphere of life aboard, in harbour and at sea, and convey the idiom and accents of his speech.

Before and after each voyage the ship underwent considerable repairs, sometimes even involving the replacement of the timbers and masts. The *Antelope* may, in fact, have been an old ship, since repairs had to be carried out on parts of the interior which even a rough passage should not have been expected to damage. Perhaps this was why Walter and his partner had a new ship built in Norway and bought a second-hand one. At any rate, her need for constant maintenance has left us with interesting references to the structure of the *Antelope* herself. Whatever specialist skills were employed there was always the need for a band of workmen for general labouring and the carriage of goods and materials. In the autumn of 1595 before sailing for Dieppe the ship was eleven weeks on the stocks in an unnamed shipyard, possibly Burntisland, undergoing repairs during which the ship's boy was paid to keep an eye on her. He may even have lived on board during that time, and during the twenty days before repairs began, for which he was given his 'meat'. After work was finished there was the customary drink-money to the men who 'brocht the schepe abone the watter efter scho cam off the stockis', with 25s to the crew after she had been rigged. At Danzig in 1597 the main and mizzen masts were renewed and a plank and two long timbers replaced. In Norway a sawyer was paid to saw the pillars of the cabin-bunk (coye)[7] and six deals were bought 'to laye our medmest doors'.

The most important craftsman on board was James Logan the carpenter, or timberman, whose work was so essential to the ship's seaworthiness that in Danzig the skipper once paid for a licence permitting him to work on two holy days. The timberman might work for anything up to two weeks before the ship sailed. He was assisted by John Henry and some temporarily-employed timbermen in foreign ports, where deals were bought for emergency repairs. These included deals 'to lyne our portes and casellis',[8] the gun-ports and the wooden castles, fore and aft, which were such a distinctive feature of ships at this time. Logan took particular charge of cargoes of timber, supervising their inloading. On one occasion he was given 4s, with a chopin of wine to the poor, 'at the losing [unloading] of his temer'. Loading and unloading was as good a reason for a drink as any. The masts were not made by the timberman, although he may have undertaken repairs. There are many references to their replacement or maintenance and payments to the labourers who carried them to the ship and helped to put them in position. In Danzig a quantity of small nails was required for the mizzen mast, with a long iron band and iron bolts for the main mast,[9] although there are also references to the more commonly-used 'welding', or woolding, a few turns of rope wound round the joints of the masts.[10] In Dieppe a new mast was bought, and payments were made 'for our mast pounding' and to 'the crane master' when it was erected on board. At home John Morell was paid 28s for 'making of our mastes' and the large sum of £8-10s 'for making of our tope mastes', that is the separate top-masts which were a comparatively new device. Morell's man was paid £5 for two weeks' work, whereas two men working with the timberman for the same length of time received only £7 between them.

If sound timbers meant seaworthiness, stout and well-made sails meant speed and mobility at sea. The need to repair the sails and make new ones was quite frequent and represented considerable running costs. None of the named hired crew is designated sailmaker, although it was usual to have one on board larger ships. On the other hand, there is evidence that maintenance of the sails was carried out by local craftsmen. When the *Antelope* arrived in the Newhaven of Dieppe on one occasion 5s was paid 'for upe careing of our saillis and to the sail sewer'.[11] Whether the French sailmaker took a pessimistic view of the state of the sails or not, Walter noted immediately below this entry the cost of canvas for a new topsail and mainsail, 63 and 90 ells of canvas respectively, costing £38-5s, which was more than double the amount the skipper realised from the sale of a web of 30 ells of cloth, £18.[12] Before leaving for Norway on one occasion the cost of making a new topsail alone, with the canvas, twine, and tar, was £22-8s. We can see why there were frequent purchases of pieces of canvas and twine to patch the sails. One interesting, undated entry refers to the payment of 5s to the sail sewers 'for cesing [? casing] of our gafes', which may refer to the short-gaffsail in common use in Holland by the 1630s, an early form of fore-and-aft sail which was developed for smaller craft.[13]

In Dieppe two iron chisels were bought for the skilled task of caulking, in this case the orlop, or lowest, deck, in order to render the ship watertight.[14] Teased-out hemp known as oakum was driven between the deck planks, tightly packed and sealed with hot pitch. In more recent times caulking was a trade in its own right but the *Antelope's* timbermen did the job in the 1590s, receiving 27s for their dinner afterwards. Underneath this is the rueful entry, 'to the serjeantis for ane onla [fine] for wirking in ane haly day that we knew not of'.[15] Rope, like sail-canvas, was costly and had often to be renewed before setting sail or on reaching harbour. In Norway the skipper bought 11½ stones of 'takell to rek

[rig] her', which cost him £20-15s. A great cable by which the ship's anchor was operated was bought in Norway, possibly for the new ship. Getting it aboard for a trial and back ashore, where it was stored until required, was a strenuous exercise:

> 'Item, for ane cabill and ane cordell thar [i.e. Norway] . . . 45 stane at 51 gros the stane is 76 gudlyngis [guilders]. For weying and dounbering, and cabar [lighter] fie, and drinksilver to the boyis, in grit mark, for two grett winding blokis, 50 gros . . . For fraucht of the cabill and cordell hamwart [homewards], £4 10s. For culling [?coiling] the cabill aland [? on land] and bering up of the cordell to my hous, 6s 8d'.[16]

Pieces of 'takell' were bought for particular purposes – for the halyards to hoist the yards when setting sail, 120 fathoms to be used in loading the cargo, for 'keyes' to tighten the rigging, for braces in working the yard-arms and rudder, a small marline to protect the surface of heavier ropes, and the 'welding' to wrap round the joints of the masts. While loading up in a French port Walter twice borrowed a fender, the bundle of rope used to keep the ship's side from being damaged on the harbour wall.

It is not surprising that the much-used blocks, which landsmen knew as pulleys, had to be continually renewed, or for that matter the ship's pump, partly made of iron and standing on feet, [17] or the rudder for which, in Dieppe, the skipper bought 'ane lang band of irone to gang abowt the heid' and later had it repaired, after a voyage to Norway, with over 12 stones of iron.[18] Before setting out on one voyage he had the *Antelope's* compass checked ('for tuiching of owr compeses'),[19] and on another occasion bought a new one, with 'neyt glassis',[20] the sand-glass used to time the night watches. Payments were made before departure to the men who collected and manhandled the anchor to the ship. In Danzig a new anchor-stock, the cross-piece, was made and 'sanded'. In the second-hand market which operated among fellow-seamen, Walter once sold a skipper an anchor for £43, sending it home to him from London. Numerous small pieces of equipment, all very necessary in their own way, came on board with the provisions, such as besoms, shovels, and baskets. All provisions came in their own 'carry' specially made from wood or canvas, the most vital of which was the 'watter carry', made of wood strengthened with bands of iron.

For safety in time of war and against the ever-present pirates, merchant ships usually travelled in convoy and carried guns. The armament features in Morton's memorandum book alongside the cost of repairs and provisions. 'Our irne wark' was how he usually referred to the guns: 'for dounberring of our irne wark and the haill pouder'. Wood and iron was used in the making of the gun-ports and wrights were paid for 'syllrein [? making ceilings for] owr gowner rowmes and making of bedis'.[21] A piece of ordnance was bought in England, on return from Lisbon, and 'wheels to owr peses [pieces]' were made in Dieppe. Ten barrels of gunpowder were taken on a voyage, with a 'pair of balenses to waye owr pouder withall', and 'ane siff to siff owr powder'.

The fact that repair and replacement materials, sometimes in quite small quantities, were bought in foreign ports suggests that not much surplus was carried on board, either for lack of stowage space or reluctance to spend money on them until absolutely necessary. This must have added to the element of risk and actual danger inherent in the seagoing trader's way of life. Yet the level of maintenance also suggests that the master and crew took pride in the appearance of the vessel, symbolised perhaps in the repairs to her flag that topped the rigging, made from three bolts of linen and proudly bearing the St Andrew's cross.[22]

The ship's company, who are referred to as 'chelder' (children) in the contemporary sense of servants, or hands, were hired for each voyage. When they were kept on to work in port this was called a 'half-hire'. The fees varied among members of the crew but, although an individual's hiring fee varied from one occasion to another, this does not seem to be related to the length of the voyage. Hiring fees ranged from £3-5s to £5-5s, compared with which Morton, the skipper, received £9 to Dieppe and £12 to Spain, perhaps the larger sums being for the greater responsibility of the longer voyage.[23] His half-hire in port was £7. The whole hires to Dieppe cost £38 10s. French seamen were occasionally hired, and once a Portuguese man was taken on in place of a member of the crew, who may have been taken ill. Arles, money in advance on hiring, were paid out when the ship was formally freighted. In addition the crew were due 'portage', reckoned in barrels, the skipper being paid 16 barrels and the others between 8 and 4, with one to the ship's boy. Apart from these basic payments and dues the company received drink-money or were treated to dinner or supper on many occasions, from the signing of the charter party to taking out the ballast or weighing the anchor.

The mariners were also supplied with a certain amount of clothing, such as their seamen's coats and hose; before leaving for Norway Morton paid for the making of 21 pairs of hose and 17 coats. He himself noted 'the count of my sarkis and nepery that I tak with me'; 13 sarks, 18 napkins (which were possibly handkerchiefs or the sailor's distinctive neckerchief, since the Scots called table-napkins 'serviettes'), a dozen 'bonet muches', worn under the bonnet, two dozen 'overlays' or the turn-down collars worn when not at sea, of which six were cambric, a dozen 'serveteris' or table-napkins, two 'bord cles' or table covers, and four 'codwairis' or pillow cases. William Gray, who may not have been a regular member of the crew but employed to undertake work on the ship, was paid at a weekly rate instead of the more usual hiring fee and fee while in port; £57 5s for 17 weeks' work and two weeks 'at hame', with 'his hat to his bounteth', or gratuity. During the voyage to Spain the shipmaster lent one of the crew, James Donnes, 40 shillings sterling 'with ane goune and ane sark till he cum hame'.

Lending money to members of the ship's company was a regular occurrence which led to complicated financial calculations in the skipper's book, the intricacies of which are probably now past unravelling. Once in Dieppe he tried writing down all the loans, of both money and clothes. Olne, the ship's man, probably the man-of-all-work, had been given '£4 off his fie' (which sound like an advance of his wages) to buy cloth, and had subsequently borrowed half a dollar. James Logan the timberman had given the skipper money to pay for extra pitch and tar but had forgotten to allow for the 'berring', the carriage. The timberman and John Jamieson had both been lent several pairs of hose and shoes, or the money to buy them, it is not clear which. It must have been tempting in a foreign port to buy fashionable clothes one could not afford. Perhaps it was these problems that decided Morton to lend £20 to a kinsman, Patrick Morton, a member of the crew, 'upoun ane plege'. It must have been difficult to maintain good relations among the workforce in the confined workspace of an early-modern sailing ship. No doubt the crew developed a group-solidarity which needed careful handling. It is significant that one hand-out of drink on the *Antelope* appears to have followed an agreement with the ship's company about the handling of the gear.

In slightly over a decade some 74 names occur among those hired. The average number on a voyage was about 12, the highest being 21 to Spain, implying a fairly large turn-over of crew members. There was a handful, however, who sailed regularly in the *Antelope* over the years. These included Andrew Hay, to whom Morton lent 40s to buy a hat and £4 'to gae to his brothir', the intriguingly-called 'John the laird', James Logan the timberman, Cornelius Lyle who went to Dieppe, Bordeaux and Spain, David Miller who indulged in some trade on his own account, as did others of the company, and who deposited with the skipper for safekeeping 15 crowns of gold, two single pistoles, and 20 crowns of 'white money', James Bad, Richard Barton, ship's man, who bore a famous seafaring name, William Calder for whom the Portuguese mariner substituted, David Douglas, John Richardson, Harry Taylor and Peter Yule. The ship's cook was Davy Rait, who took delivery of the provisions, making up barrels of meal and barley, after which he got some well-earned drink-silver. He, too, borrowed money from the shipmaster.

From the provisions put on board before sailing the cook tried to provide a reasonable diet for the company. Before leaving Dieppe in November 1595 ale, a barrel of beef, a barrel of herring, meal and bread were stowed away, and at Bruges, before leaving for Danzig, 4 barrels of bread, 5 of bere or barley, peas and 'green bread'. At Elsinore they took fresh fish on board. There were occasional losses: 'for streking [breaking open] ane last of beef that was not guid'. Butter was also taken on at some ports. Mustard seed was bought and ground, in an attempt to improve – or disguise – the flavour of the food. Corn was bought in Dieppe from a resident Scots merchant, David Scott, and his father. No doubt trade was given to a fellow-countryman whenever possible. The purchase of 'ane drinking can' and ten pounds of candle conjures up convivial scenes below decks. There are two references to passengers. Two of these came home on the *Antelope* from Königsberg, for which they paid the skipper 2 dollars, and other two who took passage to England from Lisbon owed him 6s 6d for food on the voyage; they were unnamed.

The goods taken abroad for sale were the usual Scottish exports of hides, skins, fish, salt, coal, linen and harden. Walter himself sold cloth, a 'bed' containing 134 and another 173 ells, webs of blue, grey and white cloth, and some plaiding. On 12 August 1597 the *Antelope* prepared to sail for Spain carrying a cargo of linen, harden, fish, wheat and 'twenty pairs of dubill sollit shune'. James Cooper owned two-thirds of the cargo and Morton a third. The wheat, 15 bolls of it, had cost the partners just over £111, with payments to those who had carried it to the ship and to the man who had supervised the measuring and loading of it. Prior to loading it had had to be stored in rented premises, possibly at Burntisland where Morton also had a timber yard.[24] Unbleached linen and harden were taken to Bordeaux. On 10 June 1600 the ship left Scotland for Lisbon laden with coal, arriving there on 4 July. In order to reduce the risk of loss cargoes were sometimes unbelievably small and, with individual commissions, had the character of personal buying rather than commercial trading on a large scale.

Certain people regularly used Walter Morton as a factor, several of whom were women. These included Ellen Campbell for whom he sold cloth and to whom he lent £200, Christian Cant, who gave him 42 Scots merks to buy French black cloth in Flanders, and Violet Tweedie and Violet Hodge who were possibly related to each other.[25] Morton sold cloth for the latter to the value of £418-6s-5d, a 'bed' of white Galloway wool, 130 ells of blue cloth, 3 white and 4 blue webs and 18 ells of blue, the expense of measuring and packing being 28s. Cloth was sold for both Harry Bickertoun and his wife, separately; the latter's webs were sold in Königsberg for 56 stones of hemp. Business transactions involved the handling of a wide variety of currencies, all of which had an international circulation – francs, ryals, dollars, ducats, gros, guilders and crowns. Losses are noted and faulty goods for which a 'rebate' was charged; a bed of cloth to be sold for Mark Douglas was discovered on arrival to be full of holes.

There were many contacts with Scots abroad, both with resident merchants from whom goods were bought or money borrowed, and with other factors who cleared their merchants' shares in the ship's cargo or helped to dispose of the goods. The financial transactions among these traders were complicated, not to say chaotic, at times. Robert Todd, merchant in Dieppe, gave Walter Morton 903 francs for goods, including hides, and paid part of the pilot's fee when the *Antelope* docked.[26] William Robertson, a merchant in Norway, and his wife also had business dealings with Morton. The latter was in the habit of noting items 'given' to Robertson which were still to be paid for, such as a barrel of salt, 4 pairs of shoes, a pair of white hose, the loan of a rose noble and 12½ rex dollars 'to pay ane cramer [small shopkeeper]'.[27] In spite of the fact that Robertson was often in debt to him, the master of the *Antelope* bought cloth from him and 'two irne carrys' from Robertson's wife. The names of Thomas Fairlie and James Wallace, resident Scots factors in Dieppe, turn up from time to time.

Purchases were often in small quantity, or even single items; a girdle, a whinger [dagger], a sugar loaf, two boxes of comfits, four lanterns, and two pounds of twine, bought in England for William Robertson in Norway, olive oil for Harry Bickartoun, 3½ gross of points bought in Dieppe and sent to James Mathieson in Danzig. In this way the skipper of the *Antelope* operated a small market within the European market for fellow-Scots. The only import which he brought back in any quantity was rye from the Baltic; on one occasion he purchased six lasts at £78 a last for himself.[28] Once 30 ells of Violet Hodge's cloth was sold in Danzig for rye.[29] In Dieppe Walter helpfully bought 'ane boll of rye to Adam Wilson's wife till his hame cuming'.[30] In Flanders he lent James Mene £70, with £47 to buy 15 barrels of soap. Emigrant Scots who were not doing too well must have been glad to meet a sympathetic countryman with some money to lend. White wine and claret were bought in Bordeaux, on one occasion for Ninian McMorran, brother of Edinburgh's richest merchant, bailie John McMorran, and wine was also purchased in Spain. The skipper packed small purchases of his own on board with those of other merchants, such as the 'stane of mace markit with my awen mark within Harry Bickartounis pack'. Loading up in London he once listed the merchants' packs on board, recording their marks in his book:

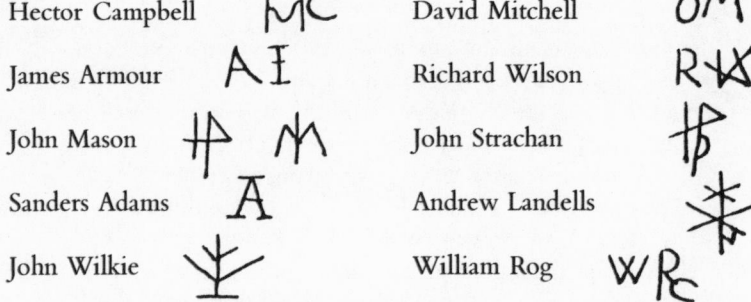

Hector Campbell		David Mitchell	
James Armour		Richard Wilson	
John Mason		John Strachan	
Sanders Adams		Andrew Landells	
John Wilkie		William Rog	

The goods were packed in an assortment of 'carrys', cloth packs, packets, barrels, pokes and pipes.

There were many duties to be paid in transporting a cargo and using foreign ports, including the custom on exports – Morton gave the dean of guild a gold piece for custom in 1595, and from 1597 onwards there was custom inwards, import duty – he paid 31s on a pack of lint from France. There was the cost of freighting the ship, £4-15s from Scotland to Dieppe, 33s from Dieppe to Danzig. Anchorage fees and 'dock silver' varied from 18d on one occasion at Dieppe to 13s 4d at home in Burntisland. Repairs to the ship prolonged her stay and caused dock silver to rise steeply. Pilot fee into harbours or up navigable rivers as at Rouen was a frequent expense, with drink-money and a meal to the pilot as well. At Fécamp 10s was spent in bread and wine for the pilot. The usual fee out of Dieppe was 3 francs, but on one occasion this cost as much as 25 francs, coinciding as it did with delay over the payment of a fine to the local serjeants. The serjeants at the ports had also to be paid, in amounts ranging from 15s to 38s, and there are references to paying the lieutenant and governor at Dieppe and the toll money at the customs house at Elsinore before passing into the Baltic. There were also the occasional expenses of a legal action, perhaps over debt-recovery. It is the reference to Morton's having sent 'owr the watter' for legal writs and at the same time to the Edinburgh merchant, William Fowler, who was handling his legal affairs, that implies that the skipper was himself based in Fife.

Financial transactions were complicated by the need to use many currencies, as already mentioned. Business demanded money-changing facilities both at home and abroad, which had its problems; in Dieppe Walter noted the 'evill silver in the chainging of my money takin with me from Scotland, 13 frankis 6s and 8d'.[31] He received, probably changed, money in Spain from 'Henderek Fernandes'. In Dieppe he counted out his money in hand, 98 crowns of the sun, 55 double ducats 'of twa heidis', 60 £5 pieces and 6 rose nobles brought from home, and 120 francs 'of white money'. His spending money – 'waring silver' – when he left home on one voyage amounted to £560 Scots. On board ship he and the clerk emptied out and counted the contents of '5 severell porses'; 400 ducats in one, 500 ducats (in ryals) in another, 'in ane ledderen [leather] pores' 225 ducats (in ryals), 'ine ane lang pores' 105 ducats and 'ine ane uthir letell pores' 80 ducats.[2]

Throughout his memorandum book the skipper wrote notes to himself about the commissions he received from his wife before he left home. She took care of their home and money matters while he was away, doing her best to get in outstanding debts and to collect rents ('hous maill') from properties which they owned. On 7 September, after leaving for Spain, he noted:
'To remember me that I left with my wyfe quhan I went to Spane, Ine gold – 44 crownis of the sone . . . .'.
In 1600 he left with her a gold piece worth £40 and a silver piece worth £25, some debts due from both men and women, and 60 crowns of gold. In Norway he noted that he had left with her £28 in a purse, £36 in a box and £60 'to serve her hous', that is housekeeping money. There were also £80 of debts 'left her to tak ine'.

When in London he sent a number of things home to his wife by various skippers and members of his own crew travelling home on other vessels: one hundred crowns of gold, a barrel of oil, 'with ane doublett of borett that I wes wont to wer at hame'; 'sum furring to yor cloks [cloaks]', and 'warp to wound abowt yor bed', sent with William Calder, a member of the crew; two hundred crowns of the sun, some cloth and 'ane glas of cerstell [crystal]', with William Blackadder, another member of the crew; one hundred crowns of the sun and a new green cloak with Sanders Duncan; and more money, some timberwork and a bible with George Hamilton of Bo'ness. On this occasion he was in London en route for Spain. Once in Spain he wrote:
'Thes is to remember me of my wyfes tornes [business] that I have

to bye to her quhane God sendis me to Londone, God wollyne [willing]

Item, ine the ferst, ane fyne bed of 8 feet of heyt and 8 feet . . . of lenthe, with ane pare of fyne courtenis therto . . .'.

Later still he made a note of the 'thingis that my wyfe hes to bye in Dieppe':

'Item, the ferst, ane steke of grograne silke,

Mar, ane ell wellenes [dress material]

Mar, ane red wylicoat

And quhan I com to Danskin [Danzig] to remember me upone

. . . ane thrie staket chandler [candlestick] . . .

Mar, 2 boutes [bolts] of whyte rebbenes [ribbons], ane bred and the othyr narowe . . .'.[33]

He had also been asked by the family's nurse to spend her silver on black cloth. The reference to a new bed, white ribbons and the nurse may suggest the imminent, or recent, birth of a child.

These detailed shopping lists emphasise the personal character of trading in this period. They also remind us of the window on the wider world which many Scots had through the activities of their seafaring kinsfolk and acquaintances, from whom they were able to bespeak all kinds of luxury items from the continent of Europe. They no doubt also waited for news of relatives and former neighbours who were now resident in France, the Low Countries, and the Baltic region. Their language was sprinkled with vocabulary from across the North Sea and the English Channel. Not only luxuries but necessities came home in the *Antelope* and her sister vessels of the merchant fleet, since the 1590s (of which Walter Morton has left this personal record) were a time of bad harvests, epidemics, and dearth in Scotland, necessitating the import of additional grain supplies chiefly from the Baltic.

Life was dangerous on the high seas, from the depredations of pirates and the complication of war in the shipping lanes. In this period of hostile relations between England and Spain Scottish ships were among those used by English merchants who persisted in trading with the Iberian ports in spite of the international situation. Walter Morton's presence in London both on his way to and from Spain suggests that he may have been in this carrying trade for English merchants. Just as the latter defied their government's prohibitions in time of war, so Scottish merchants, factors, and skippers frequented the wine ports of Catholic Spain in spite of the denunciation of their traffic by the ministers of the kirk. Where good business was to be done they could easily settle with their consciences. It was said that the wealthy merchant, John McMorran, was disliked because he persisted in shipping to Spain the victual which the ordinary people of Scotland badly needed in these hard times. What for Walter Morton was 'business as usual' is for us a fascinating glimpse of his way of life, all the more real for having been left to us in his own words.

WALTER MORTON

Notes

1 M.P. Rooseboom, *The Scottish Staple in the Netherlands* (1910); S.G.E.Lythe, *The Economy of Scotland, 1550-1625, in its European Setting* (1960), 235.

2 Shipmaster's Account Book (S.R.O.), RH 9/1/5, cited hereafter as Account Book.

3 S.G.E. Lythe, *The Economy of Scotland*, 129.

4 *Ibid.*, 131-2.

5 A. McGowan, *The Ship: Tiller and Whipstaff* (National Maritime Museum, 1981), 30.

6 Account Book, fo 25.

7 *Ibid.*, fo 50v.

8 *Ibid.*, fo 16.

9 *Ibid.*, fo 16.

10 *Ibid.*, fo 15v.

11 *Ibid.*, fo 37v.

12 *Ibid.*, fos 5v, 37v.

13 *Ibid.*, fo 53.

14 *Ibid.*, fos 15,16.

15 *Ibid.*, fo 15.

16 *Ibid.*, fos 65, 68.

17 *Ibid.*, fos 2v, 61.

18 *Ibid.*, fos 15, 58.

19 *Ibid.*, fo 1v.

20 *Ibid.*, fo 14.

21 *Ibid.*, fo 19.

22 *Ibid.*, fos 2v, 3v.

23 *Ibid.*, fo 36.

24 *Ibid.*, fo 8v.

25 *Ibid.*, fos 27, 48; fos 40v, 45v, 68, 77.

26 *Ibid.*, fo 42v.

27 *Ibid.*, fo 57v.

28 *Ibid.*, fo 43v.

29 *Ibid.*, fo 38.

30 *Ibid.*, fo 43.

31 *Ibid.*, fo 44v.

32 *Ibid.*, fo 33

33 *Ibid.*, fo 46v.

CHARLES MURRAY

Messenger-at-Arms

CHARLES MURRAY'S work kept him constantly on the move, in particular, along the roads of Perthshire, Stirlingshire, Clackmannanshire, Fife and parts of Angus, with periodic visits to burghs such as Edinburgh, Perth, Stirling and Dundee. The few major highways were regularly used by people in a hurry, such as messengers-at-arms. Many routes were simply well-worn tracks which, reasonably firm in dry weather, reverted to bog in wet seasons. With no administrative authority responsible for their maintenance, the roads were eternally patched by those through whose lands they passed, largely for their own convenience and that of their tenants. Parliament did legislate from time to time, stating that the width of the highway should be 20 feet and urging landholders to cause their tenants repair the roads between 'bere seid tyme' (April) and haymaking (July) or between that and the harvest.[1] Roads leading to parish churches were to be kept in especially good repair; petitions to the General Assembly for the erection of new parish kirks often mention the hazards of getting to the kirk in wet or snowy weather or across bogs or flooded rivers. A grant of tolls was sometimes an incentive to maintenance, a source of income which some inhabitants of Kinross-shire attempted to tap in the early 17th century; they pointed out to the lords of council the poor state of part of the main route from Perth to the Forth ferries, called 'the Gullets', at the west end of Loch Leven, offering to repair it if they might be allowed to collect a toll of 2d from pedestrians and 4d from horsemen during the eight days before and after the four fairs at Perth.[2]

Much travel was on foot even over quite long distances. Servants carried letters and messages, as well as small quantities of commodities, between friends, families and business associates. Footrunners, employed by authorities, were regularly paid to run on their business; the chamberlain of Melrose abbey who was based at Mauchline, an important location on the road from Ayrshire into Lanarkshire, paid a band of runners to go on his business as far away as

Dunfermline, Dumfries and Glasgow, while the burgh of Linlithgow retained the runner known in the records as 'Black Breeks', presumably from his livery, to run regularly between that burgh and Edinburgh, on one occasion receiving an extra payment in the name of an official who 'was nocht ther, to rin back agane'. Within each barony or estate well-worn routes led to kirk and mill, the smithy and the laird's house, and to fishing cruives, coal heuchs, salt pans and fords. Through each farmtoun ran the loan leading to the arable land, the commonty and the more distant summer sheilings on high ground.

Goods in quantity were carried on pack horses, singly or in file, with the bulky, canvas-wrapped packs strapped to the animal's back or, in creels, to its sides. The owner or his servant, either on his own mount or on foot, did his best to guide the horses over the firmest ground or the narrow bridges. Chapmen also rode with their packs of small-wares, as much in danger from robbers as from the condition of the roads. Merchant goods, or merchants themselves, went in convoy for safety and even humbler neighbours from the rural settlements would journey together to market. At certain times of the year, such as haymaking and harvest, the start of the milling season or at Whitsunday and Martinmas when the rents, including the grain rents, were paid, carts, sleds and the slow-moving wains must have held up people who were in a hurry, although these farming activities were not supposed to block up the main highways; during a dispute over the use of a Berwickshire road a distinction was made between work-roads for carts and wains and those roads leading to kirk and market and further afield.

The passage of important personages along the public highway must have caused a diversion, in more senses than one, accompanied as they would be by a train of servants, baggage horses and even men-at-arms. Queen Mary on her progresses must have been seen by many of her subjects outside the burghs, such as the inhabitants of a whole string of baronies on the coast of Ayrshire in the summer of 1563, including those living on either side of 'the Quenis streit' of Kilwinning which, then as now, formed part of the public highway leading to Eglinton and the royal burgh of Irvine. Visitors to Scotland, or Scots who for some reason found themselves outwith their own 'country', would hire a horse at a change-house, with a guide to run alongside on foot, for 2d a mile.[3] These change-houses did offer a somewhat spartan accommodation, and refreshment if required, but inns on the English pattern, primarily intended for accommodation, were rare. An unnamed fellow-messenger of Charles Murray's has left behind a memorandum of his expenses when going to Dumfries, with a trumpeter, to make a proclamation; a chamber with two beds for one night, 6s 8d, 'every single bed' (probably the straw-filled mattress) 2s, a pint of wine 6s 8d, a pint of ale, 8d, corn, straw and stable fee for the horses, 13s 4d, total £1-9s-4d.

The messenger-at-arms was a public servant, an executive officer of the law who operated from his home, and was thus, like the notary, a man linked to the nationwide legal system. He was so-called because he wore the livery and carried the insignia of the authority who employed him, and in Charles Murray's time he was paid 13s 4d a day when carrying out his duties. Much of the business which he discharged arose from debt and attempts to recover it, a process known in law as diligence. While the purpose of his many journeys was a civil matter, to confront debtors or others who had failed to honour a legal obligation with a demand for payment or performance, his job was not without its risks and even dangers, for people who resisted the demands of the law sometimes resorted to violence. More than one messenger found himself imprisoned, some are known to have been killed, and many were assaulted in the course of their duties. The messenger was, of necessity, literate since he had to read his instructions and endorse them for return to his authority after he had carried them out. He had to know the part of the country where he operated so that he could find those he was searching for. The most important officers-of-arms, of whom Charles Murray was one, were the royal messengers whose instructions arrived in the sovereign's name sealed with the signet. Others were employed by local courts such as those of sheriffs, lords of regality, barons and burghs.

The rules of office, which were drawn up and applied by the court of the Lord Lyon King of Arms who appointed all officers-of-arms, obliged the messenger to 'intertene ane horse for serving of the king and leidgis'. He had to have a silver blazon of the royal arms and carry a wand of office, which in the case of royal messengers was red and measured three-quarters of a yard. The wand, the sign of his authority, had to be carried at all times; if he arrived without it the sheriff was empowered to challenge him at the head court of the sheriffdom and to fine him 40s which was passed on to the crown. If he was obstructed in the course of his duties, ('deforced'), the messenger broke the wand in token of the fact that authority had been violated, adding another offence to the offender's charges. He had also to equip himself with a lockable pouch in which to carry the royal letters and other papers, and a horn on which he blew three blasts before making public announcements: 'eftir thrie severall blastis of the horne and thrie severall oyezis'. He also required his own signet, without which his record of having carried out his instructions was invalid.[4]

After his qualifications had been 'tried' the messenger was formally admitted, giving security or caution for the performance of his duties. A surviving admission of a messenger, Jerome Lindsay, is signed by the Lord Lyon, David Lindsay of the Mount, son of the poet Lord Lyon, at the Mount on 1 September 1597, Patrick Guthrie of Pitmouness standing surety.[5] Since the post carried considerable power, rules were laid down to protect the lieges from 'oppression' by messengers who might be tempted to use their authority for private ends:[6] they must not charge anyone other than those specifically named in criminal letters or summon to a jury anyone not named in the dittay-roll, and then not more than 45 persons; when arranging for the confiscation of a debtor's goods they must not take labouring animals, such as horses and oxen 'in time of labouring, albeit they be not actually in labouring'; and the tenant's own goods, or those given to him by the landlord with the ground (steelbow goods) could not be confiscated for the master's debt. If a messenger was deprived of office for an offence this was publicly announced at the mercat cross nearest to his dwelling place.

Diligence was not simply a legal process on paper but a series of incidents that took place publicly in the neighbourhood. It began when the creditor purchased royal letters under the signet (a small royal seal affixed to the letter) in order to begin the process of debt-recovery. These letters, prepared and presented for sealing by a writer to the signet, recited the creditor's complaint and his petition to the crown for means to make the debtor comply, and were addressed to the messengers-at-arms authorising them to charge the debtors to pay. The simplest letters, known as letters of four forms, commanded the messenger to charge the debtor four times at forty-eight hour intervals. If the debtor remained obstinate after this he was publicly denounced rebel against the royal authority, and his moveables were poinded (pronounced 'pinded') for the creditor's benefit. If this failed, attempts were made to arrest his person by authority of letters of caption and, as a last resort, his heritable property was apprised (valued) and adjudged to belong to his creditor, who soon afterwards would receive a charter of apprising and become the proprietor.[7] A record of all this business was kept in registers of horning and poinding, begun by acts of the Scottish parliament; for the sheriffdoms in 1579 and 1581, the stewartries and regalities in 1584 and 1597, and a general register covering the whole country in 1597.

A personal record of how one messenger carried out his duties is preserved in Charles Murray's book which he carried from 1570 to 1574, a fairly uncommon survival.[8] The book, which is written in a large, rather careless hand, is incomplete, lacking a clear beginning and end, and the entries are not in strict chronological order. The fact that there are only sixty-six entries covering five years and that the business relates almost entirely to a particular type of debt suggests that the book does not represent the whole of Murray's activity as a messenger. The business in question was payment of the 'thirds of benefices', a tax on ecclesiastical revenue which was partly intended to sustain the Reformed ministry. Murray probably kept this personal record in connection with the salary due to him for charging and denouncing the debtors of the collector of the thirds for Perth and Strathearn, David Murray of Kerse. The collection of the thirds was not simply a matter of public administration but one which affected a wide variety of people in social, material and financial terms: the surviving benefice-holders of the pre-Reformation church, the poorly-paid ministers and other clergy of the Reformed church, the nobles, lairds and more prosperous farmers who had leases of the teinds from which the thirds were deducted, and the tenants who had the teinds lifted from their crops, as we saw in the case of the farmers of Melrose. The situation was full of vested interests, hardship, harrassment and complicated accounting machinery. Before following Murray on some of his journeys and in order to understand why he is found knocking at the doors of all kinds of habitations, from those of the cottages of the parishioners of Auchtertool to the great yett of the Earl of Atholl's lodging in Dunkeld, it will be helpful to look at what was involved in the thirds arrangement.[9]

At the Reformation the ideal of the religious reformers was that all the revenue of the old, proscribed church should be transferred to the new. The Reformation parliament of 1560, however, while it commissioned the Reformed church as a spiritual force did nothing towards its material endowment. It proved impossible to dispossess those who held benefices drawn from the teinds and church lands; some noble families, such as the Erskines and Hamiltons, regarded certain monasteries as pieces of family property; many parsons and vicars, drawn from the ranks of the nobility and lairds to whom they had leased their teinds, shared their families' attitude to church revenue. It would have been beyond the power of a sixteenth-century administration to dispossess the existing benefice-holders without cutting across the vested interests of those whose support it needed; Queen Mary's half-brother, the Lord James Stewart, for example, had held the revenues of the rich priory of St Andrews since childhood. Besides, it is doubtful if the government could have coped with the task of extricating the teinds from the complicated system that had evolved and handing these over to the Reformed ministry. As a result the entire pre-Reformation ecclesiastical struc-ture was left in being, to the great encouragement of religious conservatives. Numbers of clerics who had been in possession of benefices and prelacies (bishoprics, abbeys and priories) before the Reformation, and who declined to take office in the Reformed church, continued to be known as 'parson of X' or even 'archdeacon of Y' until the end of their lives, in recognition of their prop-erty rights.

This was to the great discouragement of the first generation of Reformed clergy who struggled to make ends meet in the parish manse. By 1561-2 it was felt necessary to make some positive provision for them even at the expense of the 'auld possessouris' of benefices, as a result of which the arrangement of the 'thirds' came about. In a sense it was a return to the old device of ecclesiastical taxation for government–approved purposes which had characterised the reign of Queen Mary's father, James V, and the regency of her mother, Mary of Guise. By this arrangment two-thirds of the benefice were retained by the holder for his lifetime and the remaining third, collected by the government's agents, was shared between the crown and the ministers. The amount to be collected was about £76,000, whereas the total revenue of the pre-Reformation church had been in the region of £300,000 as against the crown's patrimony of only £17,500. Provision for the work of the new kirk was thus meagre – two-thirds gone to the devil and the other third shared between God and the devil, as John Knox expressed it. The only alleviating circumstance, and an important one, lay in the fact that over half the clergy of the Reformed church had been in orders before 1560, many of these being benefice-holders who were allowed to retain two-thirds of their livings under the thirds arrangement. It was hoped that as the benefice-holders died off their livings would be granted to the parish ministers, but this did not often happen, the benefices instead passing to relatives and friends of the late holders, to relatives of influential landholders or to crown servants. As to the division of the third, John Knox remarked that 'the gaird and the effairis of the [royal] kytcheing wer so grypping that the minsteris stipendis culd nocht be payit', to which William Maitland of Lethington, the secretary of state, replied that if the ministers were supplied to the extent that they demanded there would not be enough left for the Queen to buy herself a new pair of shoes at the end of the year.

It is not surprising that the payment of the thirds from a multitude of individuals was often in arrears, and the fact that the accounts of the collectory were not audited until years afterwards did nothing to improve the situation. The long annual lists of those at the horn for non-payment bear witness to the part played by messengers in the attempt to bring debtors to account, without much success. The dislocations of the civil war years of 1568 to 1571 brought complaints from the regional collectors that their authority was largely flouted. In 1570 and 1571 at Aberdeen, charges to debtors could not be followed up by denunciations at the horn 'be resoun of the greit trubillis and inobedience that wer within the saidis boundis . . . the officiaris wer stoppit to mak the denunciatiounis' and 'wer violentlie put away fra the mercat croce of Abirdene'.[10] Some improvement for the ministers came about gradually as a result of pressure from the General Assembly and the government's determination to overhaul the machinery of the collectory after the revolution of 1567: at that time an end was put to arbitrary royal gifts from the thirds, the ministers' right to succeed to lesser benefices when these fell vacant through the death of the holder was recognised, the practice of assigning thirds to particular ministers was established, and they were given liberty to collect their teinds directly from the parishioners. In an attempt to end absenteeism patrons were compelled to present qualified men to benefices, and all presentees to benefices were required to serve as ministers and readers. In 1573 came a test act by which all holders of public office (both ecclesiastical and lay), were required to take an oath of obedience to the crown and the Reformed church establishment which resulted in a number of deprivations among the remaining Catholic clergy and the acquisition of their benefices. One thing remained constant, however – reluctance to pay, whether on the part of the benefice-holder who resented the loss of part of his living, or of the parishioners with their long habit of resistance to the deduction of the teinds.

There is nothing in Charles Murray's book to indicate where he lived, but he appears to have had close connections with the family of the collector for Perth and Strathearn, David Murray of Kerse which lay in Strathearn. He took the collector's servant, William Murray, with him to Angus as a witness when he charged the laird of Fintry's brother to pay the third of the vicarage of Alyth, of which he was tacksman,[11] and he was accompanied by the collector's brother, Thomas, when he called at Dudhope castle to charge James Scrymgeour, constable of Dundee.[12] Patrick Murray of Woodend in Madderty parish, Strathearn, a relative of the collector, once carried money to Edinburgh for him.[13] Murray was usually attended by his assistant, 'my boy Collen', who also transmitted money to the collector and gathered witnesses to the delivery of charges and denunciations at the horn. When he was on his way to Edinburgh in August 1572 Colin accompanied him as far as Burntisland, where he was given 2s 'at his hame passin'. They had dined at Kinross on the way, dinner costing 2s. Charles Murray himself continued on the road, paying 12d at the ferry, and having arrived in Edinburgh bought himself a new pair of spurs at 30d, a pair of gloves and a bonnet at 2s each, a pair of shoes at 5s 6d, a bag at 3s, and paid 2s 'for the making of tua billis'.[14]

Much of his activity was centred on the parishes of the Ochil foothills, Dollar, Muckhart and Fossoway, with journeys over into Fife, including the parish of Auchtertool. At other times he worked his way along the Tayside towns of the barony of Dunkeld and those belonging to Scone Abbey, by way of Abernethy, and as far east as Invergowrie and Dundee. He was compelled to travel at all times of the year, whatever the state of the roads. The very end of December 1571 found him in the Angus parish of Liff, on the Perthshire border, and by 1 January 1572 he was in Dunkeld. His travels in spring and summer, such as to Balquhidder in April, must have been more pleasant. An itinerary compiled from his book gives some idea of his travels.

1570

May	25	Dudhope
July	1	Moncreiff
November	13	Dollar
—	25	Alloa

1571

February	15	Abernethy
—	19	Dunkeld
—	20	Cargill
March	22	Dunblane
April	4	Dunblane
May	8	Innerbus, Craigmakerran (lands of Scone abbey)
—	24	Liff, Invergowrie
June	13	Liff, Invergowrie
—	14	Liff, Invergowrie
—	17	Dunkeld
—	30	Fintry
August	1	Culross
—	4	Dundee
—	6	Megginch
—	11	Kilspindie
November	9	Invergowrie
—	20	Craigmakerran, Innerbus, Ardgilzean, Liff, Balgarvie

December	20	Auchtertool
—	28	Kirktoun of Liff, Invergowrie
—	29	Craigmakerran
1572		
January	1	Dunkeld
—	8	Liff
—	10	Castle Campbell
—	26	Touch, Stirling
March	2	Callander
—	3	Callander
—	10	Rhynd
—	26	Dollar
April	20	Auchtertool
—	27	Balquhidder
August	6	Auchtertool
—	8	Tulliallan
November	12	Dunblane
—	13	Dunblane
—	14	Dunblane
—	17	Castletoun of Muckhart
December	3	Murthly, Dunkeld
1573		
January	15	Dudhope castle
April	18	Kincardine castle in Menteith
August	30	Kilspindie
November	18	Auchtertool
1574		
January	6	Auchtertool
—	12	Auchtertool
—	16	Castle Campbell
February	14	Abernethy, Moncrieff, Gask

This itinerary does not take account of those places for which no date, or at least no year-date, is given, or of the occasions when a date is given but no location, only the name of the person charged or denounced. This applies particularly to Murray's repeated visits to the parishes of Dollar and Muckhart, many of which are undated.

A large number of those whom Murray formally charged to pay the collector of thirds were benefice-holders. It was not his business to enquire into their reason for non-payment, but one motive may have been continued adherence to the Catholic religion and a conscientious objection to handing over part of their livings to the Reformed church which they had declined to support. This is likely to have been the case with the knot of cathedral clergy in Perthshire who gathered around the two recusant bishops, William Chisholm of Dunblane and Robert

Crichton of Dunkeld. On 17 June 1571 the messenger charged Mr Andrew Abercrombie, then acting as factor for his brother Robert, treasurer of Dunkeld cathedral, who had left Scotland and joined the Jesuits in 1562. The Abercrombies belonged to the Catholic family of Abercrombie of Murthly from whose laird Murray confiscated the rents belonging to the subdeanery of Dunkeld, the subdean being Mr Richard Haldane, a close friend of the laird.[15] Mr Stephen Culross, *alias* Wilson, who was found at home by the messenger when he went to charge him on 12 January 1573, was a canon of Dunblane cathedral and vicar of Glendevon, for which he had failed to pay his third since 1568. Culross, who was a kinsman of the bishop of Dunblane, had leased his benefice of Glendevon among three landowners and an Edinburgh lawyer. He enjoyed a pension of £100 granted to him by Queen Mary out of her share of the thirds and he had spent some time in Europe in the 1560s when he was in touch with the Jesuits.[16] Sir John Learmonth, chaplain of the altar of St Blaise in Dunblane Cathedral, who was put to the horn for non-payment in January 1570, was a known Catholic,[17] as was also sir William Blackwood, vicar of Auchterarder, whom Murray charged to pay his third on 25 November 1570 and who was reported ten years later, during a visitation of Dunblane, to be 'a prest in papistrie'.[18]

The procedure for charging debtors was that the messenger called at the dwelling place, and if the debtor could be 'personally apprehendit' he was given a copy of the letters before witnesses. Charles Murray does not record being offered violence, but on several occasions the debtor refused to take a copy, a fact which was duly endorsed on the letters and noted in his book: John Semple, parson of Muckhart, James Scrymgeour of Dudhope, tacksman of the teinds of Benvie, Alexander Colville, the commendator of Culross abbey, and John Steel, parson of Dollar, who had leased his teinds to the Earl of Argyll, owner of the near-by Castle Campbell.[19] If the debtor could not be found, a copy of the letters was fixed to the door or gate, again in the presence of witnesses. Murray did this at the Earl of Atholl's dwelling house in Dunkeld in November 1571.[20] Alternatively, a copy could be left with someone in the debtor's name to be passed on to him; 'upone the 26 day off [January 1572] Chargit Setoun of Towcht at his duelling place and delyverit ane cope to Robert Ramsaye in Strivelin [Stirling] quha refusit the samyn, for the vicarage off Loge [Logie]'.[21] The vicarage was held at that time by Robert Seton who had leased the teinds to his brother the laird of Touch. In February 1572 Murray charged the vicar of Dollar, sir Henry Balfour, but, unable to find him, handed a copy to the elderly reader of the parish, Robert Burn, formerly the curate.[22] A year later when Balfour was deprived for adherence to Catholicism and refusal to take the oath of loyalty to the new religious establishment Burn was granted his vicarage.[23] A copy of letters charging sir John Semple for the parsonage and vicarage thirds of Muckhart was handed to the minister there, Mr James Paton.[24]

In the case of letters of four forms, which required four charges at forty-eight hour intervals, the messenger would have to spend over a week in the area if it were distant from his home base. His job must have involved many overnight stops. Each time he executed a charge he endorsed the fact on the letters, including the names of the witnesses and adding his signet. If the debtor refused to pay after the final charge the messenger then proceeded to denounce him rebel publicly at the head burgh of the sheriffdom concerned, preceding the denunciation with three blasts on the horn to attract witnesses to his action. There was sometimes quite a lapse of time between the final charge and the denunciation. For example, Murray charged the parishioners of Auchtertool on 20, 21 and 22 August and put them to the horn in the following December and January.

The next stage in the process of diligence was to arrange for the poinding of the debtor's moveables, of which there is only one example in Murray's book: 'Chargit . . . in lykwayis sir John Wryt for his threidis extending to £18. And arreistit his cornes at the kingis and kirkis instance . . . befoir witnes, John Glen, Thomas Nevin, and Thomas Broun with otheris dyvers'.[25] This was the most dangerous part of the proceedings, when the officer-at-arms and his assistants ran the risk of being deforced by the debtor and his sympathisers. Even Abbot Quintin Kennedy of Crossraguel Abbey was accused of having 'plainlie deforced' Robert Campbell, messenger, when he attempted to carry off the abbot's poinded goods. In 1557 Alexander Cooper of Wester Bridgend, Kilwinning, another messenger, was set upon by twelve men acting on behalf of John Mure of Rowallan, who drove off the cattle he had poinded and attacked him and his servants.[26] A messenger was empowered to pressgang local men and officers of local courts into helping him with this task, as a result of which he was sometimes the victim of collusion between these people and the 'rebels' whose goods he poinded.

In some places Murray was obliged to charge, and even put to the horn, whole communities. At other times he confronted individuals, from the powerful, earl of Argyll to a tenant farmer. He might find himself picking his way over the muddy tracks leading to the steadings of a farmtoun or knocking at the outer gate of a stronghold, such as Tulliallan, Gask or Castle Campbell, or at the door of the archdeacon's manse in the cathedral close at Dunblane, which was still inhabited by the small enclave of Catholic clergy. In mid-November 1572 he stood at the Burnside of Dollar and charged the parishioners to pay the third of the parsonage and vicarage teinds to their minister, Mr James Paton, to whom it had been assigned but had not been paid from 1567 onwards.[27] In name of the parishioners he delivered a copy of the charge to Patrick Kirk, officer to the earl of Argyll, George Drysdale, and Thomas Scotland. On the previous and following days he charged the parishioners of Muckhart similarly to pay Mr Paton's third.[28] His list of their names in the execution of his charge has given us a useful roll of the inhabitants of some of the settlements in the parish: Adam Hutton, smith, Simon Hutton, John Sharp, Anne Paton and her son-in-law, Andrew Cunningham and Isobel Paterson, all in the east toun of Pitgober; John Somerville in Hiltoun; Agnes Seton and John Donaldson her husband, 'for his interest', a couple occupying a holding which Agnes had inherited, Robert Cunningham and sir William Alexander, all in the wester toun of Pitgober; John Paton in the middle toun; sir William Cunningham in the Law; David Brady, John Johnston in Wester Bellelisk; Janet Menteith in Muckhart mill; Robert Paton in Cowdoun; Robert Masters, Thomas Marshall, Andrew Kirk, James Marshall, Bessie Masterton and Robert Marshall, younger, her son, Bessie Alexander and Walter Hutton, her husband, for his interest, all in Blairhill; Adam and John Hutton in the Mure; Thomas Hutton in the Moss; John Hutton in Balrodry, and Mr John Hutton in Easter Bellelisk. In May 1571 and at intervals afterwards the messenger charged the parishioners of Liff and Invergowrie to pay their share of the abbacy of Scone, putting the men of Invergowrie to the horn at the cross of Dundee in August that year. The parishioners of Auchtertool in Fife were charged for their contribution to the third of Dunkeld, for which they were put to the horn from 1571 to 1573 in company with the earls of Atholl and Argyll – the diligence process was a great leveller.

The brief entries in Charles Murray's book, the lists of personal and place names, cannot of themselves recreate the individuality of those whom he encountered or the sights and sounds of the roads he travelled, but other records can bring them to life.[29] The whole business with which he was involved, the collection of the thirds, was an indictment of the failure to provide for the resident parish ministry in the early years of the Reformed church. At Muckhart, where for lack of a pastor in 1586 'the Sabboth is not dewlie observit' but the minister of neighbouring Fossoway parish, it was explained, 'repares unto thame now and thane',[30] the surnames of the elders and deacons include not a few of those whom Charles Murray had charged a decade earlier. Most of the Muckhart men were portioners, proprietors of their holdings which they would have subfeued from the earl of Argyll whose father had had a grant of the lordship of Muckhart a generation before. The inhabitants of the parish of Liff in Angus and the lands of Scone Abbey mentioned in the messenger's book – Craigmakerran, Innerbus, and Ardgilzean – were also first-generation owner-occupiers, having feued their holdings from the Abbey of Scone.[31] As tenants they had had a long tradition of non-payment of teinds to their reprobate landlord, Patrick Hepburn, bishop of Moray and commendator of Scone; their new independence was unlikely to make them more co-operative. At Dollar, where the messenger-at-arms was a periodic visitor, the parishioners were nearly all tenants of the earl of Argyll at Castle Campbell. Thomas Scotland, one of those to whom Charles Murray had delivered a charge in 1572, accompanied the General Assembly's visitor on an inspection of the manse in 1586 as one of the 'honest men' of the parish.[32] Patrick Kirk, the earl of Argyll's officer, another recipient of letters from the messenger as a representative of the neighbours of Dollar, was a tenant in the Burnside who left £379 of moveable goods when he died in 1585.[33] He does not seem to have had his own work-oxen but had a few cattle, 33 sheep, and his own barn and kiln.

Although the families of men like Kirk, Scotland, and Simon Hutton in east Pitgober, who had his own plough-team but left only £174-6s-8d when he died, were tenants and small feuars, they were substantial enough to appear among the elders and deacons of their parishes. They found themselves sitting with local lairds on the kirk session, which to first-generation Protestants must have seemed like a spiritual version of the barony court in which they were accustomed to sit in the jury. However, when it came to accepting the King's commission to put down wrongdoing in the parish, part of a national policy, it was felt that lairds were more suited to the exercise of this public office; at the visitation of Aberuthven parish in 1586 it was said that 'anent the accepting his majesteis commissione for the punisment off vyce, etc. . . . ansurit nane present meit to accept the same seing thai ar all bot commonis, bot willis [wishes] my lord Montros, thair maister, to be pressit thairwith as maist meit in this boundis . . .'.[34]

The personal circumstances of some of the clergy who are mentioned in the messenger's book are also revealed in other records. Robert Burn, reader and former curate at Dollar, to whom Charles Murray had handed a charge in 1572 intended for the absentee recusant vicar, was disciplined for his shortcomings during the visitation of the parish in 1586.[35] After having served the parishioners of Dollar for about 40 years the old man was deprived on charges of failing to read distinctly, allowing congregational discipline to lapse, and for being 'giffin to drunkines and intemperance'. He denied the last two charges but excused the first 'be ressoun off his gret aige and other infirmities'. There were few clergy left in 1586 who like Burn had been in orders before the Reformation. In June 1571 the messenger handed a copy of letters of four forms to the laird of Inwar, Robert Naismith, charging him to pay teinds to the minister of Monedie, Mr Thomas McGibbon or Robertson. Having ignored the warnings Naismith was put to the horn on 1 August.[36] Mr McGibbon, then a comparatively young man, was of a studious turn of mind with an interesting library in his Perthshire manse. He loaned books to friends – the wife of one of these passed on his Greek dictionary to a third party – and towards the end of his life gave them to various 'godlie men' in pledge for loans of money. The books included not only Calvin's *Institutes* and his *Commentary on the Book of Exodus*, the commentary of Musculus on Genesis, and a Hebrew grammar, but classical authors including Cicero, Pliny, Virgil, and Ovid.[37]

Murray was obliged to charge a number of substantial landholders, including Peter Hay at Megginch castle, the laird of Moncreiff's son, Lord Oliphant at Gask, and the laird of Kilspindie who was charged in 1571 to pay the bishop of Dunkeld's mails from the parish of Cramond, although the third was remitted to the vicar of the parish, Mr Thomas Scott, because 'the boittis of Crawmond wer nocht sufferit to laubour . . . in respect of the trublis [the civil war]'.[38] On 8 August 1572 the messenger charged James Blackadder at his dwelling, Tulliallan castle, which then stood nearer to the River Forth. The laird kept a herd of brood mares on the Mains of Tulliallan, and across the drawbridge and behind the great protcullis and barred door, on which Charles Murray knocked in the King's name, were the homely signs of any other habitation, loads of peats and turfs and even some bee skeps 'about the place'.[39]

Charles Murray was in close touch with the collector of the thirds for Perth and Strathearn, David Murray of Kerse, sending money on to him to Edinburgh and to Kintocher where the collector had a house. He also put the archdeacon of Dunblane to the horn at one time for non-payment of stipend to the reader of Foulis Wester, David Murray, a kinsman who witnessed the collector's will when he died, a comparatively young man, in 1577.[40] The family had connections with the parish of Foulis Wester, where the collector asked to be buried in the parish kirk. Two business letters from him to the messenger have survived, tucked into the latter's book. Written in haste, undated, they are a little difficult to follow in certain details but they show that the messenger was not merely the executant of other people's orders but that he knew the state of affairs behind each piece of diligence and kept his own records of what had been executed, with which the collector expected him to compare and check all communications from the collectory. The collector once sent him drafts of arrears of payments drawn from the principal records kept by himself, 'to lat yow se thame so that I may send na executionis apone thame again [a second time]'. He asked Charles, when he came east by Abernethy, to contact some other messenger and ask him to deliver a copy of a charge to the laird of Moncreiff for his son 'for sa mone [many] yeris restis of Dunbarny as ye may reid as is restand yeirlie sen [since] the 1566 yeir'. He added a familiar request to stand by for further instructions: 'be nay way fra heim [home] on Monday, Tysday quhill [until] I maik yo . . . advertisment tilbe [to be] in the toun with me on Wodnesday nixt or [before] I raid away that day till Edinburgh'. He ended, 'reid this draught, and oney that ye have not chargit mon [must] be chargit. Committis yo till god, be yours, David Murray in hast'.

The other letter is a brief note: 'ye sall deliver this berar the . . . letteris for the thridis I geif yow [th]at I may caus Jhon Meikill coppe thame this neicht and send it [be] tymis the morn till my ladie Drummond. I pray yow be dilligent for my bissines in the toun and heist yow hame with silver. Committis yow till god, be youris, ye wat quhay [you know who]'. Charles Murray must have accumulated a good deal of paper in the course of his duties, of which the fragment that has survived is a personal record of his work. Even more paper must have passed through his hands; the literally thousands of diligence papers, hornings and poindings, inhibitions, arrestments, adjudications and captions that have accumulated in collections of family papers are a testimony to the continual activity that kept him and his fellow-messengers constantly on the roads of Scotland.

CHARLES MURRAY

Notes

1 P. Hume Brown, *Scotland in the time of Queen Mary* (1904), 58.

2 *Ibid.*, 59-60.

3 *Ibid.*, 64.

4 *Acts of the Parliaments of Scotland*, II, 22.

5 Miscellanous Collections (S.R.O.), GD 1/182/5.

6 Sir Thomas Hope, *Major Practicks* (Stair Society), II, 171-3.

7 For the full range of diligence documents, see P. Gouldesbrough, *A Formulary of Old Scots Documents* (Stair Society) 1985.

8 Register House Series, RH 11/1/2; cited hereafter as Messenger's book.

9 G. Donaldson, *Accounts of the Collectors of the Thirds of Benefices*, 1561-1572 (S.H.S.), Introduction; cited hereafter as *Thirds*.

10 *Ibid.*, xxxii.

11 Messenger's book, fo 15v.

12 *Ibid.*, fo 12.

13 *Ibid.*, fo 1.

14 *Ibid.*, fo 11v.

15 *Ibid.*, fo 15: *Register of the Privy Seal*, V1, 2241 (Abercrombie); Messenger's book, fo 24v (laird of Murthly); *Ibid.*, fo 19v: *Thirds*, 253 (Haldane).

16 Messenger's book, fo 2v: *Thirds*, 100: *Register of the Privy Seal*, V1, 492, 1441: J. Kirk, *Visitation of the Diocese of Dunblane*, 1586-1589 (S.R.S.), 24, cited hereafter as *Visitation of Dunblane* (Culross).

17 Messenger's book, fo 13v.

18 *Ibid.*, fo 8v: *Thirds*, 16: *Visitation of Dunblane*, 38.

19 Messenger's book, fo 2v (Semple); *Ibid.*, fos 11, 13v (Scrymgeour); *Ibid.*, fo 19v (Colville); *Ibid.*, fo 18v (Steel).

20 *Ibid.*, fo 19v.

21 *Ibid.*, fo 19: *Thirds*, 255.

22 Messenger's book, fo 19v.

23 *Register of the Privy Seal*, V1, 2240.

24 Messenger's book, fo 19v.

25 *Ibid.*, fo 8v.

26 Register of acts and decreets, xx, fo 345.

27 Messenger's book, fo 9

28 *Ibid.*, fo 9.

29 Two sources in particular have been used: the Edinburgh Commissariot, Register of Testaments and *Visitation of Dunblane*.

30 *Visitation of Dunblane*, 25.

31 M.H.B. Sanderson, *Scottish Rural Society in the sixteenth century*, 89-94.

32 Messenger's book, fo 9; *Visitation of Dunblane*, 20, 91. Thomas Scotland was one of the kirkmasters of Dollar parish who handled funds for the maintenance of the kirk fabric.

33 Messenger's book, fo 9; Edinburgh Register of Testaments, CC8/8/19, fo 273v.

34 *Visitation of Dunblane*, 47.

35 *Ibid.*, 19.

36 Messenger's book, fos 15, 16; *Register of the Privy Seal*, V1, 1253 (his ultimate escheat).

37 Edinburgh Register of Testaments, CC8/8/31, fo 153.

38 *Thirds*, 274.

39 Messenger's book, fo 23; Edinburgh Register of Testaments, CC8/8/29, fo 37v.

40 *Ibid.*, CC8/8/6, recorded 14 April 1578.

ROBERT LEGGAT

Parish Priest

and the parishioners of Prestwick

ROBERT LEGGAT, a non-graduate cleric who may have been born in the parish of Prestwick where he served, firstly, as Catholic parish priest and, secondly, as Protestant reader, represented the face of the church as most 16th-century parishioners knew it – simple, familiar and accessible. The parish kirk of St Nicholas, the walls of which survive, stood on the edge of the sand dunes where the townsmen of the small burgh harvested the bent grass which they used for thatching and other purposes, a peaceable focal-point of community life. The priest himself came from the same peasant stock as the parishioners, freemen of the ancient burgh, husbandmen and craftsmen. Not being a university graduate entitled to the designation 'Master', he was accorded the honorific 'sir', in the same way as 'Father' is used in modern times; he was 'one of the pope's knights', as the contemporary phrase went.

In order to place his role in its context we have to recognise the 'management' and 'workforce' aspects of the pre-reformation church's staff-structure. Those who were destined for the management class usually, although by no means invariably, went to university and thereafter found employment in diocesan administration, the church courts, or the universities. Many of them entered royal service, receiving government appointments in the central administration, diplomatic service or the secular law courts. Their income, apart from the emoluments of office, came from their benefices or livings, property-units from which the income was paid in cash or kind drawn from the teinds. These teinds, which had originally been intended to support the parson and the parish service, had been relentlessly diverted over the centuries through 'appropriation' to ecclesiastical institutions such as monasteries, prebends [livings] in collegiate churches and cathedrals, cathedral dignities and university colleges.[1] The holder of the teinds, whether an individual such as a cathedral canon or a corporate institution such as an abbey, became the legal 'parson' who then paid a vicar, usually with a lesser share of the teinds, to 'serve the cure' of the parish. In time, however, even the vicarage teinds were effectively removed from local use by being granted to a non-resident vicar who did not discharge parochial functions. Instead, a deputy was paid a salary, usually a small one, to act as parish priest. These deputies, or 'curates', were the unbeneficed workforce, of whom sir Robert Leggat was one.

The largely graduate management, the beneficed clergy, controlled policy through the provincial councils of the church, when these met, or more often diocesan synods, and by the attendance of prelates in parliament. They were also the executive, through the diocesan machinery, the local evidence of which was the visitations by the deans of Christianity, deputies of the bishop's archdeacon who had oversight of the diocesan clergy. The beneficed clergy also controlled the funds, voting taxes to the government from church revenue, imposing taxation on the church on the valuation of their livings and fixing the amount of the curates' salaries. In terms of material resources, education, job-opportunities and experience of the wider world they were far removed from the working parish priest. Unlike him, a number of them may never have been fully ordained to the priesthood, or may have been able at least to postpone the final step for much of their careers. It was the parish priest who had to implement their edicts and orders at local level and who was first in the parishioners' line of fire when they chose to resist clerical demands, particularly of the fiscal sort. He became involved in the family and legal disputes of the community, often trying to sort these out, he wrote out and read legal documents for his mostly illiterate flock, and was in his turn dependent on their generosity to eke out his meagre salary. Like most essential services that of the parish priest was both appreciated and criticised. Yet he was also a special, almost magical, person, especially at the altar of the normally small, plain parish kirk when at the parish mass he made God present before their eyes in the host. He baptised their children into the Christian community, married them and sent their souls with a blessing into the next world. His attitude to his beneficed superiors would repay study, if the records would suffice; whatever the inequalities that separated him from them, they were united in their identification with an all-embracing institution which not only provided the means of spiritual grace, but was a cohesive element in the familiar social order.

Training for the pre-Reformation priesthood was an essentially practical business resembling an apprenticeship. There was no equivalent to the modern seminary. Clerical students, having received the tonsure, the distinguishing mark of the cleric, at an early age, attended the local grammar and song school and learned their job by serving in the church. Since the canonical age for full ordination was twenty-four, a clerical trainee was still unfledged, so to speak, at an age when other young men in the community had become journeymen craftsmen or might have inherited the family farm. The first rung on the clerical ladder after ordination might be appointment to a chaplainry. Although the term chaplain might be used simply to mean priest, it usually denoted service at one of the many altars in a large church or the altar of a private chapel. The doctrine of purgatory and belief in the efficacy of prayers for the dead multiplied the number of such altars, with their dedications to many saints and popular forms of devotion, and added constantly to the number of masses to be said at each one. In practical terms the altar chaplain had several employers; the family of the founder of the altarage or chapel, for whom prayers were said on stated occasions according to the terms of the endowment; those who had since founded an 'obit' at the altar for themselves and their families, which required prayers to be said on the anniversary of death; and, in the case of most burgh churches, such as St John's at Ayr, there were the magistrates who acted as patrons of certain altars and generally laid down rules for chaplains employed in the burgh kirk.

The terms of a burgh chaplain's appointment could be extremely detailed, loaded with duties and restrictions. Remuneration was on the whole small, in the region of £5 to £13 at Ayr, which was on a level with that of the more poorly-paid parish curates. Besides, payment was sometimes difficult to obtain. The most common method of paying chaplains was to ear-mark a ground-annual from burgh property so that very many burgh tenements were burdened with annuals payable to altarages. Often the chaplain had to go round asking for his annuals when they fell due, and they were often in arrears. Sometimes the chaplains of a church as a body paid someone to collect the annuals for them. Poor remuneration caused many chaplains to practice as notaries, as Gavin Ross did at St John's, Ayr. Others acquired more than one chaplainry.

The job itself, vital though it was, was monotonous and repetitive in practice. Chaplains often lived 'on the job' in a chamber in the church building and the living accommodation of some of them may still be seen, such as the chamber over the altar of St Katherine in St Michael's parish church, Linlithgow. They were not always given long-term appointments; at Ayr sir Thomas Andrew was appointed chaplain in 1538 for three years, receiving as his fee £4 from the common purse of the burgh, 5 merks from the glovers' incorporation, and a merk from an annual bequeathed to his altar.[2] In May 1542 there was a wages dispute between the magistrates of Ayr and the chaplains of the burgh church when it was enacted that the treasurer was 'not to gif ony money of the commoun purss to ony chaplain of the queire of Aire in tyme cuming . . . howbeit thai [the chaplains] had augmentatiounis befoir, becaus the bailies . . . has utheris thair commoun warkis on hand mair necessair to be done, to waire [spend] these gudis upoun, and alsua has certane causis and faltis to lay to the said chaplainis chargis'.[3] When they were not at their altars the burgh chaplains were expected to assist the curate at mass and to sing in the choir. Priests who had not yet acquired an altarage also assisted at the services, in addition to the choristers, sometimes on a very short-term basis; in 1509 sir John Bollock was 'feit for a yeir to sing in the queir and keep messe and evinsang, for thrie merkis of the commoun purss'.[4] In the 1540s one of the chaplains at Ayr acted as schoolmaster. Chaplains, more than any other clergy, had the character of employees of the local secular authority, hired and fired by the magistrates who handed them their equipment on appointment – altar vessels, vestments, and service books – and took it away again when they moved on.

The name of Robert Leggat appears fairly regularly as a witness to legal documents drawn up in and around Ayr between 1524 and 1531. In these he is called chaplain without being associated with a particular church or altar. In all but one case he was witnessing the legal transactions of Adam Wallace of Newtoun, an influential local proprietor who was 'oversman' of the burgh of Prestwick in 1514, which may suggest that he was attached to Wallace's service as his chaplain and, possibly, clerk, a post that in some respects was preferable to that of a chantry priest, as the altar chaplains were called.[5] Wallace's legal business was done in Ayr itself, in the burgh court, in the barony court of Alloway, the parish church of Monkton, and the tower of Newtoun which lay between Ayr and Prestwick. It may have been Wallace's influence that gained sir Robert the appointment of curate of Prestwick, which he held by the autumn of 1525, although the appointment would be made officially by the abbey of Paisley to which the teinds of Prestwick parish were appropriated.

To be made curate meant promotion and added responsibility for chaplains. Some of them retained their altarages after appointment because of the small salary attached to a parish cure, often the bare minimum of £13-6s-8d recommended by the church councils. Generally, however, promotion to curate was reckoned to be a full-time job, requiring the surrender of any chaplainries previously held by the priest. When sir Richard Miller was appointed to 'the office of curatrie in the kirk of Aire', he was required to hand over to the bailies the books, chalice and vestments of the altar of St Peter at which he had served 'or he be dischargit his fie'.[6] His predecessor, sir Henry Hunter who was curate of Ayr for almost forty years, had been promoted from chaplain in 1506. With the cure of souls came the responsibilities of saying the parish mass on Sundays, feast-days and other set occasions, baptising, calling the banns of marriage and performing the marriage ceremony, visiting the sick, administering the last rites to the dying, conducting burials, carrying out disciplinary measures against parishioners when necessary, including the reading of 'letters of cursing' from ecclesiastical creditors against their debtors, and pronouncing the sentence of excommunication against the recalcitrant. The parish priest was also charged with the difficult task of enjoining confession and meting out penance just before the Easter communion, the annual occasion on which most parishioners took the sacrament. His need to remind them, almost simultaneously, of the Easter offerings did nothing to create a co-operative mood among them. In addition to all this he would read aloud, at an appropriate moment during the service, all kinds of public announcements, sacred and secular.

The church which was the centre of sir Robert's work stood almost within sight of its neighbour, the parish church of Monkton, in this densely-populated part of Ayrshire. Although a simple building it was much larger and more substantially built than the houses and premises of the freemen that surrounded it. In an era when sacred and secular were not distinguished from each other as they are today, and all life was lived within the Christian commonwealth, Catholic or Reformed, the kirk was a functional as well as a hallowed place which bore the marks of the life that flowed around it. The freemen parked their carts against its walls, their pigs broke through its dykes and roamed in the kirk-yard – two men who were reprimanded for allowing this retorted that 'the falt was in the kirk dyk and not in thare swyne'[7] – a kiln and barn were built against the kirk dyke, a piece of common land next to it was farmed by the local smith, and the burgh court sometimes met 'at the kirk end'.[8]

The Christian framework of everyday life was apparent in the arrangements for transactions of all kinds among the inhabitants. The freemen paid annuals from their holdings towards the upkeep of the church's fabric and the lights that burned on its altars, some of which may have been maintained by lay confraternities; 'St Andrew's lycht', 'Our Lady lycht', the 'the rud [holy rood, or cross] lycht' and the lights on the high altar which was dedicated to the church's patron, St Nicholas. The repayment of borrowed money and the payment of debts was fixed for Ascension Day, 'the Conceptioun of our Ladie', St Andrew's Day and 'the nativitie of our salveour callit Yuyll'. A dispute over the non-payment of tocher was to be 'endit at Prestwick kirk upoun Sonday next to cum eftir the conversioun of Sanct Paul eftirnoyne'. The burgh court was held 'on the nixt law day eftir Pasche [Easter]'. The accounts of the burgh treasurer sometimes included purchases for the church, such as a chalice and vestments. The saints had real personality; rent was paid from a rood of land next the kirkland to the chapel of 'our Ladie of Grace . . . and to Thomas Best in hir name'.[9] God in his providence always had the last word in an agricultural society; Sandy Finlay, newly made a freeman of the burgh, promised to pay his rent to the authority 'gif [if] God sendis him hony'.[10]

The names of other curates and chaplains, with all of whom sir Robet would be in contact, appear in the burgh court book and other records, including sir William Reid, curate of Symington, sir David Neill, curate at Monkton, sir Richard Miller, curate at Ayr, and sir John Fair, chaplain. Reid managed to engage in trade in defiance of the prohibitions of church councils, at one point owning a share in a ship's cargo. Miller, who moved from chaplain to curate at St John's kirk, Ayr, in 1551, occasionally appeared as a 'forespeaker' in Prestwick burgh court. Monasteries tended to move unbeneficed curates around their appropriated parishes; sir David Neill served at Largs in the 1530s and at Monkton in the 1550s, both of which parishes were annexed to Paisley abbey.[11] The chaplain sir John Fair, who often turns up as a witness in the 1530s in company with sir Robert Leggat, was a notary as well as a chaplain and chorister in St John's kirk, Ayr. He occasionally drew up a notarial instrument at sir Robert's request. In his youth, in 1519, Fair had had a legal dispute with a layman whom he injured in the eye with the ball during a game of tennis.[12] Clerics were sometimes caught up in even more serious incidents; in 1530 sir Robert Leggat himself had a running dispute with George Simpson, one of the bailies of Prestwick, whom the recently-appointed curate had wounded in a quarrel, 'with effusion of his blood accidentally'.[13] The curate objected to one of the witnesses, a woman, on the ground that she was closely related to Simpson, and the bailie, for his part, refused to accept the decision of the arbiters, who included sir Robert's colleagues, sir Henry Hunter, sir William Reid and sir John Fair, saying that 'he never wished to be nor could be in friendship with sir Robert' – a poor recommendation for the gospel of reconciliation. Whatever his relations with individual freemen, however, the curate was sufficiently trusted by the community to be made clerk of the burgh court, an office which he held from Ocotber 1528 until November 1570 shortly before his death, with a break in 1554 when sir David Neill deputised for him. From the records of the burgh court with which he was associated for over forty years we get a vivid picture of the life of his parishioners.

Prestwick, which was an ancient settlement even in Queen Mary's day, was proud of its long connection with the royal Stewarts which dated from the days before they became rulers of Scotland, and predated the foundation of the near-by royal burgh of Ayr. It was the head-burgh of Kylestewart, hereditary lands of the Fitzalans, Stewards of Scotland, Queen Mary's ancestors, and was in existence in 1165, for Walter Fitzalan mentioned 'my burgh of Prestwick' in the charter which he granted to Paisley abbey sometime between that year and 1173.[14] Repeated royal minorities in the 15th and 16th centuries deprived the burgh for much of the time of a personal link with the Prince and Steward of Scotland, the sovereign's oldest son, from whom the freemen properly held. Important local occasions were the meeting of the Stewart's court on the Moothill of Prestwick at which the burgh was represented. Although the charter of re-erection of 1600 confirmed Prestwick's status as a burgh of barony, it was not, like other burghs of barony, dependent on a landed proprietor but paid its rent, which the inhabitants called 'the Stewart maill', directly to the exchequer; in a sense it was a 'royal burgh' with a difference in that the Stewart sovereigns were its hereditary landlords.

The freemen or burgesses had a strong sense of both individual proprietorship and community identity. Freedom was inherited, like burgess rights in royal burghs, by both men and women; in a list of twenty-five burgesses five were women, apparently in their own right. A widow kept her husband's freedom during her widowhood and, on the other hand, a man acquired a holding in the burgh in right of his wife's freedom. New burgesses, as distinct from those who inherited their rights, qualified for freedom after having lived in the burgh for a year and a day, and on payment of 5s to the fabric of the church and 3s 4d to 'the commoun profit of the toun', on taking the oath. Women could apply for a freedom in this way, like Christian Pettigrew whom the bailies and community 'maid . . . burges of Preswik with ane consent and assent . . . to the quhilk the said Cristiane gaf hir greit aith to be leill and trew to the profit of the said burghe, with all othir that efferis [belongs] to the samyn, as use of burgesry aw to be maid'.[15] A burgess's heir on inheriting paid only 'in spyce and wine' when taking the oath. The freeman's land, like his burgess right, was held heritably, for which he paid a rent of 3d a rood.

Like many small royal burghs and all burghs of barony, Prestwick was village-size by modern standards. The number of freemen was never large; between 70 and 80 are named in 1470, 63 in 1507, as few as 31 in 1559, although these lists, drawn up for specific purposes, may be incomplete. When the freemen's wives and families, servants, apprentices, dependants and the unfree inhabitants are taken into account there may have been about 3-400 inhabitants about mid-16th century. As a trading precinct, however small, the burgh had its market cross, tolbooth and four ports at which toll could be levied on goods coming to the market. There was a weekly market on Tuesday and a fair on St Nicholas's Day (6 December) and the day following. Stallholders, who were mostly unfree, were allowed to sell their wares in the street on market days. These included women, one of whom, Isobel Allanson, was accused in court of 'sclandering of the officiaris of the towne and speciali of the stentaris [those who taxed the stall holders] the quhilk scho denyit'.[16] The volume of business was probably very small, the freemen and their families supplying their own wants from the handful of burgh craftsmen and the produce of their own holdings, purchasing additional items in Ayr. There are a few indications, however, that the freemen may have sold their surplus produce to outside merchants, most likely in Ayr. In 1549, for example, a Prestwick freeman, Adam Miller, sued an Ayr merchant, Robert Campbell, for failure to pay him in full for a quantity of hides.[17] The new freeman already referred to, Sandy Finlay, who intended to pay his rent in honey, may have been beekeeping on a large enough scale to sell to merchants; honey certainly occurs in the inventories of merchants' booths in this period.

The entries in the burgh court book have preserved the names of the working parts of the settlement and its landmarks, such as the common vennel that ran through the town, bounded by dykes which were kept in repair by those freemen whose holdings lay alongside it. A list of the burgh roods speaks of those on the west side of the town lying between the vennel and the gallows, and those on the east that extended from the vennel to the ford over the Prestwick burn. Pieces of ground took their names from owners, or former owners; 'Dame Alis holme', 'John of Daillis land', and 'the Templir acre' belonging to the Knights of St John. Other plots took their names from the location; 'the Brigg greyne' and a portion of land on 'the hidder syd of the burn callit the Burn Cruik'. Holdings were commonly small, consisting of a house and two or three roods, and in earlier times were divided, or delt, annually in quarters or dales, then the dales into rigs. The rigs were then allocated by lot among the freemen, rig and rig about, separated by unploughed strips called baulks so that no freeman's rigs all lay together. In

1572 the allocation was set for every 19 years but later reverted to a yearly pattern. The maintenance of boundaries – good neighbourhood – was of the utmost importance; 'to kep ilke nychtbur fra skayth [damage] under pain of 12d'. The exchange or sale of holdings was carefully monitored by the burgh court and freemen were forbidden to take leases from proprietors outwith the burgh – purchasing of lordship; 'ony man or wemen that is burges, inhabitant or outwith the burgh, that purchase lord, lard [laird], gentillman or ony othir, temporal or spirituale' paid 40s to the repair of the kirk of St Nicholas and lost their freedom for good.[18]

Authority lay with two bailies, who were chosen annually and had their expenses paid, presided over by an oversman, occasionally designated 'provost', who also changed from year to year and was often a local laird.[19] All freemen attended or were represented at the court, women almost certainly would send a proxy. While this looks 'democratic' on the surface it was arranged simply to give maximum support to the preservation of the burgh's privileges and the enforcement of internal rules by mutual consent. The life of the self-supporting, tightly-regulated small community changed little between the series of statutes that were drawn up in 1470 and King James's charter of confirmation in 1600. In mid-16th century it must have been of great benefit to the community's spiritual director, the curate, to sit in on the deliberations of the burgh court, hearing the public recital of his parishioners' misdeeds and complaints while he took minutes of the proceedings.

The main business of the inhabitants was husbandry, growing their crops on the burgh roods and pasturing their stock, under the watchful eye of the herd and his assistants, on the common pasture. Each freemen had a grazing allowance, or 'sowme', in proportion to the extent of his arable land. Repeated statutes called for 'dykis fensabile to beistis', but there were numerous court actions for compensation for 'eittine corne'. In spring and autumn poultry that 'multitud', such as hens and their chickens, capon and cocks, were not to be allowed free range 'till destroy and wast thar nychtburis seid',[20] only one of many neighbourhood problems that arose in days when farmers operated as close to one another as gardeners do now. Pigs were generally unwelcome because of their destructive habits; each freeman was allowed to have only one 'and that to be in bande fra Beltane to Luxmes [St Luke's Day]'. The inhabitants kept both cattle and sheep. Plough animals and equipment may have been shared, although there are references to individuals having their own harrows and peat-sleds. There may have been common byres and barns, although William Simpson accused John George of having taken away his barn 'of twa cupil' from his land, to which John replied in court that he had taken it as security for 3s that William owed him.[21]

There were local resources which the inhabitants shared, the most valuable of which were the moor and peat-bog which were used for building-turfs and fuel respectively. Use of the peats was strictly regulated.[22] Digging began on St Laurence's Day in August, when all freemen or their servants were expected to dig their own share of the peats and transport them to the town in sleds. Freemen were forbidden to lease or sell their share of this common property, whether the peat bog, the moor, or the common grazing without consent of the bailies and whole community. Having dug their peats they were instructed to replace the sand taken out during working, failure to do so resulting in a fine. The bent grass on the sand dunes was also communally harvested.[23] Cutting began on the day after Lammas, for which each freeman provided four 'hukis', or shearers, and two mowers to gather up the bent. They were fined if they began to work before sunrise. The salt-pan belonging to the burgh was leased out. Some freemen may have operated salt-pans on a small scale; Agnes Caird accused Andrew Walker in court of having 'kept nocht hyr nychburscape, in the bigging of ane salt pane hous betwix thaim' and of using her coal to fire it. By 1576 the burgh's coal heuch beside the salt-pan was leased to Michael Wallace, the provost of Ayr, who would operate the whole complex and employ local labour. As in all baronies the inhabitants were obliged to take their crops to the local mill; in 1514 Martin Miller, miller of the new mill of Prestwick, having acquired a house and land in the burgh, was made a freeman.[24]

There were craftsmen in the burgh who supplied the community through the market, including tailors, shoemakers and weavers. There seem to have been a number of weavers to judge by the references to looms. In July 1538 John Underwood accused John Miller, weaver, of failing to hand over a loom which Underwood had bought from him for 30s.[25] The weavers wove yarn for individual orders. In October 1561 John Gardner complained in court about a defect in the weaving of two sacks of yarn by Gilbert Henderson. In reply Henderson explained that 'his wyf warpyt thame and put in twa threddis with hyr awin hand'.[26] In 1564 Janet Dowyk accused John Dunlop of 'putten away of hyr dochtyr Katrene MacSpadane', although she had apprenticed Katherine to him for four merks and a firlot of meal. Weaving seems the most likely craft for which the girl had been apprenticed to the craftsman.[27] The women span the wool into yarn at home; a brother and sister once quarrelled in court over possession of a spinning wheel, probably their late mother's, which he claimed as part of his heirship goods but which she wished to use.[28]

Domestic surroundings and personal possessions are glimpsed in court actions for recovery of stolen goods, or arising from executry business such as claims to heirship goods – the best of each category set aside for the heir – or 'bairn's pairt' of a parent's estate. On one occasion a son and daughter laid claim to a lamb, ewe, 3 bolls of bere, a pot, a pan and a horse. In 1565 John Dunlop, probably as an executor, accused Robert Martin of withholding heirship goods: a loom worth 4 merks, a large pot, an ark for storing meal, a meat board (for taking meals at), a vessel board, a 'warpene fat' or trough in which yarn was laid for warping, a 'chair stool' and a mortar, all of which had belonged to Martin's mother.[29] Accusations of theft often resolved themselves into cases of disputed ownership. Robert Andrew was able to demonstrate his right to goods which a cleric and probable relative, sir Martin Bannatyne, had accused him of taking over: two wooden, iron-bound doors, a plank, a bench, two 'dishburdis' (table for holding vessels), and a girdle and 'bakstule' used in making bread.[30] Household goods as well as smaller items were sometimes pledged for a loan of money; in October 1565 Gilbert Henderson, the weaver already mentioned, accused Janet Cunningham, in whose house the burgh court occasionally met, of keeping from him a 'huyk' or sickle, a mantle, a sack, a broken pint stoup and a hempen tether but Janet replied that she held these items as 'woddis' or pledges and she had some counter accusations about his cattle having eaten her crops. The wife of one freeman pledged a silver ring with a neighbour for a loan of 2s.[31]

When a debtor failed to pay, goods to the value of the debt were arrested in the creditor's interest; in October 1571 a forespeaker for Margaret Leggat demanded three quarters of a stone of wool, a kirtle, 'ane wyndou claith', two sacks, a pot and a kist which had been arrested in the hands of John Guthrie by an officer of the court. She certainly acquired a useful selection of goods. The homes of the freemen had few luxuries, simply the necessary bedding, seating, and cooking utensils. The pots and pans, being made of metal, and the farm stock were among the most valuable possessions, while items which we might be inclined to value most were comparatively far down the scale of market prices. The mid-16th century court cases cited provide the following list, although the condition of individual items would affect the value given:

loom	£2–13s–4d (second-hand, £1–10s)
a kirtle	1–10s
a kist	18s
a horse	13s–4d (in most testaments worth about £4–£6)
a warping vat	12s
a mantle	10s
one boll of bere	9s
a pot	9s
a vessel board	8s
a sack	8s
a chair-stool	4s
a mortar	4s
a pan	2s
a stoup (measure)	1s
a sickle	8d

There are no references in the court book to sir Robert Leggat's own circumstances while he was curate of Prestwick. The details of his dispute with bailie Simpson are recorded in the protocol book of Gavin Ross. Sometime before January 1548, however, he received an addition to his income and further promotion in his clerical status when he was granted the benefice of the vicarage of Ayr, possibly about the same time as Mr David Gibson, canon of Glasgow cathedral, became the parson.[32] Leggat was in the unusual, although not unique, position of being the working parish priest of one parish and the absentee vicar of another. He may not have been an entire absentee, however, since Ayr was only a reasonable ride away. Later developments suggest that he was well known to the magistrates of the royal burgh. As vicar of Ayr he was the immediate superior of his old friend, sir Henry Hunter, who as curate of Ayr since 1506 must by now have been an old man by contemporary standards. The previous vicar, Robert Montgomerie, had belonged to one of the many branches of the Eglinton family, which was the social background of many parsons and vicars. Sir Robert Leggat, on the other hand, was a local man from a humble background who, because of the proximity of Prestwick, was virtually on the spot. Perhaps it was felt that his varied experience as private chaplain, parish priest and clerk to the community of Prestwick would be of value in strengthening the authority of the ageing curate of Ayr.

The 1530s and 1540s were unsettled years in the religious life of Ayr and district as the old phenomenon of anticlerical criticism was reinforced by a growing attachment to Protestant belief in certain circles, and a desire for positive reform of the church. In 1533 Walter Stewart, the brother of the laird of Ochiltree who was an early adherent of Protestantism, was accused of 'casting doun ane image in the kirk of Air', in fact the statue of the Virgin Mary on the church of the Observant Franciscan friary.[33] It appears that a number of people besides Stewart were involved in the incident, and that others in neighbouring, although unnamed, parishes were in sympathy with them, having 'sowed Lutheran errors, asserted them both in private and public and had read the new testament in English and other writings containing heretical opinions'. It is a great pity that the loss of evidence compiled during this and other heresy cases has deprived us of information on the extent of religious dissent at this time. Walter Stewart himself recanted in public, but in 1537 the authorities were still 'serching of the heretiks of the west land' and a summons to appear before the central courts was issued to the men from Ayr, also unnamed. That Stewart's target had been the Franciscans' kirk suggests that they may have been at the centre of a controversy over attitudes to Lutheranism, as most heretical opinions tended to be called at this stage in Scotland; the fact that two years later, in 1539, one of the friars, John Willock, left his order and went to England, to return over twenty years later to help to organise the reformed church, adds to the picture of internal divisions. A heresy trial in Glasgow in 1539 resulted in the burning of two heretics, a Franciscan friar called Jerome Russell and a young man named Kennedy, who probably belonged to Ayrshire.[34]

In the year 1543, in the early months of which the Governor, the earl of Arran, was encouraged by the reforming party to pass legislation permitting the reading of the new testament in English, there appear to have been two camps in the burgh of Ayr over the matter of positive reform, for when the Franciscan

John Routh preached publicly against the introduction of the English new testament he provoked a riot. When Routh was sent for by the Governor, then at Glasgow, to answer for his denunciation of the act of parliament he was accompanied by bailies William Nisbet and Robert Shaw. The burgh treasurer paid the expenses of his journey, including a horse and some clothes; no doubt the Franciscan monastery on whose behalf he had preached his sermon declined to bear the expense of his appearance before the secular authority.[35] The next landmark in the emergence of Protestantism in the area was the visit to Ayr and Kyle of Mr George Wishart, who had come west to avoid the attempts of Cardinal Beaton to arrest him for defiance of a prohibition against his public preaching.[36] Influential lay support for Wishart in the east of Scotland enabled him to take the pulpit in some churches. Archbishop Gavin Dunbar of Glasgow, on the Cardinal's instructions, forestalled him in St John's kirk in Ayr, delivering a somewhat negative address in an attempt to defuse a potentially explosive situation. Wishart decided to avoid confrontation and preached to a larger audience at the market cross. He then moved into Kylesmure and the parish of Galston where he taught at the house of Campbell of Cessnock. At Mauchline the sheriff of Ayr, Campbell of Loudoun, refused him entry to the church and Wishart again preached in the open air, to great effect. In the wake of his tour of Kyle some lairds tried to push forward practical reforms, and the impatient among them, who included John Lockhart of Barr at whose house the reformer had stayed, proceeded by violent means. In 1550 Lockhart and Charles Campbell of Bargour were denounced rebels for non-compearance to answer charges of 'theftuous and violent carrying off . . . furth of sundry parish churches, religious houses and chapels within the shires of Lanark, Renfrew, and the stewartries of Kyle, Carrick and Cunninghame, sundry eucharistic chalices, altars, and ornaments of the mass, and also for casting down and breaking choral stalls and glazed windows in the years 1545, 1546, 1547 and 1548'.[37]

Alongside this forceful criticism and open support for Wishart's teaching there continued the evidence of the conventional forms of popular piety particularly in the foundation of 'obits' or anniversary masses for the dead at the altars of the burgh kirk of Ayr. However, these began to fall off in the 1540s and only appear occasionally in the Obit Book of the church after 1543, the year of the Routh riot.[38] In any case, the generosity of the burgesses had for some time been diverted to the friaries to the annoyance of the diocesan clergy. Even donations to the Dominicans, however, whose register survives, fell off in the 1530s and 1540s until property tended to come to the friary through individual members of the monastic community, who had inherited it and passed it on to their house.[39] In the burgh kirk itself relations were strained between the magistrates and the clergy, especially the chaplains, although these and the choristers had experienced substantial increases in fees in this period. As we saw, fees were frozen during a dispute in 1542. Just before the Reformation the religious establishment at Ayr was costing the burgh about 41% of its income, in a period when the council's resources were already being strained by the burgh's contribution to the cost of the war with England, through taxation and the requisition of ships by the government.

When the movement for religious reform fused with the military resistance to the Queen Regent's French-backed government in the late 1550s a number of Ayrshire lairds and gentlemen, publicly led the the the earl of Glencairn, a second-generation reformer, took an active part in events. This must have been reflected in public opinion in the burgh of Ayr, for in the 16th century there was no clean-cut division between urban and rural society, landed and civic leaders. Many burgh merchants and craftsmen were the town-dwelling relatives of landed men, with whom they were constantly in touch. Besides, many clerics were related to both; bailie John Kirkpatrick, for example, who was on the side of reform and attended the Reformation parliament of August 1560, was the brother of William Kirkpatrick, monk of Kilwinning abbey and first minister of that parish. The growth of reformed opinion in Ayr has still to be studied in detail, but that it had reached considerable strength by the late 1550s is demonstrated in the early steps taken to introduce certain Protestant forms of worship and religious practice. By the spring of 1558 the magistratres were ready to take the first steps in this direction, and they turned to sir Robert Leggat, curate of near-by Prestwick and holder of the vicarage revenues of Ayr, to assist them.[40]

In May 1558 sir Robert Leggat put himself formally under the jurisdiction of the magistrates of Ayr, and shortly afterwards took on the duties of curate of that parish in addition to his own; he later sued an Ayr parishioner for failure to pay him burial dues incurred that year. He replaced sir Richard Miller, sir Henry Hunter's successor, who had become curate of Ayr in 1551, who must have been unwilling to co-operate with the magistrates in the changes which they planned. It is reasonable to suppose that sir Robert *was* amenable and already supported reform, even Protestantism, and that if that were so his attitude may already have communicated itself to the parishioners of Prestwick. He himself may have shared the views of the Wallace lairds, relatives of his old patron, Wallace of Newtoun, three of whom signed the Bond of Ayr of 1562 together with Mr Michael Wallace, provost of the burgh.

In 1559 the Ayr magistrates obtained their first Protestant minister, nearly a year before the Reformation-settlement was formally ratified by parliament. He was Christopher Goodman, an Englishman who had been a colleague of John Knox at Geneva. In November 1559 the newly-appointed schoolmaster, John Orr, was given the added responsibility of reading the common prayers and administering the sacraments according to Protestant practice, 'in absence of Christopher Goodman, quhilk salbe bot 8 or 9 dayis at the maist at ance . . . sua the said Cristopher wais nocht to be oft absentand himself thairfra'; the reformed minister was denied the luxury of non-residence from the start. On 11 May 1559 George Cochrane, the organist and master of the song school, handed over to the bailies the keys of the organ loft, 'protestand that through his non-service in the kirk of Ayr in tymes coming as in tymes bygane it be nocht allegeit that he of benevolence left the said cure for ony opinioun but be virtue of his discharge foirsaid'. In the midst of the landslide Cochrane was probably anxious to make the termination of his contract of employment as regular as possible but, in fact, his 'opinioun' brought him the appointment of reader at the church of St Quivox.

In the spring of the same year the magistrates began to discharge the chaplains of the burgh kirk; masses for the dead were no longer held to be efficacious, according to Protestant teaching. On the day of the organist's removal from his post the burgh court heard the complaint of sir John Sinclair, chaplain, whose fees were in arrears. Having got the bailies' promise to send the burgh officer to demand payment of his annuals, Sinclair then objected to the magistrates' intention of discharging him, alleging 'that there was no fault presentlie fund to him quhairthrow thay micht now discharge him of his office in the kirk and stall permitted to him'. Sinclair, who had been inducted in 1551 and was now trying to hold the council to the letter of their contract with him, had spoiled his case by non-residence. When he came before the burgh court again the following October they were able to charge him with 'absenting himself furthe of the said kirk and service uset be the remanent chaplains thairintill, to the number of fyftene or sextene dayis togidder nocht regarding his promise contenit in his allegeit act of conductioun [induction] that he suld serve dailie in the said kirk . . . and latelie hes maid thaim na service be the space of ane yeir and an half . . . quhairfoir the saidis bailies . . . ar nocht astrictit nor halden to observe thair pairt of the samyn to him, first brekker foresaid'. In a final attempt to hold on to his living Sinclair appealed to the bailies on 26 May 1560 to be allowed to keep the liferent of his chaplainry, saying that he had been unable to perform his duties lately for lack of vestments in which to say mass; a few days previously he had asked sir Robert Leggat the curate for a loan of vestments only to be told that he could not have them as 'the bailies and dean of guild had forbidden him, because thai had dischargit thair chaplainis of the said kirk and thair service'. Sinclair's prolonged absence from Ayr may have put him out of touch with the radical changes in the burgh church, but it is more likely that he was simply trying to hold on to his property rights in his chaplainry according to the letter of the law. The reference to sir Robert's responsibility as curate at a time when a Protestant minister was in charge, and a reader of the prayers had been appointed, is a unique glimpse of the coexistence of the two ecclesiastical systems; it is almost as if the minister represented the parson, hitherto non-resident, with the vicar-curate as his assistant.

The position of unbeneficed chaplains faced with the termination of their specialist service and the loss of their livelihood was perhaps the most pitiable of that of the lesser clergy. The magistrates eventually agreed to allow sir John Sinclair the liferent use of his chaplain's annuals; in 1573 he was said to be receiving £20, the same amount as the reader of the parish. The case of sir Alexander Kar, son of an Ayr burgess and a chaplain for at least twenty years, is a human document of the Reformation;

> 'the bailies and inquest [jury] in consideratioun of the lamentabill
> bill of support and supplicatioun gevin in be sir Alexander Kar, hes
> grantit . . . him to haif yeirlie of the tounis commoun purse £10 of
> fie and support . . . in tyme cuming, he keipand the paroche kirk
> of the said burgh honest and clein, ringand the bellis yeirlie, and on
> ilk day neidfull to the commoun prayeris and preiching – and
> cumand the morne to the said kirk and thair openlie in presence of
> the haill congregatioune sal confess his offences done to his God
> and neightbouris and sal surlie promit [promise] nocht to comit sic
> error nor offence in tyme cuming: and willinglie to amend, sal with
> his hart renunce the devill, the paip and all thair warkis, otherwayis
> he to haif na fie of the toun'.

It is possible that Kar had peristed in his former duty of saying private masses, perhaps at the request of founding families and private patrons. The unique transitional duties of sir Robert Leggat must have afforded him many opportunities for discussion with perplexed and in some cases resentful former colleagues about the changes that were taking place.

Within a year of Christopher Goodman's appointment as minister he moved on to St Andrews, and his place was taken at Ayr by Robert Acheson who was lodged with a burgess, Robert Rankin, when he first arrived; the burgh treasurer paid for the coal and candle and bought shoes for him and his servant.[41] For the accounting year 1561-2 he was given a coat of French black cloth costing £3. In 1563 sir Robert Leggat was made a reader in the Reformed church and moved back to full-time charge of Prestwick parish. In the Reformed church the minister was fully qualified to preach, to administer the sacraments of communion and baptism, to perform the marriage ceremony and conduct burials. Readers, who were only permitted to read the common prayers during the service and homilies from the English Book of Homilies, helped to maintain a parish service in those parishes which at first had no settled, full-time minister, and they also assisted in those parishes to which ministers were provided. It proved impracticable to realise the reformers' ideal of weekly communion, partly because of the medieval habit of infrequent communion and partly from lack of fully qualified ministers. The ordinary Sunday morning service, which resembled the contemporary English service in structure and even content, began with an act of confession of sins, psalms and lections, followed by the main part of the service – a sermon followed by a long intercessory prayer and concluding with the Lord's Prayer and the Apostles' Creed.[42]

His new status would officially debar sir Robert from a number of his former functions, such as celebrating the communion, baptising and conducting burials. However, in many areas where ministers were few and the incumbent was the former parish priest or other cleric familiar with the parish, who already knew his parishioners well, these official rules were sometimes breached; people were grateful for the prompt service of a pastor in the matters of marriage, baptism and burial, especially if he was already known to the family. The terminology of functions was sometimes loosely used, and sir Robert Leggat is designated 'minister' in Prestwick burgh court book in 1570.[43] The prohibition against preaching was less of a problem since many pre-Reformation clerics of the lesser orders – those most likely to become readers – had not been in the habit of doing so anyway.

It has been estimated that over half the clergy in charge of parishes after the Reformation, in whatever capacity, had been in orders in the pre-Reformation church, very many of them in the parishes with which they were already associated. Sir Robert had some friends and colleagues in nearby parishes of Kyle. His neighbour, sir David Neill, who had been curate of Monkton until at least 1556, was moved to Largs as a reader, a parish in which he had also served as curate almost thirty years before. At Monkton itself sir John Wylie, preceptor of the local chapel of Our Lady of Kyle, was made minister, suggesting a familiarity with Reformed teaching, although he seems to have been demoted to the office of reader a few years later. His family belonged to Monkton parish. The parish of Symington did not fare so well; sir John Miller, the curate, became reader, but not until after sir Robert Leggat's death. The Dundonald parishioners were still asking for a minister in 1565; the man appointed reader in 1567 was Robert Burn, ex-prior of the Irvine Carmelite Friary.

Sir Robert himself continued to act as clerk of the burgh court at Prestwick where his former subordinate at Ayr, sir Richard Miller, occasionally appeared as a forespeaker on behalf of pursuers. In October 1562, just before he returned to Prestwick as reader, the bailies granted him permission to cut peats in the common peat moss 'wyth castar and ane stykar' for his lifetime; David Blair of Adamton, oversman of the court, signed this act in his favour.[44] A year later the minister of Monkton appeared in the Prestwick court on behalf of his nieces, to whom he was tutor, about their rights to part of the same moss. In 1567 the court stated that no freeman must sell any of their share of the peats except 'sir Robert Legat' – the old courtesy-title probably stuck to him throughout his lifetime. Perhaps he and his parishioners may have experienced some of the excitement engendered by Queen Mary's progress through Ayrshire in the summer of 1563, when at one point she and her entourage rode from Eglinton down the coast to the burgh of Ayr; as the Steward's vassals they had a personal link with the Queen. The last entries in sir Robert's hand in the court book are dated November 1571, shortly before the end of his life. His continuous local service does much to redeem and perhaps helps to qualify the reputation of the sometimes maligned parish curate – 'sir John Latinless' – in this difficult time of change.

ROBERT LEGGAT

Notes

1 On the subject of appropriation, see I.B. Cowan, *The Parishes of Medieval Scotland* (S.R.S.) 1967.

2 A. MacKenzie, *An Ancient Church: St John's Ayr*, 43.

3 *Ibid.*, 37.

4 *Ibid.*, 52.

5 J. Anderson and F. Grant, *Protocol Book of Gavin Ros* (S.R.S.), eg. 717, 736, 896, 1123, 1152.

6 A. MacKenzie, *An Ancient Church*, 42-3.

7 *Records of the Burgh of Prestwick* (Maitland Club), 52.

8 *Ibid.*, 20.

9 *Ibid.*, 9.

10 *Ibid.*, 67.

11 M.H.B. Sanderson, 'Some Aspects of the Church in Society in the Era of the Reformation' in *Records of the Scottish Church History Society* xvii (1970), 91, 98.

12 *Protocol Book of Gavin Ros*, 330.

13 *Ibid.*, 1069, 1073, 1074.

14 D. Murray, *Early Burgh Organisation* (1932), 58.

15 *Records of Prestwick*, 20.

16 *Ibid.*, 29.

17 *Ibid.*, 61.

18 *Ibid.*, 14.

19 *Ibid.*, 74.

20 *Ibid.*, 17.

21 *Ibid.*, 20.

22 *Ibid.*, 19.

23 *Ibid.*, 23.

24 *Ibid.*, 44.

25 *Ibid.*, 54-5.

26 *Ibid.*, 66.

27 *Ibid.*, 68; as early as 1486 Elene Walker had complained upon James Allanson that his daughter had come into her house and 'distrobillit hir weblumys'.

28 *Ibid.*, 70.

29 *Ibid.*, 69.

30 *Ibid.*, 23.

31 *Ibid.*, 71.

32 *Protocol Book of Henry Preston* (S.R.S.), 6.

33 D. Calderwood, *History of the Church of Scotland*, I, 104.

34 J. Knox, *History of the Reformation in Scotland*, ed. W.C. Dickinson (1949), I, 27-8.

35 G.S. Pryde, *Ayr Burgh Accounts* (S.H.S.), 90.

36 J. Knox, *Reformation*, I, 61-2.

37 R. Pitcairn, *Criminal Trials*, I.*353.

38 J. Paterson, *Obit Book of the Kirk of St John the Baptist, Ayr, passim*

39 *Charters of the Friars Preachers of Ayr* (Ayr and Galloway Archaeological Association), 1881.

40 Information on the progress of the Reformation at Ayr comes from Ayr Burgh Court Books (former S.R.O. B6/12/2,3).

41 *Ayr Burgh Accounts*, 33.

42 G. Donaldson, *The Scottish Reformation* (1960), 83.

43 *Records of Prestwick*, 71-2.

44 *Ibid.*, 66.

MARK KER

1517-1584

Metamorphosis

MARK KER was a Borderer from Teviotdale in the Scottish Middle March. It was the habit of his family, the Kers of Cessford, and their kinsmen the Kers of Ferniehirst, to lead a double life. At one and the same time they were feudal landholders and the almost tribal leaders of a powerful kin-group known as the 'surname'. The head of the house of Cessford in the 16th century was often the Warden of the Middle March, public administrator for the crown in his troublesome home-country, and at the same time Border reiver in his own interest. On days of truce he worked out peace formulas with his counterpart, the English Warden, and in his own time pursued private feuds, notably that against the Scotts, sometimes to the death.

Mark himself ran true to the family pattern. As a pre-Reformation ecclesiastic, who nevertheless took part in the family warfare, he acquired a choice piece of church property, Newbattle abbey, at the eleventh hour and, having backed the new religious establishment, shed his clerical skin to emerge as a landowner and secular official, building the fortunes of his family, literally, on the foundations of his former abbacy. Even the narrative of his career that can be traced in the surviving records is a success story.

He was the second son of Sir Andrew Ker of Cessford and Agnes, daughter of Sir Patrick Crichton of Cranston Riddell, a match arranged by Sir Patrick after buying the legal disposition of the young laird of Cessford's marriage from the crown, for just over £460, in 1507. Mark was born in 1517, in Edinburgh castle of which his maternal grandfather was governor; the grandest fortified house in the country was certainly a prestigious beginning. In 1526, when he was nine years old, his father was killed, cut down by an Elliot in the service of Scott of Buccleuch while the latter was being pursued by the Kers. As a younger son in a landed family Mark was expected to support himself from church livings, and, having graduated master of arts from St Andrews university, he obtained a papal dispensation to hold benefices although still under the canonical age, and from

January 1536 he held what was virtually the family benefice of the Maison Dieu, or Hospital, at Jedburgh, successfully winning his case against a rival claimant to the rents.[1] In December 1547 the pope provided him to the abbey of Newbattle,[2] the material assets of which included not only good farmland but coal workings and salt pans, representing an estimated annual rental of around £1,400. At the time of his appointment, however, the abbacy was held by the ageing abbot, James Haswell, who lived on for another ten years, Mark Ker being correctly designated commendator.

Although not drawing the abbey revenues as yet he established a personal connection with Newbattle, living partly there and partly at Edinburgh in the 1550s. In 1552 his kinsmen took their revenge on the laird of Buccleuch by murdering him in the High Street of Edinburgh. Mark may have been with the attackers; his brother-in-law, John Home of Cowdenknowes, with whom he was often associated, was said to have shouted to one of the Kers during the assault, 'Strike! Ane straik for thy father's sake!' In 1555, the year in which parliament tried to reduce the friction between the Scots and the French forces in the country by an act against 'speaking evill of the quenis grace [Mary of Guise] and the Frenchmen', Mark Ker and his brother-in-law, Home, were accused of killing one French soldier and wounding others during a fracas in Newbattle itself.[3] Abbot Haswell must have had gloomy thoughts about the future of the monastery in the hands of his obstreporous successor. Summoned to court for his part in the crime, Mark donned his clerical hat and asked to be repledged, judicially transferred, to the court of his 'ordinary' judge, the archbishop of St Andrews. The representative of the archbishop of Glasgow contested his custody since his benefice of the Maison Dieu lay in the archdeaconry of Teviotdale, to which Mark replied that he had resigned that living. There is no formal record of his having been further prosecuted.

His connection with Newbattle, both before and after he took over personally, was mainly concerned with the management of the abbey property. In 1549 he had received the pope's licence to exercise the office of commendator in spite of not having taken monastic vows or the Cistercian habit – a virtual exemption from ever having to do so, and from taking part in the internal, spiritual life of the monastery. He was designated Commendator in January 1557 and came into actual possession of the property on the death of Abbot Haswell that year. He immediately set about raising capital on the estates by granting a number of feu charters of abbey property for down-payments which were said to be earmarked for repairs to the fabric of the monastery, which had sustained damage during the English invasions. Time was to show that the commendator had grander designs on the fabric than mere repairs. Abbot Haswell had granted a handful of charters in the 1540s and 1550s, mostly to small tenants, but Mark Ker's feuing programme bears more clearly the signs of estate-management for profit. He alienated some territories *en bloc* to lairds such as Borthwick of Glengelt, Blackadder of Tulliallan, and his own nephew, Alexander Home, son of the laird of Cowdenknowes, who received feus of Prestongrange and Newtongrange in Lothian and Gartsherrie in the abbey's detached barony of Monkland in Lanarkshire, all substantial properties. Over the years he also feued smaller holdings to tenants, mainly in and around the towns of Newbattle and Easthouses. The bulk of his feuing programme was carried out before 1560, indicating a deliberate attempt to develop the property as soon as he got his hands on it.[4]

The arrival of a new-style head of the monastery may not have upset the monks too badly at first, although in a year or two their relations with the commendator were to deteriorate badly. In the 1550s they were regularly involved in estate business outside the monastery: the cellarer, Thomas Reid, is found receiving the statement of a tenant, who was acting as tutor to a young relative, with regard to the latter's property; James Harvey, another of the monks, went to the house of a tenant in Masterton to protest about the non-payment of teinds; the subprior, Andrew Langland, acting as the abbot's commissioner, absolved a tenant and his wife from the sentence of excommunication which they had incurred for debt. In some ways the monastic discipline had been relaxed; as elsewhere the monks received their individual 'portions' and possessed their own chambers and yards. The theory was that they only had the use of the latter, but these yards were treated almost as pieces of property. This was demonstrated in the test-case of a yard belonging to the monk, John Liddell, who in 1554, in providing for his niece when she married his servant, Robert Dickson, gave the latter 'his full power and . . . gudewill . . . to intromett with the fructis [fruits] growand in his west yaird within the abbay of Newbattle assignit to himas use is', with liberty to occupy and cultivate it.[5] A few years later, after dene John Liddell had died, the monks complained in the court of session that Mark Ker refused to give the now vacant yard to another member of the convent, George Simpson, who was without one, claiming that it was customary for vacancies to be filled in this way. No matter how customary it was the monks could not arrange the business without the commendator's concurrence; they were now finding it difficult to dislodge Robert Dickson and his wife from what had been her uncle's possession.

A more serious internal dispute occurred in 1552 when the monks found it necessary to extract an agreement from James Acheson, the properous Edinburgh merchant to whom Abbot Haswell had leased some acres near Musselburgh and from whom he had been buying goods 'on the house'. Acheson agreed not to 'furniss ane reverend fader in God, James, abbot of the said abbay with ony merchandis or guidis without thair consent excep wine, ceir [wax], irn, salmond and abulzements for the abbatis bodie, nor ony otheris in his name, and that he [Acheson] sall ressave thankfull payment of the sowme of £1,000' owing by the abbott and convent 'in greit and small sowmis as thai pleis'. The merchant also promised not to sublet the land which he had leased from the abbey.[6]

The new commendator did not cut himself off from the possibility of acquiring non-ecclesiastical property. As early as 1542 and on several occasions thereafter he was named as next in line to succeed to the family's properties after the direct heirs of his brother, Sir Walter Ker.[7] This may seem a good distance away from the succession, but for the relatives of those who pursued blood feuds or, for that matter, were obliged to apprehend desperate Border thieves in the name of the law, the possibility of succeeding as head of the house was by no means remote. In the later 1550s the Kers were identified with what has been called 'the party of revolution', which combined the elements of Anglophile politics, or at least collaboration with the English, and demand for reform of the church establishment.[8] Not all adherents of this 'party' showed both these characteristics, but there were those who did. One family in this category, with whom Mark Ker came to associate in the 1550s, was that of the Leslies, George 4th earl of Rothes and his sons, some of whom had been involved in the assassination of Cardinal Beaton in 1546. In January 1557 Mark Ker witnessed a charter granted to the earl's son, Robert Leslie of Arderseir, by Robert's half-brother, David Paniter, bishop of Ross.[9] Of more personal significance was his association with the earl's daughter, Helen Leslie, who had borne him a son, Mark, by February 1558, when his father granted him a charter of the lands of Coitlaw and Gledhouse belonging to Newbattle abbey. Helen Leslie was already the widow of Gilbert Seton, younger of Parbroath, to whom she had been married in the autumn of 1542 and by whom she had a son, David, and a daughter, Janet. She is one of the pre-Reformation concubines who lived to become a respectable wife, of whom there must have been far more than we shall ever find in the records, some of whom may even have been transformed into ministers' wives.

In developing his property, maintaining his place in the house to which he belonged, and even founding a family of his own, the Commendator of Newbattle was behaving more like the layman he was at heart than the kirkman he claimed to be and, technically, was. The dividing line between clerical and lay in those landed families who had invested in the patrimony of the kirk, through commendatorships, before the Reformation came had been blurred for some time, and may have become more so from 1557 onwards as the speed of events increased. It does not need hindsight to see that many people with something to lose as well as those who hoped to gain at the church's expense expected some kind of crisis from about 1557 onwards; the sudden increase in capitalising on church lands by feuing, whether to lairds or husbandmen, is particularly eloquent. So are the conciliatory tactics of the Queen Regent and the belated attempt by Archbishop John Hamilton to initiate a measure of reform from within the church, which suggest that both the political and religious establishments were on the defensive.

As if to underline how they thought of themselves as landed folk, Mark Ker and Helen Leslie had their portraits painted sometime in the 1550s.[10] The date 1551 that now appears on the half-length companion portraits traditionally believed to be theirs, and attributed to Willem Key, is misleading and probably too early. In 1551 Mark Ker was in his 35th year according to the records, although papal documents are often approximate in the matter of people's ages, not 40 years of age as stated on his portrait.[11] He would be 40 in 1557, which may have been the date orginally on the paintings but misread or inadvertently altered in a later touching-up. The year 1557 is very near to the time when he and Helen probably began to live together; one wonders how far they regarded the arrangement as a quasi-marriage, calling for commemorative portraits, like those of Jane Gordon and the Earl of Bothwell nine years later. The red-haired, bearded Commendator wears subdued but undeniably secular dress: a dark cloak, doublet and bonnet, with a narrow frill at the neck and wrists of his shirt. He wears a ring with the device of a skull on the forefinger of his left hand, and holds, in the same hand, what is either a glove or a document. Helen wears a simple, dark gown, with rose-coloured sleeves and a narrow turned-down collar and turned-back cuffs of open-work, a fine coif under her linen cap and a natural hairstyle parted in the middle. In her left hand she holds a piece of music to which she points with her right forefinger. The only words clearly readable above the musical notation are ' . . . in eodem', but if more could be made of this item it might add some personal detail to what is known about her.

The Commendator sat in parliament in November 1558, and probably in the provincial council of the church, convoked by Archbishop John Hamilton at the Queen Regent's instigation in March 1559. At this gathering there were attempts to implement certain reforms such as better payment of the parish priesthood (as well as a stricter supervision of them) and an alleviation of the unpopular customary 'kirk dues' demanded from the laity, especially death-duties; these efforts to placate the laity and lower clergy pinpoint the areas of dis-content. The council refused to consider the introduction of vernacular services, which would have been a further gesture of conciliation in the laity's direction, and the gathering met under the threat of the mysterious 'Beggars' Summons', which foretold the violent dispossession of the orders of friars at the coming Whitsunday.

The progress and success of the Reformation-rebellion has been chronicled elsewhere. One aspect of the final months of the movement which has not often been pointed out but has recently been emphasised is the diplomatic ability of the leading 'rebels', the provisional government of the 'Lords of the Congregation', to be 'all things to all men' until victory was assured.[12] Having gained the promise of English military help by the treaty of Berwick in February 1560, they laid emphasis on the religious issues thereafter, as the idea of political rebellion was distasteful to their ally, Queen Elizabeth. When at Leith in April 1560 a bond was signed by some 140 persons to set forward the Reformation, care was taken in deploring the presence of the French to protest loyalty to Queen Mary and King Francis. Religious conservatives, including the nervous prelates who were concerned about the fate of their livings, were reassured with patriotic emphasis on ridding Scotland of the French. Even those most concerned about the religious issues would not have taken part in a revolt against the native Scottish monarchy, loyalty to which was now a habit of two hundred years. It consoled those who were prepared to abandon their Catholic practice but not their ecclesiastical revenues, of whom Mark Ker was evidently one, that parliament when it met in August 1560 ratified the Reformation in the theological sense, but made no move to confiscate the revenues of the proscribed church for the endowment of the new. This same circumstance, which left the entire pre-Reformation ecclesiastical structure in being, encouraged the religious conservatives among the clergy to hope for a Catholic reaction. Nevertheless, the estates carried through radical legislation without reference to the sovereigns and with questionable legality, something they would not have risked had they not been confident of wide support.

Mark Ker signed the Band of Leith of April 1560, in company with the lairds of Cessford and Ferniehirst, and attended the Reformation parliament four months later. During Queen Mary's personal reign he set out to give the Newbattle estates the character of a private property, meeting with local opposition in the process. His attempt to remove one tenant, Andrew Champnay, disappears from the court of session record before a decision was reached, but the fact that the case lasted at least six months suggests that the tenant, or at least his advocate, Mr John Spence, did not give up without a fight. Spence argued that the Champnay family, having held their land for thirty-two years, could not be evicted except for a crime or non-payment of their dues: 'becaus of the consuetude of the said barony of Newbottill, ane tenant beand anis rentallit, be vertew of the said rentale hes tytle and ryt to the landis . . . ay and quhill [always until] the same be forfaltit [forfeited] in ane court'.[13] In 1560 John Blackadder of Tulliallan and Alexander Home did a deal with the Commendator, the details of which are unknown, whereby they resigned lands which he had earlier feued to them – Easthouses, Westhouses, and Newtongrange – in favour of his son Mark, heritably, and to Helen Leslie in liferent.[14] The suggestion that this change of proprietor may have entailed changes in cultivation, perhaps a move to farming with direct labour, is found in an action raised in name of the young Mark Ker in 1569 calling for the removal from Easthouses of the tenant, Agnes Turnbull, widow of Thomas Home in Dalkeith, 'herself, servandis, cottaris, hyndis and gudis [stock]'.[15]

In 1567, by which time the Commendator and Helen Leslie were married, James Gifford, younger, of Sheriffhall complained to the privy council that his family's kindly tenure of the revenues of Newbattle mill had been violated by their being feued 'ower his heid' to Mark Ker's wife and children.[16] A rather different kind of court action, in 1562, reminded the Commendator of his lawbreaking past when one of the former monks of Holyrood abbey, Stephen Litster, sued him for £80 which he claimed to have spent on Ker's sustenance when the latter 'wes in ward about nyne yeris befor in the place of Halyrudhous', possibly after the killing of Scott of Buccleuch in Edinburgh in 1552.[17]

He treated the monks of Newbattle abbey very shabbily indeed. In January 1563 four of them – John Harvey, Thomas Guild, Adam Scott and George Simpson – complained to the privy council of their eviction from the place of Newbattle in 1560, saying that although the Commendator drew the abbey revenues he 'wald nevir gyf thame worth ane pennie to leif upoun'.[18] Since being turned out they had got into debt in trying to sustain themselves. Both parties compeared before the lords of council who ordered Ker to pay the brethren £20 recompense for what they had already spent and £20 a year each 'until order be taikin'. Evidently he failed to carry out the order, for the following year the same four monks sued him for non-payment of the portions which they claimed were theirs by use and wont. The trouble was that unscrupulous superiors knew that portions, like individual chambers and yards, were not part of the monastic constitution and that directives for their payment, even from the law courts, were difficult to enforce. During this case the monks, like those of other monasteries who brought many similar actions against their superiors in the 1560s, supplied interesting details of their provision. They each claimed 13 bolls of malt and 3 bolls 1 firlot of wheat, with 6s a week for 40 weeks of the year and 3s-6d a week during Advent, Septuagesima, and Lent, £6 of 'habit silver', 5 stones of cheese and one of butter, with a chamber and yard. Their common allowance extended to 3s a head for wine and meat for 23 days and a common yard. The Commendator had failed to pay not only their portions but their special Lent allowance of 1 boll of pease, 40 bolls of oats to the brewer and baker, a side of beef and leg of mutton between Easter and Lammas, and a leg of mutton, from the marts, between Lammas and Fasternse'en, or Shrovetide. The convent had their own servants, including steward, cook, pantryman, brewer and maltman, whose allowances were also in arrears, and 120 loads of coal a year for their common fire. They had the right to the money-rent from the lands of Craighouse.[19] When the Commendator sent in his returns to the collector general of the thirds of benefices about this time he mentioned the deduction of £240 a year to 'sex agit, decraipit and recantit monkis', but their complaints continued to reach the courts for several years.

Mark Ker's removal of the monks and their servants from the abbey was probably linked with his plans to transform the monastic buildings into a private residence, something which was also being done at the nunnery at North Berwick by Alexander Home, son of the laird of Polwarth, who built a 'New Wark' on to the conventual buildings there in the 1560s. From archaeological evidence at Newbattle it appears that the earliest secular building was superimposed on the monks' living quarters, including the dorter of which the south half of the undercroft is the only remains of the medieval abbey above ground today.[20] Two 16th century window surrounds, now set in a wall in the heart of the present house at first floor level, are the only surviving features of the Commendator's new residence. Between them is a panel bearing the initials 'M.K.L.N.', with the date 1580; Mark Ker signed as 'Mark Lord of Newbotill' long before his son was granted the title 'Lord Newbattle' in 1591. The year 1580 may have seen the completion of the new building at Newbattle, just four years before the Commendator's death. The house may have been erected more for prestige than everyday living, more associated with Mark Ker himself as 'unsufructor of the abbay of Newbotill' than a family home, hence his own initials only on the walls. At any rate, the family had a house at Prestongrange, comfortably furnished, to which Helen Leslie retired towards the end of her life. Few estate records, apart from charters and leases, survive for Newbattle for the period of Mark Ker's lifetime. His returns of revenue already referred to list 59 tenants in the town of Newbattle, itself, with possibly between 300-500 inhabitants in the settlement altogether. The estates stretched from 'Prestoun be the se' in the north to Romanno grange and Crawford muir in the south, with Monkland barony in Lanarkshire, a local area whose name was resurrected in the reorganisation of local government in 1975. Mark Ker made his brother, Sir Walter Ker of Cessford, his bailie or chief executive officer of his lands, to hold the barony courts. The chamberlain or chief financial officer was a local man, John Kirkpatrick, who served him for many years 'verey lawfullie and discreitlie'.

If the years of Queen Mary's personal reign were occupied with his property interests, the reign of King James VI saw Mark Ker make a place for himself in public life. By 1569 he was a member of the privy council, during the regency of the earl of Moray who, like himself, drew revenues from an ecclesiastical estate, the rich priory of St Andrews. In the same year Ker was made an 'extraordinary' lord of session, in the supreme civil court, one of a group of additional judges chosen for their political experience to sit with the 'ordinary' lords of session who were professionally-trained lawyers, an arrangement which derived from the traditional practice of mixing trained lawyers and privy councillors, who were often feudal magnates, on the judicial bench. In 1572 he was one of the commissioners chosen by the newly-appointed Regent Morton to negotiate peace terms with Queen Mary's remaining supporters in the last months of the civil war, negotiations which ended in the so-called Pacification of Perth, followed by remissions to many Queen's men. Disputes arising from this settlement 'south of Tay' were to be resolved by the Commendator of Newbattle, Lord Boyd, and Sir John Bellenden of Auchnoule, justice clerk.

At first Ker was numbered among the supporters of the Regent Morton, in company with his old confederate and brother-in-law, Home of Cowdenknowes, but as time went on they became dissatisfied with his style of government, their antagonism towards him being aggravated by a quarrel between Morton and the laird of Cessford, whose habit of independent action as Warden of the Middle March was unacceptable to the Regent. In 1578 the Commendator was one of those chosen to carry on the government on Morton's resignation of the regency. In 1580 the Kers were among those who gathered around the King's second cousin, Esme Stewart, Lord of Aubigny, who was created Duke of Lennox soon after his arrival in Scotland from France that year. Lennox quickly became a focal point for those who were disillusioned with Morton, and by mid-September 1580 Bowes reported to the English government that he counted Lords Ruthven, Lindsay, and Herries (Mark Ker's son-in-law), the commendators of Dunfermline, Newbattle, and Inchcolm, and the lairds of Cessford and Cowdenknowes among his supporters.[21] Mark Ker, always with an eye to the main chance, had supported both Morton and Lennox during their ascendancy and was on terms of personal friendship with the latter. Although he continued to sit on the privy council and act as an auditor of exchequer, he withdrew from active politics after the ultra-Protestant *coup* known as the Raid of Ruthven, an attempt to 'rescue' the King from the company of Lennox whom some suspected of fostering sympathy for Queen Mary and even of collaboration with the Catholic party. Lennox, having fallen from power, left Scotland for France in 1582.

Mark Ker's must have been one of the most affluent families around the court of King James VI. In addition to their houses at Newbattle and Prestongrange he and Helen Leslie, in 1577, took the lease of a commodious lodging on the north side of the High Street of Edinburgh, 'a litill beneath the salt trone in James Bannatyne writeris clos heid', from a merchant, James Marjoribanks, for £40 a year.[22] The house consisted of an 'ovir hall with chalmer in the end of the samen, tua chalmeris abone the hall, ane kitcheing and ane litill chalmer abone the kitcheing, with tua sellaris, togidder wyth my myd foirchalmeris upoun the foirgait, and the ovir foirchalmer into the loft hous abone the samen'. Their household goods, spread among the three residences, were valued at the then enormous sum of £1,000 (much higher than those of some contemporary nobles), suggesting an extremely comfortable standard of living.[23] The silver tableware included silver basins and lavers, saltcellars, trenchers, cups and spoons. There was a clock which had been acquired from the laird of Cessford and, at Prestongrange, a fashionable 'buffet' or sideboard, used partly to display silver, the gift of Esme Stewart, Duke of Lennox; Prestongrange also had a fine painted ceiling, completed in 1581.

In addition to the rents and feu-duties from the abbey estates the Kers drew substantial income from the coalheuchs of Prestongrange, from which Helen Leslie once tried to remove the leaseholder, the laird of Cockpen, the salt pans, which were also leased, and the sale of the wool from the large flocks of sheep; there were over 3,000 in pasturing at Lethenhopes at one time. In 1583 the wool fetched over £900: when it sold for £2-6s-8d a stone. Both the Commendator and his wife handled large sums of money. At the time of his death Mark Ker had in his possession, 'in cunzeit gold and silver', over £6,000 in a variety of coinages: Portuguese ducats, rose nobles, angel nobles, English ryals, 44s pieces, rydars, pistolets, crowns of the sun and five three-merk pieces 'cunzeit be King James fyft'. At the same time Helen Leslie had custody of £1,441 as well as the money realised from the wool sales. The Commendator was able to lend money: 3,000 merks to his advocate friend, Sir John Shairp of Houston, for which the latter had pledged 1,000 crowns of the sun, and 300 merks to the laird of Ferniehirst. The teinds of the kirks appropriated to the abbey of Newbattle were leased, predictably, to the Commendator's relatives and friends: the parsonage teinds of Newbattle parish to his brother, Sir Walter Ker of Cessford, the vicarage teinds of the same parish to an Edinburgh burgess, George Adamson, those of Bathgate to William Home of Prendergast, Heriot to John Borthwick of Rashaw, those of Cockpen still being paid directly by the parishioners.[24] The teinds or their money equivalent brought in over £1,400, yet the Commendator was habitually in arrears with the payment of the 'third' from his abbacy, being listed among those 'at the horn' for non-payment from 1562 to 1572[25] and having his third remitted in 1567-68, the year in which Queen Mary was deposed and the Regent Moray assumed the government in name of James VI.

From their considerable wealth Mark Ker and his wife provided for their family. Helen's son, David Seton, succeeded to his father's lands of Parbroath in Fife. Her daughter Janet married Hamilton of Samuelston, and between 1565 and 1568 she and her husband received three charters of Newbattle land from her stepfather.[26] Mark Ker had a natural daughter, Margaret, who married John Crawford of Roughsalloch in Lanarkshire before 1557 when their son had a charter from Mark Ker,[27] making her contemporary with Helen Leslie's first family and indicating that she was born when Ker was young. Mark, the eldest of the Ker sons, was made gentleman of the bedchamber to James VI in 1580 and Master of Requests the following year. In 1581 his father resigned the commendatorship of Newbattle in his favour, retaining the liferent,[28] the only post-Reformation case of a son acquiring his father's prelacy, accomplished in the way that a laird transferred his property to his heir during his own lifetime. He had a house on the abbey lands of Morphat and was also known as Ker of Prestongrange. Andrew Ker of Fenton, named in the *Scots Peerage* as the second son, was granted the abbey lands of Romanno Grange and later became administrator of the revenues of the abbey of Kelso. George, who became a Roman Catholic, was involved in the alleged plot of the northern Catholic earls in 1592 to cause a Catholic reaction in Scotland with the help of Spain. The youngest son was William, who lived until 1613; and the only daughter, Katherine, married William Maxwell, 5th Lord Herries, who as a Catholic gave protection to a cell of recusants and their ministering priests in and around Dumfries and New Abbey in the 1580s and 90s.

Mark Ker died at Newbattle on 19 August 1584. Eight days previously he had made his will in the presence of Lord Herries, his son-in-law, Alexander Home of Gartsherrie, his nephew, his faithful chamberlain John Kirkpatrick, and his good friend, Mr John Shairp of Houston. He died a rich man: his net estate of £16,046-5s was on a level with that of some of the capital's richest merchants or the greatest of the nobles. It was far beyond that of most lairds, whose estates, so far as their testaments have been examined, only occasionally exceeded £2,000. He had certainly done better than many holders of public office whose salaries, paid from various sources, were often in arrears and unreliable, and whose expenses were great: Sir Louis Bellenden of Auchnoule, the justice clerk, left only £606-15s-8d. It need hardly be said that he lived, materially speaking, in another world from even the most prosperous of the farmers on his estates, the most successful of whom might leave between £5-600. It is significant that while others owed him over £2,600 he himself was in debt for only £349-4s-8d; his income had kept ahead of his expenditure. He made 'his weilbelovit spouse' and their younger sons his executors, she to have the sole managment of his estate and money. To his son Andrew he left his 'deidis pairt', that is the third of the estate remaining after wife's and children's thirds had been deducted and all debts paid, 'in respect of the necessitie of his effairis'. At the same time he left a number of legacies: £1,000 to his granddaughter, Agnes Maxwell, with 1,000 merks to her father, Lord Herries, a quantity of silver ware to his daughter, Lady Herries, and to Helen Leslie over and above her wife's third part or terce. He left 100 merks to his natural daughter Margaret, whose husband, John Crawford of Roughsalloch, acted as his bailie in the barony of Monkland, and £100 to their son, John. There were bequests to his servants, who thus go down in history: Henry Lyle, the cook, David Spence, the steward, John Brown, keeper of the stable, James Wright, brewer, George Tait, gardener at Prestongrange, David Gibb, the household's baxter, Cuthbert Ferguson and Robert Watson, grieves at Newtongrange and Prestongrange respectively, and Ninian Liston, barony officer at Newbattle. He commended his chamberlain, John Kirkpatrick, to his oldest son, Mark, leaving him £200 'though not equivalent to his service'.

Helen Leslie outlived her husband for ten years, living in the house at Prestongrange of which she had the liferent. The Mains of Prestongrange was farmed directly, rather as it had been in medieval times as one of the granges of Newbattle abbey; the presence of 17 drawing oxen and over 400 bolls of grain from the recent harvest on the Mains when Helen died, on 26 October 1594, suggests fairly intensive cultivation. Helen dictated the details of her own inventory, executory and latter will, making her sons Andrew and William with their sister Lady Herries her executors. She made a classic statement of her protestant faith in her will, committing 'hir saull in the handis of the almytie God, certanelie hoiping that be the merreitis [merits] and passioun of Jesus Chryst the samyn salbe ressavit to the eternall bliss and joy of hevin'. She asked to be buried in Newbattle 'besyd hir umquhyll darrest husband in sik maner as salbe thot maist expedient be hir wyse freindis hoiping alsua be the mercie of God that on the day of ressurrectioun the samyn [her body] sall ryse and be placit wyth the elect'. She signed her will, in her own hand, 'Helen Leslie Setoun'.[29]

She must have had mixed feelings about her family's fortunes in her later years. Her son George, caught during the alleged popish plot of 1592 in possession of the papers known as 'the Spanish blanks', revealed details of his fellow conspirators' plans under torture. He is not mentioned in his mother's testament and, apart from his legal share of her moveables, received no personal legacies;

she left 1,000 merks to her son, David Seton of Parbroath, £1,000 to her daughter Janet, wife of Hamilton of Samuelston, and 1,000 merks to Janet's daughter. Whatever their religious differences she remained on intimate terms with the recusant family of her daughter Katherine Ker, Lady Herries. She must have been gratified, however, with the progress of her son, Mark Ker, in whom the final transformation of the family property was completed and who in so many respects followed in his father's footsteps. It had long been planned that he should do so. In 1567, possibly the year in which his parents formally married, Queen Mary in the last weeks of her personal rule had granted him the right to hold the commendatorship of Newbattle should his father die or resign the property;[30] this was almost the language of the papal curia which continually provided to livings under these conditions, the death or resignation of the current holder. In 1580, with his father's formal resignation, keeping the liferent, Mark became what in lay terms would have been the fiar of Newbattle. In 1584, the year of his father's death, he had a ratification from King James of the 1567 letters under the great seal, establishing his right to the property, and at the same time he took his father's place as an extraordinary lord of session and privy councillor. On 28 July 1587 he was granted all the lands belonging to the abbey of Newbattle in spite of the Act of Annexation by which the crown assumed direct superiority of all land that had belonged to the church. In this respect he was one of the small, closely associated group of favoured royal courtiers and servants who, having been granted immunity from the 1587 Act, were soon to have their former ecclesiastical properties transformed into temporal lordships. In 1591 Mark Ker, younger, was created Lord Newbattle, and in 1606 1st earl of Lothian. He died three years later leaving a net estate of nearly £37,000, more than double the amount left by his father a quarter of a century earlier.

Having transformed the nature of their property in parchment terms over the years, the Kers had also realised the process in stone and lime. The house which they built and gradually embellished is a rare example in Scotland of a house which took its name, in the manner of so many English country houses, from the monastic foundation on which it was built.[31] In the early years of the 17th century Sir John Scot of Scotstarvet, writing from his own little tower house, commented on the phenomenon of Newbattle:

> 'And the father and son did so metamorphose the buildings that it
> cannot be known that ever it did belong to the church, by reason
> of the fair new fabric and stately edifices built thereon; . . . instead
> of the old monks has succeeded the deer'.[32]

MARK KER

Notes

1 Lothian Muniments (S.R.O.), GD 40/1/ 167, 177, 181.

2 J.B. Paul, *The Scots Peerage*, V, 453.

3 R. Pitcairn, *Criminal Trials*, I, *378; it was in giving evidence at his apprehension that Mark Ker gave details of his early life, including the fact that he had been born in Edinburgh castle.

4 For the pattern of feuing at Newbattle, M.H.B. Sanderson, *Scottish Rural Society in the sixteenth century*, 65-6, 128-9.

5 Protocol book of Thomas Stevin (S.R.O.), B 30/1/5, fo 93v.

6 *Ibid.*, fo 67.

7 *Register of the Great Seal*, III, 2649, 2784; IV, 912.

8 G. Donaldson, *All the Queen's Men*, Chapter 3.

9 *Register of the Great Seal*, IV, 1225.

10 At time of writing these portraits, owned by the National Gallery of Scotland, are on display at the Scottish National Portrait Gallery, Queen Street, Edinburgh. Helen was a half-sister of Agnes Leslie, lady of Lochleven and later countess of Morton; the young Mark Ker was therefore moving in the same reforming circles as William Douglas of Lochleven in the 1550s.

11 Lothian Muniments, GD 40/2, Portfolio IX, 21.

12 G. Donaldson, *All the Queen's Men*, 34-6.

13 Register of acts and decreets, xviii, fo 273.

14 Lothian Muniments, GD 40/3/51, 89.

15 Register of acts and decreets, xliii, fo 38.

16 *Register of the Privy Council*, II, 590.

17 Register of acts and decreets, xxiii, fo 129.

18 *Register of the Privy Council*, I, 228.

19 Register of acts and decreets, xxxii, fo 386v.

20 C. McWilliam, *Lothian* (The Buildings of Scotland, Penguin, 1978), 344-50.

21 G.R. Hewitt, *Scotland under Morton*, 74.

22 Lothian Muniments, GD 40/3/558.

23 Testament of Mark Ker, Edinburgh Commissariot, Register of Testaments, CC8/8/ 16, fo 79.

24 Books of Assumption (S.R.O.), E 48/1, fos 114-18.

25 G. Donaldson, *Thirds of Benefices* (S.H.S.), 114, 130, 135, 274, 278, 285-6.

26 *Register of the Great Seal*, IV, 1771.

27 Register of Abbreviates of Feu Charters of Kirklands (S.R.O.), i, fo 267.

28 *Acts of the Parliaments of Scotland*, 111, 276.

29 Testament of Helen Leslie, Edinburgh Commissariot, Register of Testaments, CC8/8/29, fo 280. In 1593 her son's wife, Lady Newbattle, was visited by a deputation from the church authorities who suspected that mass was being said in her house; they found no evidence. In 1595 Mark, Lord Newbattle, was himself summoned to appear before the synod of Lothian and Tweeddale to answer questions about his religious beliefs, possibly because of his younger brother George's known Roman Catholicism.

30 *The Scots Peerage*, V, 45.

31 Culross House is another example, built by Edward Bruce, Lord Kinloss, a title derived from another ecclesiastical property, after he had acquired the Lordship of Culross.

32 Sir John Scot of Scotstarvet, *The Staggering State of Scottish Statesmen*.

GLOSSARY

The following definitions apply only to the period and context of this book. Variations in meaning and usage should be checked with the help of dictionaries or reference works on specific themes, such as maritime or costume history.

Appropriated	— annexed, in the sense in which parochial revenues, especially the *teinds* were appropriated to monastic and other ecclesiastical institutions.
Annualrent	— annual payment of rent; interest on money.
Archdeacon	— ecclesiastical dignitary charged with supervision of the diocesan clergy.
Arles	— earnest-money paid to a servant on being hired.
Aumry (aumbry, almery)	— free-standing cupboard or pantry.
Avoyd	— to remove or clear from.
Bailie	— chief executive officer of a barony or regality.
Barony	— basic unit of local government in landward parts of Scotland; lands held of the crown might be erected into a barony.
Benefice	— ecclesiastical living.
Bill	— the document used to initiate legal proceedings.
Bill of lading	— certificate of loading of a ship which bound the master to deliver the cargo.
Body (bodies)	— the stiffened bodice of a woman's dress, sometimes referred to in the plural.
Bombasie	— fabric, a mixture of wool and silk or wool and cotton.
Bond	— written legal obligation to repay money or perform a service.
Bowgang	— dairy farm.
Buccasie	— buckram, a linen fabric.
Buffet	— sideboard.
Burd (buird)	— table.
Burret	— a coarse woollen fabric.
Burrs	— looped tags on the shoulders of a garment, such as a doublet.
By	— without, eg. 'by the avis of', without the advice of.
Caddes	— cotton wool or flock used to pad garments.
Cannel	— cinnamon.

Caravel	— method of constructing a ship by laying the timbers flush against one another; a ship built by this method.
Carriage	— customary haulage service required from tenants.
Carry	— a container, eg. 'a wattir carrye'.
Caulking	— rendering a ship's deck timbers watertight with a mixture of oakum and pitch.
Caution	— security (pronounced as in 'nation').
Chamberlain	— chief financial officer of a barony or regality.
Chamlet (camlet)	— a fabric, a mixture of wool, silk and cotton having a watered appearance.
Charge	— to publicly order a debtor to make payment or defaulter to obey a court order.
Charter party	— contract between shipmaster and merchant when a ship is hired.
Child(ren)	— servant(s), e.g. 'chamber child', a personal or body servant.
Clinker	— method of ship construction in which the timbers overlap.
Collectory	— central office concerned with the collection of the Thirds of Benefices.
College of Justice	— original name for the Court of Session.
Commendator	— the holder of the revenues of a monastery not elected internally by the community and often not a monk.
Commute	— to turn a payment in kind, eg. grain, into a money equivalent.
Confraternity	— a religious association of lay persons in pre-Reformation times.
Conjunct fee	— joint holding of heritable property by a husband and wife.
Cottar	— the holder of a cotland, usually under a husbandman and owing labour-services to him, but sometimes holding directly from the landlord.
Crear	— a standard trading vessel.
Cruck-framed	— the wooden, inverted-V shaped, framework of a tenant's house.
Cummer	— godmother; bother.
Cunzie	— coin; 'cunziehous' was the mint.
Curia	— the papal court.
Dantellis (Dentelles)	— scalloped edged lace used as edging for ruffs.
Defalcations	— authorised deductions from income, allowed for in a chamberlain's accounts.
Deforce	— obstruct in the course of duty.
Diligence	— legal procedure, usually associated with attempts to recover debt.
Dittay (roll)	— indictment; roll of accused persons.
Dorter	— monastic dormitory.
Entry silver	— payment made at the beginning of a lease.
Escheat	— to legally confiscate goods; the goods themselves.
Factor (rix)	— a person appointed to manage property or legal affairs on another's behalf.
Ferme	— rent, commonly the rent in kind, the greatest part of which was in grain.
Feu-farm	— form of heritable tenure in return for an annual feu-duty in money, in place of the old feudal ward-duty; in the 16th century it replaced leaseholding on many church estates, turning tenants into owner-occupiers.
Forespeaker	— an advocate who appears in court in company with his client during a law suit and speaks on his behalf.
Frame	— to compose legal documents and record them in the public legal registers.
Frieze	— a woollen cloth with a heavy nap on one side.
Fustian	— a fabric of cotton and flax or flax and wool, with a silky finish, used as a substitute for velvet.
Gear	— moveable goods.
Gif	— if, eg. 'gif neid beis', if need be.

Girnel, Girnall (=Giruel, Girnall)	— granary.
Goods (gudis)	— farm animals, stock.
Graith	— equipment.
Grange	— a monastic farm.
Grassum	— a down-payment or periodic payment to a landlord.
Grogram	— a silk material in taffeta weave having a coarse grained texture.
Harden	— a heavy quality linen.
Herezeld	— death-duty on a husbandman's moveable estate, usually an animal.
Hind	— a farm worker.
Holland	— a fine quality linen.
Horning	— public denunciation of a debtor or other defaulter, who is thereafter liable to be escheated.
Husbandman	— the most substantial of the rural tenantry.
Inlaik	— loss, damage or failure, often used in estate accounts with reference to loss of crops.
Intromit	— to handle or deal with funds or property.
Jupe	— a fitted, sleeveless garment worn over the doublet, more or less equivalent to the English jerkin.
Kane	— customary payment from tenants, usually in poultry or farm produce.
Kiln	— a structure for the drying of grain.
Kindness (kindly tenancy)	— a claim to customary inheritance on the basis of kinship with the previous holder.
Knaifship	— perquisites of the miller's servant.
Liferent	— right to use a property during one's lifetime.
Maill	— rent, commonly money-rent.
Mailling	— literally, a piece of land for which maill is paid; a holding.
Multure	— tax on grain ground at the local mill.
Neighbourhood	— mutual obligations among members of a community, particularly a burgh; usually associated with the need to observe the boundaries of holdings.
Oakum	— teased-out hemp packed between the deck planks of a ship and sealed with pitch to render it watertight.
Oker	— usury.
Orlop deck	— the lowest deck in a ship.
Outland	— overseas, eg. 'outland men', overseas traders.
Overlay	— a turned-down linen collar.
Oxgang	— division of arable land; nominally the amount that one plough team could work in a year.
Oy	— grandchild or nephew/niece, the relationship being determined by the context and known details about those concerned.
Pament	— paving; to pave
Pasvelour	— a velvety-textured material which may have been of a purple colour.
Pettycommons	— the common fund of a monastic community.
Plaiding	— a heavy woollen material.
Plant	— to assign ministers to churches.
Pledge	— security for a loan or debt.
Pockmantie	— a travelling bag or case.
Poind	— to confiscate in the name of the law.
Poldavie (canvas)	— a coarse linen mainly used for lining.
Portion	— a monk's personal allowance from the monastic revenues.
Procurator	— advocate in the law courts, ecclesiastical and secular.

Prolocutor	— an advocate who appears in court in name of his client. (see also, *forespeaker*).
Provision, provide	— The final stage on papal authority, in a senior ecclesiastical appointment.
Rantering	— repairing garments.
Recusancy	— religious dissent which involves the practice of the proscribed religion.
Regality	— unit of local government in which the landholder, unlike the situation in a *barony*, enjoyed certain exemptions from royal authority.
Register	— public record kept by government and law courts into which both official business and the texts of private rights are registered, or recorded; the act of recording in the register by a clerk.
Rental	— rental book or rent-roll of a landholder; the working rental or check-list of rents and dues compiled by a chamberlain; the written title of a tenant who held his holding for life.
Repledge	— to judicially transfer a person to another court.
Rests	— arrears of rent or other payments.
Riding books	— the record of the 'riding', or collection, of the teinds.
Russet	— a coarse woollen homespun fabric.
Serjeant	— an inferior officer of a court, eg. barony court.
Shanks	— stockings.
Silver	— money.
Security writ	— term used to describe the title of someone who holds land in security for another's debt to him or her.
Skaith	— damage or loss in the legal sense.
Sowme	— share of grazing.
Steading	— farm buildings; originally, the farm or holding itself.
Steilbow	— a customary tenure under which the farmer received stock and seed with the land.
Stemming	— a woollen or worsted fabric.
Stenting	— stiffening material.
Tack	— lease.
Teinds	— tenth of the produce of the land in a parish divided between parson and vicar, in practice mostly leased out.
Thaik(ing)	— to thatch; the thatching material.
Thirds	— tax, equivalent to a third of income, paid by benefice-holders after 1562; shared between the crown and the ministers of the reformed church.
Timberman	— ship's carpenter.
Tocher	— dowry.
Tonsure	— the shaving of the crown of the head of a cleric.
Toun	— a rural settlement, sometimes called a farmtoun.
Turn	— a service, in the sense of doing someone's 'turns' for them.
Tweel	— (?) twill.
Usufructor	— Possessor of revenues, literally, the fruits.
Wad (in)	— pawned.
Wadwife	— money-lender and pawnbroker.
Wadset	— to grant away land as security for debt; a wadsetter was a proprietor who held land in security until the debtor paid.
Wardigaird	— a receptacle for clothes.
Whinger	— a short stabbing sword.
Woolding	— rope wound round the joints of a ship's masts.
Wyliecoat	— petticoat.

SELECT BIBLIOGRAPHY

This is not a definitive bibliography on the period, but simply a suggested reading list for those interested in the background to the themes of this book. Manuscript sources used and additional printed works will be found in the footnotes.

Cowan, I.B. *The Scottish Reformation* (Weidenfeld and Nicolson, 1982).

Cowan, I.B. and Shaw, D eds., *The Renaissance and Reformation in Scotland: Essays in Honour of Gordon Donaldson* (Scottish Academic Press, 1983); subjects include the law, government, the church, society and education.

Donaldson, G. *Scotland, James V to James VII* (The Edinburgh History of Scotland, Oliver and Boyd, 1965 and 1978). Reprinted, Mercat Press, 1987.

Donaldson, G. *The Scottish Reformation* (Cambridge University Press, 1960).

Donaldson, G. *Mary, Queen of Scots* (E.U.P., 1974); *All the Queen's Men* (Batsford 1983).

Fraser, A. *Mary, Queen of Scots*, (Weidenfeld and Nicolson, 1969).

Gouldesbrough, P. *A Formulary of Old Scots Documents* (Stair Society, 1985).

Lynch, M. *Edinburgh and the Reformation* (John Donald, 1981).

Lythe, S.G.E. *The Economy of Scotland in its European Setting, 1550-1625* (Oliver and Boyd, 1960).

McRoberts, D. ed., *Essays on the Scottish Reformation* (Reprinted from the *Innes Review*, 1960); contains many pioneering articles on the intellectual contacts between Scotland and Europe.

Murison, D. *The Guid Scots Tongue* (Reprinted by the Mercat Press, 1984).

Rae, T.I. *The Administration of the Scottish Frontier, 1513-1603* (Edinburgh University Press, 1966).

Robinson, M. ed., *Concise Scots Dictionary* (Aberdeen University Press, 1985).

Sanderson, M.H.B. *Cardinal of Scotland: David Beaton, c. 1494-1546* (John Donald, 1986).

Sanderson, M.H.B. *Scottish Rural Society in the Sixteenth Century* (John Donald, 1982).

Simpson, G.G. *Scottish Handwriting* (Aberdeen U.P., 1986).

Wormald, J. *Court, Kirk and Community: Scotland, 1470-1625* (Edward Arnold, The New History of Scotland, 1981).

INDEX

The index contains only the most important references to people, places and themes closely associated with the subjects of the book.

Aberdeen, 36, 49, 51
Aberlemno (Angus), 9
Acheson of Gosford, Alexander, 25, 27
— , Euphemia, second wife of Sir John Shairp, 27
— , Robert, minister at Ayr, 163
Airlie castle, 4
Andrew, sir Thomas, chaplain, 151
Arbroath, 5, 6, 7, 14
Arran, 2nd earl of, James, 160
Auchterhouse (Angus), 62, 63, 68
Auchtertool (Fife), 145
Ayr, 151, 152, 155, 159-63
Ballindalloch (Angus), 26-7
Balquhidder (Perthshire), 141
Beaton of Balfour, John, 11
— of Melgund, David, 7, 8, 9, 11-12, 13, 15, 16, 17, 18, 19, 20
— , Agnes, 7, 13, 15, 17, 19-20
— , Mr Alexander, archdeacon of Lothian, 7, 8-9, 14, 15-16, 17, 18, 19, 20
— , Cardinal David, and Marion Ogilvy, 3, 4-6, 7-9, 12-13; career, 5, 7-8, 10-13; in France, 8, 16; alliances of, 11-12; death of, 20, 56, 169; and heresy, 34, 160
— , Elizabeth, 7, 11, 14-15, 17
— , George, 7
— , Mr James, 7, 8, 15, 16
— , John, 7, 16, 17
— , Margaret, countess of Crawford, 7, 11, 13, 18
— , Mr Walter, 9, 13
— ⸲, William, embroiderer, 86
Blainslie (Roxburghshire), 104, 110
Blair of Adamton, David, 164
Bollock, sir John, chaplain, 151
books, 146
Bothwell, 4th earl of, James, 37-41, 57, 92
Brora (Sutherland), 45, 49

building, 9-10, 28, 32, 48-9, 68-9, 78, 96, 99

Burn, Robert, reader at Dundonald, 164

— , — , reader at Dollar, 146

Campbell of Glenorchy, Sir Duncan, 72-3

— of Loudoun, [Hugh], sheriff of Ayr, 160

Carnegie of Kinnaird, Sir Robert, 14

church, post-Reformation, 139-140, 163-4

— , pre-Reformation, 5-6, 149-52

clothes, 46-7, 49, 71, 80-9, 94-5

Cochrane, George, schoolmaster at Ayr, 161-2

— , Marion, in Lessudden, 108-9, 118

Collace, Margaret, third wife of Sir John Shairp, 27, 29, 30

Corrichie, battle of, 37

Crackaig (Sutherland), house of, 48-9

Craig, Mr Thomas, advocate, 25

Craik, dene Richard, monk of Arbroath, 17, 18

Cramond of Auldbar, William, 11

Crawford, 10th earl of, David, 11, 16, 18

Crichton castle, 38, 39, 41

Dalkeith, 61, 62, 63, 64, 68, 69, 71

Darnaway castle, 36

Darnick (Roxburghshire), 104, 110

Darnley, Lord, Henry, 39, 40, 42

diligence process (for debt recovery), 137-8

Dollar (Clackmannanshire), 141, 143, 144-6

domestic life:, 9-10, 48-50, 68-71, 99-100, 101, 117-19, 157-8, 174, 175-7

Dornoch (Sutherland), 44, 46, 49, 50, 52

Douglas of Lochleven, Sir Robert, 55, 68, 71

— — , Sir William. later earl of Morton, family background, 55-6; and the Reformation, 56-7; and Queen Mary, 57-9; and King James VI, 59-60; in France, 56, 60-1; and his estates, 61, 62-8; household, 68-71; health, 70-1; children, 72-3; and Janet Fockart, 98; and Mark Ker, 178 n.10

— , George, 59

— , William 'the Orphan', 59

Dounreay (Caithness), 42

Drochil Castle (Peeblesshire), 67,68,69

Drummond of Hawthornden, John, 99-100

— — , William, 91, 99

Drygrange (Roxburghshire), 112

Dunblane, 141-2, 143, 144

Dunkeld, 141-2, 143

Dunrobin castle (Sutherland), 42, 43, 44, 48, 50, 51, 52

Eildon (Roxburghshire), 104

Elgin, 47, 49

Elliston (Roxburghshire), 109

Erskine, 5th Lord, John, 55

— of Dun, John, 73

— , Lady Margaret, wife of Sir Robert Douglas of Lochleven, 55-6, 59, 68-9, 71-2

Ethie (Angus), 6, 12, 13, 14

Europe, trade with, 120, 122

Fair, sir John, chaplain, 153-4

family, provision for, 116

farming, 62, 64-8, 104-6, 112-13, 156-7

feu ferme tenure, 110-12

Finavon castle (Angus), 14

Flanders, 105

Fockart, Janet, biographical details, 91-2; house of, 91, 96, 99, 100; business, 96-9; financial dealings, 98-101; political contacts, 99; her family, 99-100; personal possessions, 100; clients, 100-01

food, 69-70

Fowler, Susannah, 91, 99

— , William, elder, merchant, husband of Janet Fockart, 91-4, 95-7, 98

— , — , younger, merchant, 92, 99, 132

— , poet, 91, 92, 98

France, 4, 7, 8, 12, 15, 17, 31, 60-1, 98, 120-133, *passim*

Galston (Ayrshire), 160

Gattonside (Roxburghshire), 104, 110

Glasgow, 67, 159

Glencairn, 4th earl of, Alexander, 161

Goodman, Mr Christopher, minister at Ayr, 161-2, 163

Gordon of Gordonstoun, Sir Robert, 43, 44, 46-7, 48, 49, 51, 52-3

— of Navisdale, Sir Alexander, 43, 44, 46, 48, 52-3

— , Lady Jane, countess of Bothwell, later countess of Sutherland, and the earl of Bothwell, 34, 37-41, 44; family background, 34-7; and Queen Mary, 34, 36-41; contemporary comments on, 38, 41, 43, 53; and Sutherland estates, 43-5; children and grandchildren, 45-8, 49, 50; third marriage, 45-6; and local affairs, 47-8; household, 48-9, 50; religion of, 51-2; illness and death, 52-3

Hamilton, John archbishop of St Andrews, 38, 170

Haswell, James, abbot of Newbattle, 167-8

Helmsdale (Sutherland), 45, 49

Houston (West Lothian), 27-8, 29-30, 32

Hunter, Adam, tailor, 77, 79

— , sir Henry, curate of Ayr, 152, 154, 159, 161

Huntly, 4th earl of, George, 34-7, 57

— , 5th earl of, George, 37, 40, 41

Invergowrie (Perthshire), 141, 145

James V, King of Scots, 8, 10, 11, 14, 55

James VI, King of Scots, 19, 22, 57, 59-60, 91

Jesuits, 31, 51-2, 143

Kar, sir Andrew, chaplain, 162-3

Keillour (Perthshire), 62, 63-4, 65-7

Keith, Lady Agnes, countess of Moray, 41, 43-4, 71

— , Lady Elizabeth, countess of Huntly, 36-7

Kelty (Fife), 68

Ker of Cessford, Sir Andrew, 166

— — , Sir Walter, 169, 173, 175

— , Mark, commendator of Newbattle, biographical details, 166-7, 168-70; family, 169, 175-7; and Newbattle abbey, 167-8, 171-3, 177; and politics, 170-1, 173-4; standard of living, 174-6; and William Douglas, 178, n.10

— Mark, Lord Newbattle, 169, 177

Kerwood, Sarah, sweetmeatwife, 70

Kinross, 62-4, 67, 68, 69

Knox, John, minister, 23, 56, 58, 92, 139, 161

Largs (Ayrshire), 153, 164

legal profession, 23-6

Leggat, sir Robert, curate and reader at Prestwick, biographical details, 149, 152, 153-4, 158-9; clerk of Prestwick burgh court, 154, 164; at Ayr, 161-2; reader at Prestwick, 163-4

Leslie, Lady Agnes, lady of Lochleven and countess of Morton, 55, 56, 58, 62-4, 71, 98, 178, n.10

— , Lady Helen, wife of Mark Ker, commendator of Newbattle, 169-70, 171, 174-5, 176-7

Lessudden (Roxburghshire), 108-9, 110, 112

Liff (Perthshire), 141-2, 145

Lindores (Fife), 62

Linton (Peeblesshire) 62, 68, 72

Lochleven castle, 16, 36, 41, 58-9, 62, 68-9

Lyle, Janet, Lady Ogilvy, 3-4

markets, 155

Mary, Queen of Scots, first marriage, 10; in Lochleven castle, 16, 55, 58-9; deposed, 22; and the earl of Bothwell, 34, 39-40; and the earl of Huntly, 35-7; and Jane Gordon, 36-41; supporters of, 16-17, 73; and William Fowler, 92-3, 98; in Ayrshire, 164; and Mark Ker, younger, 177

Melgund castle (Angus), 9-10, 14, 16, 18-19

Melrose abbey, 103-8

merchandise, 93-5

merchants, 71-2

Miller, sir John, curate and reader at Symington (Ayrshire), 164

— , sir Richard, curate of Ayr, 152, 161, 164

Moffet, Agnes, first wife of Sir John Shairp, 27

monastic estate management, 104-6, 108, 171

money and money-lending, 25-6, 93, 98, 100-01

Monkland (Lanarkshire), 168

Monkland (Ayrshire), 152, 164

Moray, earl of, James, 35, 41, 55, 57, 139, 173, 175

Morton, 4th earl of, James, 18, 59, 173

— , Walter, shipmaster, biographical details, 120-1, 132-3; voyages, 122-5; trading methods, 130-3

Muckhart (Perthshire), 141-2, 144-5

Murray of Kerse, David, collector of thirds, 140, 147

— , Charles, messenger-at-arms, duties 136-8, 142-5, 147; biographical details, 138, 140-1, 147; journeys, 141-2

Neill, sir David, curate of Monkton, reader at Largs, 153-4, 164

Newbattle abbey. 167-8, 171-3, 177

Newhouse of Lochleven, 68-9

Newlands (Peeblesshire), 68, 72

Newstead (Roxburghshire), 110

Newton (Newton St Boswells, Roxburghshire), 104, 110

Nimmo, Patrick, tailor, biographical details, 77; account book, 77-9, 80, 86; house and booth, 78; clients, 78-80, 87-9

nurse, 70-1

Ogilvy, 1st Lord, James, 3-4

— , 4th Lord, John, 3-4

— of Boyne, Alexander, husband of Lady Jane Gordon, 37, 45-6

— , Janet, sister of Marion Ogilvy, 3-4

— , Marion, lady of Melgund, and Cardinal Beaton, 3-13; property, 6-9, 14; and the law courts, 7-8, 13-14; family, 7-9, 14-15, 20; marriage of, 14; last illness and death, 18-20

Orr, John, schoolmaster at Ayr, 161

Pettilock, sir William, notary, 7, 14, 15, 17

Pitgober (Clackmannanshire), 146

Prestongrange (Midlothian), 173, 174, 176

Prestwick, 149, 152-3, 154-64

Queensferry, 61

recreation, 71

Reformation, the, 15, 17, 57, 139, 159-64

Reid, sir William, chaplain, 153

Rizzio, David, 39, 57

Routh, Friar John, 160

Ruthven Raid, the, 60

St Andrews, 12, 13, 20, 22

St Quivox (Ayrshire), 162

Scrabster (Caithness), 45

Scroggie, Mr Thomas, 25, 30, 32

seamen, 125, 128-9

Seton of Parbroath, Gilbert, younger, 169

Shairp of Houston, Sir John, advocate, career, 22-4; clients, 24; money-lending, 25-6; property, 26-7; marriages, 27; family, 27, 29-30, 31; tenants, 28-9; illness and death, 31-2; and sir William Douglas, 72; and Mark Ker, 174-5

— , Mr James, 27, 31

— , Mr John, advocate, 27, 28

ships, 121-2, 125-8

Sinclair, sir John, chaplain, 162

Skibo castle (Sutherland), 42, 48

Somer, David, merchant, 71

standards of living, 112-119, 157-8

Stewart, Esme, duke of Lennox, 98-9, 173-4

Strathbogie castle (Aberdeenshire), 36, 41-3, 46-7, 49, 50

Strathbrora (Sutherland), 45

Sutherland, 11th earl of, Alexander, 42, 45

— , 12th earl of, John, 46, 49-50

— , 13th earl of, John, 46

tailor craft, 75-7, 79, 89

teinds, 114, 138, 149-50

tenants and tenure, 44, 62, 63-8, 108-13,171

thirds of benefices, 138-40

Todd, John, first husband of Janet Fockart, 91

— , William, 92, 98

trade, overseas, 120, 130-1, 133

travel and communications, 51, 61-2, 135-6

Tulliallan castle (Clackmannanshire), 144, 146-7

Uddart, Marion, wife of Patrick Nimmo, 77

Uphall (Strathbrock, West Lothian), 32

Vaus of Barnbarroch, Mr Patrick, judge, 26

Vayne castle (Angus), 14-15

Wallace of Newton, Adam, 152
—   , Mr Michael, provost of Ayr, 157, 161
weaving, 157
Willock, Friar John, 159
Winterhope family, in Elliston, 109
Wishart, Mr George, reformer, 160
Wylie, sir John, preceptor of the chapel of Our Lady of Kyle, minister at Monkton, 164